To RULE the SKIES

TITLES IN THE SERIES

—— •●• ——

The History of Military Aviation

Paul J. Springer, editor

This series is designed to explore previously ignored facets of the history of airpower. It includes a wide variety of disciplinary approaches, scholarly perspectives, and argumentative styles. Its fundamental goal is to analyze the past, present, and potential future utility of airpower and to enhance our understanding of the changing roles played by aerial assets in the formulation and execution of national military strategies. It encompasses the incredibly diverse roles played by airpower, which include but are not limited to efforts to achieve air superiority; strategic attack; intelligence, surveillance, and reconnaissance missions; airlift operations; close-air support; and more. Of course, airpower does not exist in a vacuum. There are myriad terrestrial support operations required to make airpower functional, and examinations of these missions is also a goal of this series.

In less than a century, airpower developed from flights measured in minutes to the ability to circumnavigate the globe without landing. Airpower has become the military tool of choice for rapid responses to enemy activity, the primary deterrent to aggression by peer competitors, and a key enabler to military missions on the land and sea. This series provides an opportunity to examine many of the key issues associated with its usage in the past and present, and to influence its development for the future.

To **RULE**
the **SKIES**

— •• —

GENERAL THOMAS S. POWER
AND THE RISE OF STRATEGIC
AIR COMMAND IN THE COLD WAR

Brent D. Ziarnick

Naval Institute Press · Annapolis, Maryland

Naval Institute Press
291 Wood Road
Annapolis, MD 21402

Library of Congress Cataloging-in-Publication Data
Names: Ziarnick, Brent David, date, author.
Title: To rule the skies : General Thomas S. Power and the rise of
    Strategic Air Command in the Cold War / Brent D. Ziarnick.
Other titles: General Thomas S. Power and the rise of Strategic Air Command
    in the Cold War
Description: Annapolis, Maryland : Naval Institute Press, [2021] | Series:
    The history of military aviation | Includes bibliographical references
    and index
Identifiers: LCCN 2020048469 (print) | LCCN 2020048470 (ebook) | ISBN
    9781682475874 (hardback) | ISBN 9781682475881 (ebook) | ISBN
    9781682475881 (pdf)
Subjects: LCSH: Power, Thomas S. (Thomas Sarsfield), 1905–1970. | United
    States. Air Force—Biography. | United States. Air Force. Strategic Air
    Command—History. | Cold War. | Generals—United States—Biography. |
    United States—History, Military—20th century.
Classification: LCC E745.P69 Z53 2021 (print) | LCC E745.P69 (ebook) |
    DDC 355.0092 [B]—dc23
LC record available at https://lccn.loc.gov/2020048469
LC ebook record available at https://lccn.loc.gov/2020048470

♾ Print editions meet the requirements of ANSI/NISO z39.48-1992
(Permanence of Paper).
Printed in the United States of America.

29 28 27 26 25 24 23 22 21   9 8 7 6 5 4 3 2 1
First printing

CONTENTS

—— •••• ——

ACKNOWLEDGMENTS

T he journey to tell the story of General Thomas Power involved many institutions and people, mostly within the small academic circle of the United States Air Force's Air University. The first group I must thank are the people who have had to deal with me the longest. I owe many thanks to Archie Difante, Maranda Gilmore, Tammy Horton, and the staff of the Air Force Historical Research Agency for their help finding and declassifying hundreds of obscure documents over many years. They are all great professionals and a pleasure to work with.

Next, I must thank the men and women of the School of Advanced Air and Space Studies, especially my thesis and dissertation advisor, Dr. Tom Hughes, for teaching me how to write biography. Any mistakes I made in technique were despite his best efforts to drag a stubborn engineer and economist into the ways of biography. Also, Dr. M. V. "Coyote" Smith, Colonel, USAF (Ret.), a mentor and friend of many years, helped me place General Power and SAC in the historical context of both the Air Force and the national space program. Thank you for taking the time to help me work through some of my ideas!

Lastly, I would not have been able to complete this project without the help of my colleagues at the Air Command and Staff College, where I have the pleasure of serving. I owe a great deal to Dr. Paul J. Springer of the Department of Research for his wealth of advice and encouragement as well as for making introductions at the Naval Institute Press.

I also greatly appreciate the help of many others outside of Air University. Joel Dobson provided me with many documents and research

I would never have been able to find anywhere else, along with some amazing insights into the Power family. George Dyson, who wrote the definitive history of Project Orion—indispensable to understanding Power as a military thinker—offered a great deal of material and encouragement. His insight led me to Dr. Robert Duffner, Air Force Research Laboratory's command historian at Kirtland Air Force Base, who graciously allowed me to search his Orion archives. I am especially indebted to Frederick F. Gorschboth, an original Project Orion staff officer, for traveling to Maxwell Air Force Base to discuss his role in the effort. To speak to one of the first Air Force space theorists, who should be known as the military father of the space Navy concept, was a great personal honor.

To RULE
the SKIES

CHAPTER 1

Introduction

———•••———

Of Insanity and Icons

On 28 April 1963, a beautiful day in Washington, D.C., the senior civilian in a nondescript section of the Pentagon bureaucracy would rather have been outside. Unfortunately, he had to be at a meeting to listen to a speaker who had been termed a "madman."

The speaker, about five feet ten inches tall and wearing a light blue service coat, was at the podium. The audience members—about three hundred senior officers and civilian equivalents—were quieting down and taking their seats. Our ordinary senior civilian sat down just as the briefer, Gen. Thomas S. Power, commander in chief of the Strategic Air Command (SAC), started speaking.

The general informed the audience that his briefing was classified top secret and that its subject was the critical role of the Strategic Air Command as the nation's deterrent force. This was no surprise to anyone in the room. The general explained that he was going to stress the importance of SAC's bomber force and the need to maintain this decisive capability. "Oh, there it is," the civilian thought. "The old general wants to defend his precious bombers! Everyone knew that the intercontinental ballistic missile [ICBM] was the ultimate weapon, but this guy wants his flying club!" Power's loud voice and aristocratic New York accent were beginning to grate on the nerves of a few in attendance.

The purpose of the military in war is to kill human beings and to destroy the works of man, Power told the assembly. And if we need to kill human beings and break man-made objects to defend the American people, we should accomplish this in the quickest way possible with whatever means we have available. If we have nuclear weapons, they should be used.[1]

The civilian sat up a little. "The lunatic actually wants us to use nuclear weapons in combat? Did not we come close enough to destroying the world over Cuba a few months ago?" The squirming and muted but noticeable objections by the crowd indicated that most of the audience felt the same way about the general's broadside.

Those who advocate for disarmament are fools, the general explained. He went further, claiming the imminent ratification of the Limited Test Ban Treaty would be a horrible mistake. "Most people think that the Limited Test Ban Treaty is a great political success, a small candle of hope in the darkness of this Cold War," the senior civilian reflected. But Power maintained that the treaty would block the United States from developing high-yield weaponry, and the atmospheric ban would keep SAC from fully testing ICBMs from launch to detonation, which Power supported.

Power got angrier as he spoke. Wars always start because someone is weak, he claimed. Trying to stay strong while disarming is like trying to dress and undress at the same time; it cannot be done! Even space must be used for military purposes, the general continued, assuring the group that the Soviet Union was not neglecting this field. Further, it was a grave mistake to tell the Russians that we would not preempt them in a war! This admission had made the Soviets' war planning much easier because they did not have to plan against a sneak attack. "Well," the civilian thought, "better that than start a war!"

A major general from Power's staff then got up and gave the formal briefing, the real reason everyone was there. He noted that SAC currently possessed 271,672 personnel, 2,424 combat aircraft, 141 Atlas ICBMs, 119 Titan ICBMs, and 372 Minuteman ICBMs[2]—certainly too much to merely guarantee assured destruction, the civilian thought. More assets would be destabilizing and redundant, yet that is what the major general from SAC now outlined for the period 1965–69, though he acknowledged that the Office of the Secretary of Defense (OSD) had recently decided for the same period that SAC would operate with a greatly reduced bomber force. That reduction, thought the civilian, made more sense than anything Power was saying.

Mercifully, the staff officer was finished quickly, and Power returned to solicit questions. A query from a well-educated young civilian prompted a fury in Power. He blamed the "computer-type minds" who know nothing about military weapons for all of the problems the United States was facing. The room fell silent but for the muffled stirring of hundreds of men. Power continued blaming the attendees for being the sort who had been selling naive aspirations to the president and the secretary of defense, getting the United States into wars and allowing tyrants to rise.

After this outburst, the general went on what could only be described as a "rambling tirade." Power became more sullen than angry. The general was tired, after thirty-seven years of military service, of experiencing the "peaks and valleys" of military preparedness. Attendees could tell Power was extremely bitter that civilian advisers, not the military, had the ear of the president and the secretary of defense. The only exact words our senior civilian remembered clearly were Power's last remark: "The computer-types who were making defense policy don't know their ass from a hole in the ground!"

With that parting shot, the nervous crowd dispersed quickly and quietly. The civilian was among the first to leave, anxious to get away from the general. Before this meeting, he thought Power was simply the worst of the ultra-conservative warmongers left over from World War II, but now the civilian was worried: "Perhaps Power was not simply a joke. Maybe Power truly was insane." And, the civilian silently shivered, that man commanded the most powerful military force in human history.[3]

So goes the conventional narrative. General Thomas Sarsfield Power did command the most powerful military force in history. The Strategic Air Command reached its zenith during Power's reign as commander in chief (CINCSAC) from 1957 to 1964, a tenure second in length only to that of Gen. Curtis E. LeMay. Power also took part in many of the Air Force's most storied efforts, from the open-cockpit biplanes of the 1920s to the mighty aerospace force of supersonic bombers, ballistic missiles, and spacecraft. However, in the nearly fifty years since his death, there has not been a biography of this important Air Force leader. Popular accounts of the history of the U.S. Air Force, the Cold War, and the nuclear arms race have very little to say about Power. His name is acknowledged in many books, but he generally is in the background of the story. He took part in the Cold War like thousands of other people, but the implication is that he did not make any mark worth studying or recording in detail.

This history is wrong. Thomas Power is the most misunderstood officer ever to wear the uniform of the U.S. Air Force. Historians have succumbed to two different but serious errors when considering the general. First, with their requirements for protagonists and antagonists, popular accounts have portrayed Power as a tyrannical sadist—the living embodiment of everything wrong with both nuclear weapons and the military mind.[4] Power was a demonic, despotic, and detested commander—the willing and able hatchet man of Gen. Curtis LeMay, who himself was one of the cruelest men in uniform. Power was virtually a mass murderer in waiting; given the chance, he would have happily started a global thermonuclear war. Demented and dimwitted, Power was also intellectually suspect, for he was only a high school graduate. The world was spared destruction only by the "Whiz Kids," those bright youngsters serving under Secretary of Defense Robert McNamara, who took control of nuclear planning.

Second, academic accounts recall Power as a carbon copy of Curtis LeMay. He emerges as LeMay's right-hand man in the firebombing of Tokyo and remains his loyal subordinate for almost two decades, faithfully executing LeMay's innovations without critical reflection. Power was a bomber boy addicted to flying, bested by the visionary Gen. Bernard Schriever and his ultimate weapon, the ICBM. Power's lackluster leadership of Strategic Air Command prompted its slow decline into irrelevance as LeMay's crown jewel tarnished into a plodding, bureaucratic freak show finally discarded and forgotten by the real Air Force. Power was also the last senior flying cadet, the final Air Force general without a college diploma, and a relic of a bygone era of barnstormers perhaps high on courage but low on intelligence.[5] Even relatively sympathetic accounts describe Power as a "sadist," because LeMay himself admitted as much—though this trait was excused because Power "got the job done."[6]

These narratives are wrong. Power's reputation is the function of both the arrogance of the intellectual class in the 1960s and the vitriol of the antinuclear movement that followed. It is also the result of Power's long tenure under LeMay and his relatively early death. Polemicists have peddled in half-truths, and historians have been uninterested in Power. As a result, history has accepted a caricature.

However, Thomas Power deserves to be seen as his own man. When we closely examine that man, we do not find what the conventional wisdom suggests. Rather than a sadistic and tyrannical man without a shred of people skills, we find a stern but compassionate man of faith, devotion, and character, deeply respected by the men who knew him well. Rather than a dim copy of LeMay, we find an innovative and daring combat commander largely responsible for the development of SAC itself. Rather than a strategic dullard easily bested by Whiz Kids, we find a man of remarkable military insight and experience who could—and did—speak intelligently and articulately. And, perhaps most relevant to an understanding of today's Air Force, instead of a man intimidated and horrified by the rise of the ICBM within his flying club, we find a man with a sharp understanding of the real value of space to the Air Force and the nation, and a man who should eclipse Bernard Schriever as the true father of the U.S. Air Force space effort. Ultimately, Thomas Power is the last, unsung founding father of U.S. airpower and the final champion of what historian Edward Kaplan calls the "air atomic strategy"—the peak evolution of the airpower visions of Billy Mitchell, Henry "Hap" Arnold, and Haywood Hansell.[7] Thomas Power was a brilliant and successful officer at all levels of command whose foundational mantra was to do whatever it took to keep America strong. To accomplish this mission, Power faced enormous personal and professional obstacles, but he overcame them to become the operational and strategic leader America needed in times of crisis.

Thomas Power's life is a fascinating tale of a relatively normal boy who, through family tragedy, personal ambition, skill, and effort, rose to become one of the most important military officers of the Cold War and the final champion of the original airpower vision that would have taken the Air Force to the stars as a true and dominant aerospace force. This book chronicles Power's life from his rough beginnings through victory in World War II and finally through the defeat of his vision by Department of Defense civilians in the Cold War. This book challenges many assumptions about the man and the leader and instead frames him as a great tactical innovator and combat leader in World War II, a superb operational innovator and leader in SAC, and a strategic prophet denied in his own time.

Little-known events in Power's life are illuminated here, such as his having to leave school to support his mother after the devastating collapse of his upper-middle class family, his chance encounter with a barnstorming pilot, and his extraordinary efforts to be accepted as an Army flying cadet. These events all marked young Power's determination and skill and laid the groundwork for his military career, the early years of which were ordinary and uneventful but likewise set the stage for his later rise to four-star rank. His early experiences show tantalizing glimpses not of an evil and dimwitted man, but of one with a highly innovative technical mind who excelled as both a pilot and an officer capable of becoming a brilliant visionary and operational commander. He flew in the Army air mail fiasco, exhibited an early interest in rocketry for warfare, and saw firsthand the aggressive expansion of Japan in Asia before World War II. These experiences transformed him from a young man whose main interests were flying, hunting, and playing golf, into a hawkish devotee of countering world aggression with overwhelming U.S. strength. Power's broken but unbowed family also influenced his career in dramatic ways—especially his wild yet determined sister Dorothy, whose strategic marriages took her from immigrant poverty to American millionaire heiress and British aristocracy.

Power was initially on the sidelines in World War II. Aching for combat, he slowly but inexorably emerged as an expert administrator and instructor, helping to operationalize the mighty Boeing B-29 Superfortress. In time, Power saw combat in Consolidated B-24

Liberators assigned to North Africa and Italy, distinguishing himself as a combat leader in multiple missions before returning to the B-29 and leading a wing to Guam to help defeat the Japanese. On 10 March 1945 Power proved his abilities as both a tactical innovator and an effective combat leader as he planned and led the first low-level incendiary attack on Tokyo, one of the most destructive military assaults in history. The efforts of LeMay and Power and the rest of the B-29 men of the Pacific theater developed a new approach to strategic bombing remarkably different from original prewar American conceptions. After earning his reputation as LeMay's best B-29 wing commander, Power finished the war as the director of operations of the Strategic Air Forces Pacific, where he was first introduced to the weapon that most defined his career path— the atomic bomb.

After the war, Power was at the center of some of the most critical junctures in Air Force history. He played a crucial role in Operation Crossroads, the early postwar nuclear tests in the Pacific. He was involved with the planning of the Berlin airlift briefly as the air attaché to London. As Curtis LeMay's deputy at SAC, Power helped guide a truly strategic air force toward the vanguard of national defense and a lasting peace.

Instead of resisting new technology, Thomas Power embraced it with a very considered and balanced approach. As commander of Air Research and Development Command (ARDC), Power oversaw some of the most emblematic defense projects of the day, including the North American XB-70 Valkyrie supersonic bomber, the ICBM, and emerging space and satellite technologies. Power made his mark in ARDC as a superior leader of technology, consolidating the space and missile programs under Gen. Bernard Schriever and beginning a far-sighted Air Force effort to understand the future of space power and the Air Force's role in exploiting space. Throughout, Power was a vociferous champion of the role of education, science, and technology in aiding the United States to win the Cold War against the Soviet Union without resorting to kinetic war.

Power is the Air Force's great unsung space hero, because he was able to see beyond existing political and technical conventions of space in the 1960s and realize that the service could not "afford to play catch-up or wait for the day when the battlefield is shaped by the heavens."[8] To ensure that the United States was ready for the space age, Power almost singlehandedly orchestrated the development of the organizations, doctrine, and equipment necessary to achieve a mature military space power for the nation. The never-before-told stories of Power's attempts to turn America's air service into a true U.S. aerospace force should alone cement him a place in space history.

As SAC commander, Power emerged as a brilliant strategic leader, helping Curtis LeMay's SAC evolve into a truly integrated aerospace force of bombers and missiles, whose determined twenty-four-hour alert crews compressed tactical warning and attack into mere minutes and could devastate any enemy within an hour. To do this, he pioneered many organizational innovations, such as alert crews, airborne alert, and the Joint Strategic Target Planning Staff. Along the way, Power led SAC through the most harrowing days of the Cold War, the Cuban Missile Crisis in October and November 1962, when SAC established an unprecedented aerial reconnaissance program while maintaining a striking force of a power never before seen on twenty-four-hour airborne alert. Throughout his tenure at SAC, Power brought his argument for overwhelming superiority in strategic nuclear power over the Soviet Union in personal messages to the American people with great charisma and connection, the exact opposite of what one would expect from a man remembered in popular history as "mean," "cruel," "unforgiving," and who "didn't have the time of day to pass with anyone."[9]

Power's drive is epitomized by his support of Project Orion, a program devoted to launching massive human payloads into space using nuclear pulse propulsion. Power's efforts culminated in the 1962 Air Force space program, an ambitious effort supported by Chief of Staff LeMay but ultimately rejected by defense secretary McNamara. Through it all, Power labored to instill an aerospace force mindset at SAC, including the development of aerospace wings and other activities meant to turn SAC into the champion of aerospace power. However, with Power's retirement in 1964, his efforts to develop the organization, doctrine, and equipment necessary to develop combat space power ended in failure, relegated to little beyond classified archives, and left for scholars to fill the human gap in space history with Bernard Schriever. But today Thomas Power deserves a more fair and full hearing, and both the Air Force and Space Force need a new appraisal of how an air and space atomic vision came to be—and was lost. This book aims to provide both.

CHAPTER 2

From Flying Cadet to Aerospace Commander

Early Life and Career, 1905–54

Thomas Stack Power, father of Gen. Thomas Sarsfield Power, was born to an affluent family in the civil parish of Seskinein, a small farming area about twenty-five miles west of Waterford City, Ireland, on 25 May 1873.[1] The family prospered in the lace industry, and here young Thomas learned his trade. As a teenager, Thomas met the slightly older Mary Alice Rice, born 12 June 1872. The couple married in 1889 when Thomas was only 16 and Mary 17. Together they moved north to Dublin, and for ten years Thomas worked in the lace trade to provide for his wife.

Near the turn of the century, the Powers decided their prospects in Ireland were limited, and they immigrated to the United States, probably for greater opportunity rather than to escape poverty. The North Atlantic sailing from Londonderry to New York in the early spring would have been a rough passage for the young couple, but they decided to embark anyway. Thomas could not remember the name of the ship they boarded at Londonderry on 11 March 1900 and marked it as "unknown" on the petition for naturalization he filled out nearly twenty years later, dated 3 September 1918. Ten days after their departure, Thomas and Mary arrived at the port of New York on 21 March 1900.[2]

It is a mystery why it took eighteen years for Thomas Stack Power to apply for U.S. citizenship, but by the time he did so, it was for himself, his wife Mary, and their three children: Cathleen (later Kathleen), born 12 July 1900, Dorothy, born 12 August 1902, and Thomas Sarsfield, born 18 June 1904. Records for young Tommy's birth year would later be either changed or corrected to 1905.

The Power family's address in the 1900 census was 500 West 166th Street, New York. By 1910 the Power family had moved one and a half miles north, to the higher terrain on the east side of the Harlem River known as Morris Heights, at 1793 Sedgwick Avenue in the Bronx. Thomas Stack earned his family a comfortable middle-class living as a merchant dealing in imported laces, silk, and other high-end cloth for ladies' garments. He was frequently gone on business trips to Europe, sailing from New York to Le Havre and Cherbourg, France, and also to Liverpool and London. By 1915 the family had moved to a residential area known as Harbor Heights in the village of Mamaroneck, in Rye, Westchester County. Harbor Heights was known to be an area where a young family could comfortably settle down in New York.[3]

Life was good for the Power family by 1915. Thomas Stack had made many contacts in the business world of fine textiles and ladies' fashions on both sides of the Atlantic, associated with such people as the famed New York dress designer Lady Duff Gordon, and continued to expand his business.[4] As an adult, Tommy's sister Dorothy recalled sailing on the ocean liners to Europe with her father as early as age ten, perhaps romantically but mistakenly recalling that "diplomatic missions summoned him to Ireland."[5] The oldest daughter, Kathleen, was apparently not as flamboyant as her sister Dorothy, but both became known as lively and vivacious young women. Dorothy, perhaps enamored with Europe from her trips with her father, once told a friend, "Someday I am going to marry a very, very rich man and I am going to have magnificent homes and servants. I am going to travel all over the world. I even am going to visit the King's palace in England. Who knows but eventually I may marry a lord or even an earl!"[6]

At some point, the family decided, possibly on the insistence of mother Mary, that the two sisters were getting too flashy, especially by the old country standards of Ireland. Even though they were both practicing Catholics, Thomas and Mary decided to enroll their daughters in Oakwood Seminary, a Quaker boarding school for girls in Union Springs, New York, where they hoped "the austere standards of living would tone down" both girls' (especially Dorothy's) taste for luxury and bring their "high spirits" under control.[7] It would be a formidable project; Dorothy, just fourteen, arrived at Oakwood with a half-dozen large wardrobe trunks filled with Paris-made gowns, forty pairs of shoes, coats, hats, and furs.[8]

Thomas Sarsfield, rather than being flamboyant like his sisters, was a studious boy. He was also known as an athlete, often "hopping trucks" to play sports against teams across town. Tommy attended Mamaroneck High School but, after a year, enrolled in the Barnard School for Boys in the Riverside section of the Bronx. The Barnard School was a private college preparatory academy for relatively well-to-do families that later merged with the Horace Mann School at the same location. Tommy was there for three years and did very well academically. He played baseball, basketball, and football—especially excelling at football—and was given the nickname "Teetie" by his fellow students.

Though the family thrived financially, there were domestic troubles. Dorothy was busy becoming "one of the most beautiful girls in New York" and, after graduating from boarding school, spent increasing amounts of time out of the house.[9] Thomas Stack traveled frequently to Europe, and he appeared to abandon the family entirely when he did not return home from a trip to Ireland in 1921. Thomas Stack and Mary divorced soon after Thomas' abandonment.

Although Tommy remained reluctant to talk about it, his father's abandonment devastated the young boy's family life. There is a record of a Mary A. Power from Westchester County being committed to the Utica state mental hospital by a relative, Kathleen Power, in 1925. Her admission record notes Mary Power as a "not cooperative, mentally ill, white female, born in Ireland late 1800s," but additional details are sealed permanently by New York confidentiality laws.[10] Whether the person committed was Power's mother is unclear, but it fits other facts, foremost of which is that neither Tommy nor his sisters bore their father much ill will later in life. The Power family members kept in cordial—if infrequent— contact throughout their lives, which might not have been expected if Thomas Stack had simply abandoned the family without cause. In any case, mother Mary was essentially the ward of either the state or her children for the rest of her life, living with Tommy for a time in 1930 while he was assigned to Langley Field, Virginia.

Without their father and his income, the family fell upon hard times. Kathleen left home soon after her father and in 1921 married Robert Ziegele and had a son, Robert Raines Ziegele, born 29 October 1922. The couple divorced after a few years, with Kathleen charging Robert with "extreme cruelty," a catch-all divorce rationale that was a contemporary version of irreconcilable differences. Also in 1921, Dorothy eloped with Adelbert Mitchell after meeting him at a junior prom at Brown University. Their marriage likewise did not last. In 1922 Tommy, unable to pay for private school and perhaps the sole supporter of his mother, dropped out of Barnard before finishing his final year of high school to earn a living for his family.

Although he was raised to think of himself as a member of the wealthier upper middle class, Tommy did not shirk hard work. Instead of going to college as he had planned, he joined Godwin Construction Company on 41st Street and Lexington Avenue in New York as a clerk. Even while working, however, Tommy did not ignore his education. World War II–era press releases relate that Tommy went back to Barnard School at nineteen and graduated in 1924, but scant evidence exists that this actually happened. In fact, Power never formally graduated high school, and he obscured this fact on official documents until he had to admit the truth on an Atomic Energy Commission security clearance application in 1957, when the likelihood and consequences of being found out became too high to bear.[11] Nevertheless, convinced he needed to go to college, Tommy enrolled in Cooper Union night classes to study civil engineering. By 1926 Tommy had become a construction superintendent. Years later, Power exaggerated that he was a "construction engineer" between 1922 and 1927, perhaps out of shame for his blue-collar employment and lack of education.[12]

There is little reason to believe that Tommy was not content to remain a construction worker in New York, but two events took his life in a different direction. First was Charles Lindbergh's historic flight from New York to Paris in May 1927. Like many people, especially in New York,

Tommy was caught up in the euphoria. Power said in a 1960 interview that he had "the natural longing to fly that a lot of youngsters get" but that it was "probably Lindbergh's flight [that] really got me to make up my mind that I was going to do something about a career in aviation."[13]

As with many fancies, roadblocks kept it from becoming a reality. Tommy was not rich, and flying was expensive, so he worked. Shortly thereafter, Tommy had his second—and personal—encounter with aviation. At a company outing, Tommy and his crew sat watching a barnstorming pilot flying in a nearby cow pasture with a World War I–era Curtiss JN-4 Jenny trainer.[14] Fascinated with what he saw, Tommy asked the pilot for a ride. The barnstormer offered flights for $10 a piece ($145 in 2018 dollars). Tommy borrowed the money from his construction crew, and the pilot took him for a ten-minute flight that included a few loops.[15] Impressed with Tommy's enthusiasm, the barnstormer took him up for a second flight and took him through a few more stunts.[16] After that, Tommy "was hooked."[17]

When Tommy found out Lindbergh had learned to fly as an Army Air Corps flying cadet for free, he decided to apply. Kathleen's second husband, Tobias Miller, was a minor hero as an infantry officer in World War I and was a captain in the New York Army National Guard. He intervened on Tommy's behalf to the War Department to appoint the young man a flying cadet. The Army was receptive to Captain Miller's recommendation, but they informed him that Tommy would have to compete for a flying cadet slot by passing an admissions test, as he could not prove having two full years of college education.

The exam was tough. Between July 1928 and June 1939, only 411 of 1,500 applicants passed.[18] Subjects included history, grammar and composition, geography, mathematics through trigonometry, and physics. Tommy's time at Cooper Union did not adequately prepare him in all of those subjects. Therefore, for months after work and on weekends, he entombed himself in the New York Public Library, studying every subject he would need to master.[19] He maintained this demanding schedule for almost half a year, but as soon as he thought he was ready, he reported to the testing center. The high school dropout passed the exam.

Flying cadet Thomas Power reported to the Air Service Primary Flying School at March Field, California, on 29 February 1928. The school there was relatively new, with its first class having entered in November 1927.[20] Power's class was only the second at the field. The class began the careers of many important airpower leaders, including Haywood Hansell, one of the later architects of the U.S. air war against Germany in World War II.

The Air Corps flying training program had just undergone a major revision when Cadet Power arrived. The six-month initial school had been extended to eight months, and cadets and flying officers (newly commissioned officers from West Point or the Reserve Officers' Training Corps attending pilot training) were sent through a battery of medical and physical tests. Before they could even touch an airplane, they were subjected to a rigorous physical examination for flyers, as well as the Ruggles orientator, a metal cage in a gyroscope operated by an instructor that tested the student's ability to control stick and rudder simultaneously in various circumstances.[21] Those skilled (or lucky) enough to pass then received four months of instruction on the standard Army Jenny training aircraft. For the second half of the course, the students were upgraded into an Army observation aircraft (the World War I–era DeHavilland with a Liberty engine) and taught the skills necessary to perform the observation mission. At the end of primary school, the graduate was "a thoroughly competent airplane pilot."[22]

Three decades later, Power recalled that the most difficult stage of primary school was the first one, the solo stage: "We soloed first and, from there, went right into an aerobatics stage which is rather surprising."[23] After the aerobatics stage, the students went through an accuracy stage. They upgraded to the DeHavilland, in which instructors focused on accuracy rather than basic flying skills, and students began formation flying and developing other skills necessary for Army aviators.

Of the one hundred students who began, forty-eight graduated in October and moved on to advanced flying school on 1 November 1928. In addition to Power and Hansell, the Kelly Field advanced school

November class included Frank Armstrong, who later became the inspiration for the World War II film *Twelve O'Clock High*.[24]

The four-month advanced flying school was the last obstacle before earning the grade of airplane pilot. All students initially received finishing training as observation pilots and aerial gunners, and Power performed well. After this finishing, each student earned his specialty as an observation, pursuit, bombardment, or attack pilot.[25] Students had no input in choosing their specialty; leaders simply "put us into whatever specialty they wanted us," Power recalled. He was placed in the pursuit specialty, where he learned with World War I–era fighter planes.[26] Unfortunately, Power was hospitalized for a month for severe lymphadenitis due to an ill-fitting boot, which swelled his entire left leg from ankle to groin, but he was able to fly enough to graduate with his class.[27]

Power and his eighty-five cohorts became the largest graduating class in the history of the advanced school since World War I, and they earned their wings and reserve commissions on 28 February 1929, a year after Power entered the Air Corps. Shortly after, Power received orders—along with Hansell and Armstrong—to the 2nd Bombardment Group at Langley Field, Virginia. Hansell, Armstrong, and Power were all assigned to the group's 49th Bombardment Squadron.

Lt. Howard E. Hall, writing in the 26 April 1929 *Air Corps Newsletter*, said of the new batch of lieutenants, "Only six of the new officers have had any training in bombardment at the Schools, the rest being Pursuit, Observation, and Attack men. It will be necessary to give these officers training in Bombardment in the Group, so it will be some time before they are ready to take part in Group Operations."[28] Power was not the only fighter pilot to be flying bombers.

The 49th Bombardment Squadron flew the Keystone LB-5A two-engine light bomber. The LB-5A had a top speed of 107 miles per hour and a range of almost 450 miles, and it could climb to 8,000 feet and carry a payload of 2,300 pounds of bombs along with its crew of five (pilot, copilot, bombardier, and two gunners) with their five .303 Lewis guns. The two Liberty L-12 420-horsepower engines that powered it proved to be very troublesome for its flight crews. Accidents were common in the 2nd Bombardment Group, which the pilots recounted with good humor when no one was seriously hurt. Soon after Power arrived, a propeller detached from its crankshaft during one flight and rendered the bomber's fuselage a "meat-box," narrowly missing two crewmen. Lieutenant Hall, in the *Air Corps Newsletter*, reported the flight as "a real thrill."[29]

Entering flying at this exciting but hazardous time, Power was not immune to the dangers. He recalled, "I must have had about half a dozen actual forced landings. But we used to put our airplanes down in one piece, then fly them out again after they were fixed."[30] Power had many close calls in his flying career, but a point of pride was that he had never "cracked up a military airplane in some 10,000 hours of flying."[31]

Power had significantly different luck in civilian aircraft on account of his sister Dorothy. At age seventeen Dorothy had become a model for Jean Patou, a famous dress designer in Paris. Referred to as "one of New York's prettiest blondes," Dorothy soon captured the attention of Harry Hall, a successful young stock broker who was very wealthy by the time they met.[32] Harry, Dorothy, and their young sons William and Henry and two servants split their time between their New York home at 21 Vista Drive, Great Neck, and Hall's colonial estate "White Hall" near Richmond, Virginia. Hall, like Power, was a pilot and aviation enthusiast (he had a $9,000 Stearman B1 canvas airplane), and the men got along very well, often flying together when Hall was in Virginia. On 11 September 1929 the men were flying together when they joined the "Mystical Order of Caterpillars"—aviators who have been forced to bail out of a disabled aircraft by means of a parachute. Shortly after taking off from Gloucester, Virginia, in Hall's Stearman, Hall and Power heard a cracking noise and saw the leading edge of the upper right wing collapse. After struggling to gain altitude "with full gun climb" and the fabric of the wings ripping off, pilot Hall finally made 2,500 feet and headed for Langley Field. Unfortunately, the entire wing cover came off and put the plane into a power spin. Power and Hall both bailed out and landed "without any trouble."[33] Eventually, Power logged over one thousand hours in Hall's Stearman B1 and Waco F biplanes.[34] He also recounted a time when a civilian engine quit and "I had to put it down in a swamp, but I walked away from it."[35]

In addition to his civilian flying, Lieutenant Power performed well in administration at the group. Power was appointed assistant operations officer of the 96th Bombardment Squadron on 6 April 1929 and of the 2nd Bombardment Group on 8 August.[36] Applying for active service, Power received his regular Army Air Corps commission on 4 September 1929, where he ranked higher than most college graduates of his flying training class.[37] In his early years at the 2nd Bombardment Group, Lieutenant Power was an aircraft commander as well as a squadron armaments officer in addition to his assistant operations position.[38]

Power, however, might not have been a superior pilot or bombardier. On 21 September Capt. Harry Pascale led a flight of five bombers to Camden, New Jersey, to put on a bombing display during a celebration marking the opening of a new airport. The five aircraft dropped sacks of salt from three hundred feet in a "bombing" competition. Lieutenant Power was the co-pilot of the bomber that finished dead last in the competition, and although he did not win any of the big prizes, which included wristwatches and suitcases, he did receive a silver pocket flask for participation.[39]

Power finally became a fully mission-ready rated pilot on 13 October 1929.[40] Averaging around thirty to forty hours of military flying a month as either a pilot or an observer, Power, like all of the flying officers, bounced around between squadrons and jobs, but even routine flying was dangerous in those days. In December 1929, a severe snowstorm forced him down while flying a Curtiss B2 Condor.[41] Besides the occasional in-flight mishap common to all prewar aviators, however, Power's flying time and military positions were largely unremarkable.

Some glimpses of Power's connection to advanced technology and his skill at flying do appear in his early career, however. Power joined an aerial demonstration team and proved to be a fearless stunt flyer. A photograph in the *Chicago Daily Tribune* on 27 August 1930 shows a Keystone bomber flown by Power in a steep bank rounding a stunt pylon only a few feet from the ground. It was a dangerous maneuver for many of the specialized stunt planes of the time. In an underpowered Army biplane bomber, it appeared nearly suicidal. The newspaper reported it was "one of the sights that sent a thrill through the spectators at Curtiss field yesterday afternoon."

In April 1931 Power was part of a 49th Bombardment Squadron night navigation experimental flight of three bombers using radio navigation to fly from Bolling Field to Langley Field, Virginia. The flyers kept in constant contact with the Langley Field radio navigation beacon as well as with 2nd Bombardment Group ground stations, which provided valuable experience for Power later.[42]

That same month Lieutenant Power received orders to the Air Corps Technical School at Chanute Field, Illinois, as one of twenty-two students in the maintenance engineering class beginning 1 October 1931.[43] The maintenance program at the Air Corps Technical School was considered the best in the nation well into World War II.[44] This was a major turning point in Thomas Power's career for two reasons. First, attendance at the technical school precluded attendance at the Air Corps Tactical School, the schooling that brought many young interwar aviators into early prominence. Instead, Power remained in operational flying units and did not attend the tactical school until just before World War II, delaying his emergence from Air Force obscurity first only in a B-29 in 1945 and significantly only in 1954 as Strategic Air Command vice commander under Curtis LeMay. Second, assignment to the technical school signified the point at which Power became intimately familiar with aircraft, from both a technical and an operational perspective—a hallmark of his later service.

Power arrived at Chanute Field in late September to begin his maintenance training. Only a few weeks later, Power learned Harry Hall was killed on 25 October when he crashed his Gee Bee Sportster Model C (which he had owned less than a month) racing in Jersey City, New Jersey.[45] There was some speculation at the time that Harry had committed suicide due to financial troubles but, given that he had little experience flying this specialized plane, in all likelihood he simply suffered a fatal accident. Fortunately for his family, he left Dorothy a wealthy young widow, providing a comfortable income from an estate worth $400,000.

Technical school instructors noted that Power's class was particularly motivated and that every man was "putting forth his best effort."[46] On 25 June 1932 Power graduated from the technical school with an 84.2 percent ("Excellent") academic record. The director of the maintenance engineering school, Capt. William Hayward, confirmed in Power's officer efficiency report that he had performed very well at technical school but rated Power as "satisfactory" across the board, noting that this "officer is inclined to take tasks quickly and sacrifice accuracy."[47]

Despite his new maintenance education, Power went back to performing squadron armament officer duties after graduating. He filled his time making cross-country flights to Selfridge Field, Michigan, and Bowman Field, Kentucky, in July.[48] Power was an assistant ordnance officer and assistant armament officer for the annual Air Corps machine gun and bombing matches at Langley on 12–14 September. His 96th Bombardment Squadron did not make the top three in the bombing competition.[49] During this period, Power was in excellent health and did not share the excesses of many in the military flying community; he admitted to smoking fifteen cigarettes a day but denied he drank alcohol, perhaps wishing to avoid his mother's liver problems, and perhaps due to Prohibition.[50]

At the end of May 1933, Power received word he was to join the Civilian Conservation Corps at Fort Devens, Massachusetts. On 14 July Power was transferred to the 118th Company, Civilian Conservation Corps, as the commanding officer.[51] Based at Annette State Forest Camp, New Hampshire, the 118th Company had two hundred men assigned to it. The company initially lived in tents, but in the few months before the onset of winter, six barracks were built, as well as a mess hall, a recreation hall, an officer's barracks, and truck shelters. Specific projects accomplished by the 118th Company included completing "the road to the fire lookout tower on Temple Mountain, the road to the fire lookout on Highland Hill in Westmoreland, the swimming pool at the Adams

Playground in Peterborough, trails up Monadnock Mountain, cabins and shelters on state-owned land, and planting over one million seedlings."[52]

Lieutenant Power was recalled to the Air Corps in February 1934 to assist in one of the most important, and tragic, operations of the interwar Air Corps. In early February President Franklin Roosevelt directed postmaster general James Farley to cancel all air mail contracts with private airlines due to widespread fraud, and the Air Corps was ordered to deliver the mail instead. While delivering the mail, the Air Corps flew in harsh winter conditions. Power was assigned to the eastern zone of operations, flying the Greensboro, North Carolina–Richmond, Virginia–Bolling Field, Washington, D.C., route. On 10 February 1934 the eastern zone had approximately eighty pilots to deliver the air mail. Only about thirty-five were qualified as "blind flyers," pilots capable of flying at night, but "of these, only 20 were really qualified to fly by instruments under adverse weather conditions."[53] Although Power was very experienced, he probably was not among the twenty qualified pilots mentioned. Nineteen of the twenty pilots were graduates of the Air Corps "Avigation" training school taught by the 8th Pursuit Group at Langley Field.[54] There is no record of Power being a graduate of this course, nor does Power mention it in any interviews. However, Power stated in a draft article that he was one of the first Air Corps pilots to be a rated instrument pilot, so it is possible that Power could have been the twentieth officer Major Jones observed as qualified.[55]

Seven officers and seven enlisted men were assigned to the Greensboro airport for flying the mail. Power was one of the four pilot officers assigned to fly, and he flew the northern route between Greensboro and Washington, D.C. Every other day he would take off from Greensboro at 5:30 p.m. sharp and arrive at Washington at 8:30 p.m. The next morning, Power would take off at 4:30 a.m. from Washington to arrive back in Greensboro at 7:10 a.m. Each flight could hold approximately four hundred pounds of mail. Before one flight, Power's picture was taken for a story in the *Greensboro Daily News* that described the pilot as "wearing a leather flying suit, parachute, radio-helmet, and has a flashlight strapped to one leg and a pistol to the other, just in case he meets John Dillinger in the upper regions."[56]

At the end of the operation on 1 June 1934, twelve Air Corps pilots were dead from sixty-six crashes. The reasons for these losses included poor Air Corps equipment (including open-cockpit aircraft with few instruments) and inexperienced pilots. More than half of the 260 pilots available to the Army Air Corps Mail Operation (AACMO) had less than 2 years of flying experience, only 31 had 50 hours or more of night flying time, and the overwhelming majority had less than 25 hours of weather or hood (simulated instrument) time.[57] Because Lieutenant Power had racked up more than 1,150 flying hours between February 1929 and September 1933 alone and had experience with night radio navigation flying since at least 1931, he was among the most proficient and veteran pilots of the AACMO.[58]

In a 1960 interview, Power looked back upon the AACMO fondly, telling the interviewer he did not volunteer for the operation: "We were assigned to it, but it was a big lark for us. In those days, we were for anything that was a little different. A young man likes that—he's got sand in his shoes, he's ready to go anyplace at any time."[59] Power reminisced in a later interview, "We had to fly all night, every other night, but we enjoyed it. And with all this flying, we used to play 36 holes of golf every day."[60]

Power recalled that his Douglas O-38 observation biplane had an open cockpit. He did have to fight "some pretty rough" weather, but was proud that "I always got to where I was supposed to go."[61] Power objected to his interviewer's suggestion that the AACMO was unsuccessful: "I differ with that. [AACMO] was finally called off, but we were flying our mail successfully." Power maintained that eastern zone operations were even more successful than the commercial planes because "we got through every time."[62] Facts suggest that Power was right. According to official records, of the 11,830 flights attempted in the eastern zone, there were 80 instances of forced landings or crashes due to weather, but not one piece of mail was lost or went undelivered during the entire operation,[63] and some pilots (such as Lieutenant Power) got through every single time.

Lieutenant Power's successful air mail flying led to more prestigious assignments in May 1934. His demonstrated skill landed him a position as one of the first instructors in instrument flying in the Air Corps, stationed at the new school at Langley Field.[64] The navigation school at Langley also received one of the first six Model A Link trainers, the Air Corps' first true aircraft simulator and a machine that actually taught students how to fly—far better than the Ruggles orientator that flying cadet Power had endured seven years before.[65] After this assignment at Langley, Power was promoted to the temporary grade of captain on 20 April 1935 and served as the commanding officer of the 2nd Wing Headquarters Detachment and operations officer of the 20th Bombardment Squadron.[66] However, in December 1935, after six years at Langley Field interrupted only by a few detached duties, Captain Power experienced the first permanent change of station of his career. He received orders to the 28th Bombardment Squadron and Nichols Field, Philippines in August 1935, and, relieved from his temporary rank on 28 December 1935, departed across the Pacific as a first lieutenant.[67] He arrived on station in February 1936. While at Nichols Field, Power stayed busy as the adjutant, mess, armament, and engineering officer of the squadron.

Since the U.S. occupation and annexation of the Philippines after the 1898 Spanish-American War, the Army had stationed troops there to defend Manila Bay and to conduct delaying actions against an adversary invasion, which the Army thought would likely occur around Subic Bay. The Air Corps garrison was meant to support the ground forces in their mission and specifically to conduct reconnaissance of the enemy, oppose and harass enemy attempts to establish air bases on Luzon or adjacent islands, conduct artillery spotting missions as necessary, and conduct joint operations with the Navy in destroying enemy aircraft and surface vessels.[68] The 28th was the only bombardment squadron on the island and could count on air support from only one additional observation and one pursuit squadron, which together comprised the remaining elements of the Philippine air forces.

Shortly after arriving, thirty-year-old Lieutenant Power and thirty-year-old Mae Ayre, an English woman from Newcastle-on-Tyne, were married by Presbyterian (perhaps due to Mae being a divorcée) minister George Wright in Manila on 3 April 1936. The two had met earlier when he was stationed at Langley and she was visiting Virginia. It took Mae a few months to be able to leave Virginia to join Thomas at his new assignment. However, when the ship Mae was traveling on neared the Philippines, Lieutenant Power flew out and intercepted it, dropping from his aircraft "an affectionate note of welcome" to his fiancée.[69] Mrs. Power helped care for the wives of U.S. pilots who were flying in China when they moved to the Philippines to escape the war with Japan.[70] Most of the Powers' time in the Philippines was happy. Recreation was a major interest of the Power family in the peacetime Philippines. Power was an avid outdoorsman his entire life, naming golfing, fishing, and hunting as his major pastimes. Many officers in the Philippines frequented the Motorboat and Gun Club in Manila's Bacoor Bay on weekends. One writer remarked that half of Nichols Field could be found at the club on any given Sunday.[71] Boating, sunbathing, and swimming were popular pastimes, but Power likely spent a great deal of time at the rifle and pistol range. Power regularly qualified as a military sharpshooter (as early as 1930 and regularly through 1944), and he undoubtedly kept sharp for hunting when he could. It was while in the Philippines that Power learned his sister Dorothy had married a twenty-nine-year-old future earl, Viscount David Field Beatty, son of the "hero of Jutland," Admiral of the Fleet David Richard Beatty, making her an English countess.

The 28th Bombardment Squadron's Keystone LB-5s were quite familiar to Power. The squadron's mission was training for coastal defense, and the aircrews spent most days on navigation, bomb sight training, and aerial gunnery.[72] Power took part in tow-target missions to fly targets for Fort Mills' live fire antiaircraft gunnery practice from 27 January to 23 February 1937, a task probably more exciting than most of the pilots wanted, given the open cockpit of the LB-5.[73] Training became much more interesting and fun for crews when the open cockpit biplanes were upgraded to Martin B-10s, the first all-metal monoplane bombers in the Air Corps, in late 1937.[74]

Lieutenant Power displayed some inkling of his talent for forecasting future weapons while in the Philippines. On 8 February 1937, writing from the 28th Bombardment Squadron office of the chief engineer, Power wrote to the chief of the Air Corps regarding the "Design of an Aerial Torpedo for use against Bombardment Airplanes." Power described his six-hundred-mile-per-hour, rocket-powered air torpedo as "a projectile mounted on the upper or lower surface of each wing of a pursuit airplane outside the arc of the propeller" that would "overtake a bomber from the rear and release projectile when directly behind and at such distance so as to enable pilot to dive out of danger radius of explosive."[75] Power received a letter about two months later from ordnance Lt. Col. Burton O. Lewis observing that similar rockets developed in World War I were grossly inaccurate and infeasible. Nonetheless, Air Corps Lt. Col. V. B. Dixon wrote, "Although the development of rocket propulsion does not warrant, at this time, undertaking the development of the type of torpedo you suggest, your interest in this connection is appreciated by this office."[76]

Given that *General* Power was widely assumed by historians to be against the development of the ICBM, Lieutenant Power's early application of rocket technology to warfare is significant. Power was thinking about rocketry as early as 1937. Also, that his idea was rejected primarily due to the rocket's inaccuracy is also interesting since Power's early misgivings about the ICBM as a substitute for the manned bomber were partly due to the ICBM's inaccuracy. Power's letter to the chief of the Air Corps is evidence that he was an innovative officer in both the equipment and tactical realms of air warfare. It would not be his last example of visionary thinking.

An incident in late 1937 foreshadowed Power's outspoken, hawkish demeanor during the Cold War. Power had visited Japan a number of times while in the Philippines, and the *Panay* incident on 12 December 1937—when the Japanese air force attacked the gunboat USS *Panay* and the tankers it was escorting, killing two and wounded forty-five more—prompted Power to predict war with Japan at some point. When questioned whether he saw much of Japanese aviation while in the

Philippines, Power in 1960 responded that the Japanese kept their aviation industry well hidden, but they made the result of their aviation very clear. Power could see that war with Japan was coming when he and Mae left the Philippines in 1938.[77]

Lieutenant Power's efficiency reports while in the Philippines were unquestionably the best in his early Air Force career. Rating Power superior in most categories and excellent in the rest, Maj. Lionel Dunlap wrote in 1936 that Power "is a superior squadron officer, always willing and eager to do his duty, unquestionable in his loyalty, superior in the performance of his duty, and a credit to have serve in my command."[78] Dunlap also mentioned Power was a "highly desirable candidate" for the Air Corps Tactical School. The next squadron commander, Maj. Lloyd Barnett, agreed, writing Power was "of high and exceptional value to the service."[79] Capt. Julius T. Flock wrote Power was "cheerful and courageous; fully cooperative . . . open-minded . . . visualizes future events, produces practical ideas . . . [and is of] superior character."[80]

The Powers sailed home on the transport *U.S. Grant* on 2 March 1938, traveling to Honolulu and finally reaching Tacoma, Washington, on 24 March.[81] The transport also held the U.S. Army's 15th Infantry Regiment that had been stationed in Tientsin, China, for more than thirty years. Japanese forces in Chin Wang Tao had combined massive political pressure and the threat of overwhelming military force to compel the regiment to withdraw from China. The Powers were shocked at seeing a once-proud Army unit withdraw in silent but noticeable disgrace. "The American troops came down with their tails between their legs and got on the boat which did not exactly make our spines tingle with pride," Power recalled years later. "Thus, it was quite obvious what was going on, and I came home convinced that we would be in a war real soon."[82]

Power tried to warn people in the United States to prepare for a war against Japan, but he recalled that few Americans knew of or cared about the Philippines. After six months of trying to get people to listen, his wife Mae advised, "Why don't you just give up? They don't even know what you're talking about nor are they interested!" After World War II, Power remembered a friend from Virginia told him, "You know when you visited us after you came back from the Philippines, we thought you had blown your rocker. But you were right, weren't you?"[83] It would not be the last time people thought Power was off his rocker.

After the Powers returned to the United States, Lieutenant Power was sent to Randolph Field, Texas, to begin his many years associated with flight training. On 26 February 1938 Power reported to the Air Corps Training Center to serve as an instrument instructor pilot for the primary school.[84] On 4 September 1939 he became a permanent captain. Shortly thereafter, he received orders to attend the Air Corps Tactical School (ACTS). However, due to the increasing likelihood of war, Gen. Henry "Hap" Arnold decided to suspend the regular nine-month ACTS course in favor of a twelve-week course that would number one hundred students rather than the traditional course's sixty to seventy. Air Corps officers over thirty-two years of age were considered eligible for "responsible assignments" should the Air Corps be rapidly expanded, and 425 officers were identified in this group (Power among them) that were not ACTS graduates.[85] While the plan helped educate as many senior officers as possible, the drawbacks to the abbreviated scheme were significant. The total number of student education hours decreased from 712 to 298, meaning the course merely presented students with "the Air Force picture for a fundamentally sound basis of employment" because there was not enough time for anything else.[86]

The ninety-nine students that began the last class ever graduated from ACTS mustered on Monday morning, 8 April 1940, to attend opening ceremonies that were described as "inauspicious." For three months Power and his classmates were taught abbreviated classes on subjects including air force, attack, bombardment, pursuit, reconnaissance, naval operations, combat orders, communications, logistics, military intelligence, staff duties, observation, antiaircraft, cavalry, chemical warfare, ground tactics, field artillery, infantry, and map reading.[87] In ACTS commander Col. M. F. Harmon's efficiency report for Captain Power, Harmon wrote he knew Power only "slightly" and that there was "insufficient observation to determine flying efficiency, special aptitude, or suitable training for high command and General Staff duty." Power's rating as an ACTS student was "Excellent (Graduate)."[88] Of note, Power stands out in his Section "B-1" ACTS graduation photo as being in the dead center of the photo with a large, bushy moustache that he wore until 1944.[89]

The students could not have helped but be underwhelmed by their experiences at ACTS. This may have influenced Power enough to shed some light on why he resisted the release of many Strategic Air Command officers to attend professional military education while he was in command. However, it might also have been Power's disregard for professional military education that caused him to almost miss ACTS altogether.[90] Power never seemed to mention ACTS, as many Air Force founding fathers did later in their careers. What seems clear is that in ACTS historical material written after the school's closing, Thomas Power is not included as a distinguished graduate, though he surely became the most successful member of the last class at the venerable institution. No other student in his class had nearly as much of an impact on the U.S. Air Force.

With diploma in hand, Captain Power went back to Randolph Field to instruct new flyers. Presaging his later interest in movies as promotional tools for the Air Force, Power was one of a group of officers that assisted Paramount Pictures in its 22 March 1941 preview of *I Wanted Wings*, his friend Beirne Lay's semi-autobiographical story of early Army pilot training at Randolph Field.[91] Many of Power's early performance reports indicated that he had the charisma and professional bearing suitable "for any and all civilian contacts or duties."[92] Now, Power had begun to be assigned these duties.

On 15 April 1941 Power was promoted to major.[93] Sensing impending war, the Army activated the West Coast Air Corps Training Center at Moffitt Field, California. Major Power was sent there to serve as assistant S-3 (operations) in May 1941, "just setting up the staff, the staff positions, and operations."[94]

This assignment was short lived. On 7 December 1941 the United States entered World War II, and the gigantic expansion of the Air Corps into the Army Air Forces commenced. One of Major Power's first duties in the war, in accordance with his efficiency reports noting his charisma and ability to work with civilians, was to appear on the "Kraft Music Hall"

show with Bing Crosby on 22 January 1942 to outline the new requirements for aviation cadets to help a recruiting drive.[95] Maj. Gen. Barton
Kyle Yount, the commander of the West Coast Air Corps Training Center,
was summoned to Washington and ordered to establish the Army Air
Forces Training Command (AAFTC) at Fort Worth, Texas. General
Yount brought Power along to Washington and then to Fort Worth in
February 1942. At AAFTC on 17 November 1942, Power became a lieutenant colonel and served as an air inspector until December. Power
was promoted to colonel on 26 June 1943 and served as training and
inspection officer until 1 August. Power concurrently was chief of the
non-pilot section and became familiar with the art of radar navigation,
which suited his technical and inquisitive nature. He was named assistant
chief of staff of the command until a new assignment took him to Salina,
Kansas, on 1 September.[96]

Yount appears to be the force that placed Power on a command track
in the Air Force. In Power's first efficiency report, Yount rated "Special
Staff Officer" Colonel Power as superior in leadership, handling of men,
and administration, writing that "with all other officers of his grade and
component known to me, I would place him in the upper third" and
that Power was "a most valuable officer for important command or staff
responsibilities in the Army Air Forces."[97] Six months later, Yount added
Power was a "diplomatic, zealous, accomplished, painstaking, and effi-
cient officer" and "one of the finest young officers in the air force."[98] Power
remembered with pride that Yount (who after the war opened up the
Thunderbird School of International Management in Arizona) had built
AAFTC "up from practically nothing to about a million and a half men."[99]
It was probably due to Power's influence that the first officer honored in
Strategic Air Command *Combat Crew* magazine's "Men Who Built the
Air Force" column was Lt. Gen. Barton K. Yount.

Colonel Power finally entered a combat flying unit on 1 September
1943 as deputy group commander of the 40th Bombardment Group
(Very Heavy) under Col. Lewis R. Parker in the 58th Bombardment
Wing, where he continued to study radar navigation with B-29 crews.

However, he was quickly reassigned to Colorado Springs, posted to A-3 (Operations) and later assistant chief of staff of the 2nd Air Force under Brig. Gen. Uzal Girard Ent from 1 October 1943 to 13 January 1944.[100] The 2nd Air Force's responsibility was to train crews for the B-29 "Superbombers" as the "Combat College of the Air."[101]

Power flourished under General Ent as much as he had under General Yount. Ent rated Power superior as air inspector, deputy commander of the 40th Bomb Group, and assistant chief of staff, A-3. Ent declared Power a "forceful and capable officer, thoroughly familiar with all phases of heavy bombardment training . . . extremely intelligent and enthusiastic about his work" and possessed of "sound original ideas."[102]

Power was in awe of the B-29 and became one of the best instructors in the 2nd Air Force, especially in the early field of radar bombing techniques, but he longed for a combat role. He got his chance when he was assigned to the 304th Bombardment Wing (Heavy) and found himself on 2 March 1944 in North Africa.

Upon arrival in the Mediterranean in March, Power became the executive officer of the B-24 wing flying out of North Africa and Italy, commanded by Brig. Gen. Fay R. Upthegrove.[103] The day Power arrived, the 304th was engaged in air support of Allied troops at their beachhead in Anzio.[104] While in North Africa, Power and his wing "operated a regular pattern from there against Ploesti and other targets."[105] Power missed the first infamous low-level raid against Ploesti on 1 August but had been over Ploesti "several times" by the time he left the 304th. "It was a pretty sporty course down there," Power recalled, "and we used to get shot up quite regularly along about that time." The 304th had little fighter escort, and Ploesti was very well defended with fighters and heavy antiaircraft batteries. Power remembered that missions "used to get quite rough. We lost a lot of airplanes over Ploesti but I was lucky. We had a hell of a lot of holes in the airplane every time we would go over there but, as long as they didn't hit you, you were all right."[106]

Many of Power's other missions with the 304th were also difficult but more obscure, bombing marshalling yards and airfields. Some were "staff officer raids" around northern Italy that were reasonably safe. Some, however, were deep into Germany and Austria, and "you had a good fight on your hands, going in and coming out." Around Vienna in particular there were many German fighters. Power remembered that the raids he took part in against Wiener Neustadt's "big aircraft factories," where almost half of German single-seat fighter production was taking place in 1944, would "generally be a pretty hot ride."[107]

Colonel Power was named deputy wing commander on 21 April and served with the 304th until 14 August 1944, when he transitioned from B-24s in the Mediterranean to B-29s in the Pacific.[108] In the few months with the 304th Bombardment Wing, Colonel Power played his small part in turning the Fifteenth Air Force into a crack bombing unit, specializing in striking oil and transportation, while also racking up scores against fighter production facilities, with bombing accuracy even better than the mighty Eighth Air Force.[109] Back at headquarters, Power also became the batting star of the wing officers' softball team.[110] Ultimately, his efforts in the Fifteenth Air Force helped to destroy the Luftwaffe in the East, robbed over half of Germany's oil supplies, and dented—but could not end—the dominance of the 304th Wing's enlisted softball team.[111]

General Upthegrove rated Power superior in his duties as both executive officer and deputy wing commander, placing him in the upper third of his officer group. Upthegrove specifically mentioned Power was an "unusually well-rounded officer, both personally and professionally."[112] Power also received decorations for his activities with the 304th Wing. He received the Air Medal for meritorious achievement in aerial flight from 15 March 1944, his first combat mission (against Cassino, Italy), to 20 April 1944, his last mission (against Monfalcone in northern Italy) as wing executive officer.[113] Power also received the Distinguished Flying Cross for leading a wing formation to bomb Budapest, Hungary, on 13 April 1944, where the formation encountered heavy flak and attack from twenty to thirty Axis fighters without Allied fighter escort.[114]

Colonel Power arrived back to Peterson Field in Colorado Springs on 23 August 1944, where he took command of the 314th Bombardment Wing (Very Heavy) on 28 August.[115] The wing consisted of four B-29 groups (19th, 29th, 39th, and 330th Bombardment Groups) training in Colorado Springs and Salina, Kansas. Colonel Power wasted no time in explaining his command philosophy and what he expected the 314th to do when they left for the Pacific. In a staff meeting with his wing's senior officers on 1 September, Power stressed four important points. First, he implored his men never to lose their sense of humor. Second, Power told his men never to be afraid of making mistakes: "It is more important to do something and do it wrong than not to do anything at all." Next, Power explained loyalty begins at the top, and that his loyalty to the wing was unwavering. Lastly, Power emphasized that the 314th was going to fight by dropping bombs on the enemy. "As long as we are doing that," Power reasoned, "we are doing a good job."[116]

After this meeting, Power went to Salina, Kansas, for three days "in connection with a critique of maneuvers."[117] Power no doubt assisted the units in Salina with his special skills in advanced training in the B-29, for which he had been developing a reputation for some time. Perhaps in response to what he saw in Salina, on 4 September he exhorted his wing's officers in a staff meeting that, as commanding officer, he expected everyone in the wing to become "radar-minded."[118]

The wing departed Peterson Field for Guam on 9 December 1944 with an intermediate stop at Hamilton Field, California. On 16 January 1945 forward echelons arrived at Guam, hopping to North Field a day later. Power and his deputy chief of staff for operations, Col. Hewitt T. Wheless, arrived on North Field on 25 January.

North Field, which later became Anderson Air Force Base, was a disaster. LeMay wrote that when Power arrived, "The only thing [Navy Seabees] had built for him was a coral airstrip down through the jungle. He and his airmen slept on that, the first night they arrived." They had to clear space for their tents the next day using only pocket knives; there were no other tools available.[119] Power and his men improved the North Field airstrip well enough for a B-24 to land on it on 3 February. Five days later, LeMay personally landed the first B-29 on the strip, with the 19th and 29th Groups landing shortly after. Any disappointment for having to build the 314th's home from scratch was partially alleviated when Power was promoted to brigadier general on 22 January 1945 (he was notified on 15 February), as he was preparing his wing to enter the fight against Japan.[120]

On 25 February the 314th Bombardment Wing flew over Tokyo for the first time.[121] It did not go well. Washington had asked the XXI Bomber Command to "put on a big effort" against Japan, but as of 20 February Power's wing had only twenty-five airplanes. The mission required skipping the normal shakedown flights for the planes and crew familiarization training phase typical with a new wing. The anticipated 25 February raid required at least twenty B-29s to fill the bombing formation, and the 314th flew twenty-four of its twenty-five crews in support.[122] Beyond that, the 314th's crews had the longest routes to fly of all the XXI Bomber Command by 250 to 300 miles, and there was some concern that the distance was simply too far and that some or all bombers would run out of fuel during the flight. In addition, the mission was hampered by poor weather from the beginning. Power recalled that at the rendezvous area, "The weather got worse and worse, and we went down lower and lower [to find clear sky], and finally we were flying right on the deck. It was pouring so hard, you couldn't see your hand in front of your face, and pretty soon airplanes started going by in every direction."[123] Realizing the danger of collisions, Power ordered his wing to begin climbing. The weather cleared at 15,000 feet. "When we popped out," Power remembered, "I found that, instead of having the people on my wings that I had started out with, I had only one wing man and about 30 airplanes, including some from other units. So we formed up again and kept on climbing." Eventually it began to snow, forcing Power to bomb Tokyo from 25,000 to 28,000 feet using radar bombing techniques.[124]

Of all the hundreds of airplanes that started out, only Power's thirty bombers reached Tokyo. Their payloads were incendiary bombs. It was the first time firebombs had been dropped on Tokyo. The weather forced the crews to rely entirely on radar bombing, and no one saw the city at all. The raid was fraught with difficulty and did not run according to plan, but the 314th Wing had been able to deliver the first of their bombs to Japan.[125]

The 25 February mission was a fiasco, but it was the genesis of perhaps one of the most daring bombing missions of World War II, with Power firmly in the lead both intellectually and physically. A few days after the raid, reconnaissance photos revealed that the bombing had, in Power's words, "destroyed about a square mile because the city was covered with snow, and you could see the blackened square mile in the pictures. *This is what gave me the idea of mass bombing and of coming in low.*"[126]

When studying the reconnaissance pictures of the 25 February raid, Power began to wonder what the damage would have been had they attacked Tokyo with a heavier bomb load and at lower altitude. Power and Wheless took the 314th Wing's specialized expertise in radar (which Power developed through recruiting the best aircrews from his time in Kansas) and developed a low-altitude flight path to Tokyo using radar landmarks. Using radar for both navigation and bombing was critical because the spring weather in Japan would get progressively worse. That meant all B-29s would increasingly rely on radar. Weather would likely preclude both accurate navigation and visual bombing, but radar navigation and the unique effectiveness of incendiary bombs for area bombing—the only type of radar bombing possible—required a new way of prosecuting the strategic air war against Japan.[127] Power and Wheless believed they had come up with the solution. "*We would not try to use our bomb-sights at all,*" Power emphasized.[128] Once over Tokyo, the formation would spread their bombers "like the leaves of a fan" and have each bomber drop its incendiary bombs at a specific time in order to get "an automatic spread."

After a few days, LeMay heard of the studies Power and Wheless were developing. Late one night, LeMay walked to the Dallas hut that Power and Wheless shared. It was almost two in the morning, but LeMay found Power on the porch. "Tom, what's all this talk about fire-bomb raids?" he queried. Power immediately started detailing what they had been working on. Wheless was eventually woken up, and the three men discussed the details of the plan. LeMay was impressed with the viability of the low-level incendiary raid and gave Power and Wheless twenty-four hours to clean it up and present the plan to the XXI Bomber Command planners.[129]

After working out the basics of the plan, they presented it to LeMay, who replied, "Looks good to me. Work it up with the Operations people and see what they think of it." After working with XXI Bomber Command's planning staff, including John Montgomery and Dave Burchinal, Power's and Wheless' plan was approved by LeMay, who ordered five such attacks, "one right after another" to form a weighted effort.[130]

The generally accepted history of World War II credits Curtis LeMay for the idea of low-level firebombing of Japanese cities. There is little doubt that LeMay had decided upon mass incendiary raids of Japanese cities as early as 15 February 1945, when he requested Brig. Gen. Lauris Norstad visit the XXI Bomber Command headquarters on Guam to discuss LeMay's new direction personally. But the low-level incendiary attacks also showcase Thomas Power as an operational tactician and innovator of the highest order.

Montgomery approached St. Clair McKelway, a *New Yorker* essayist on the island, who reported that the new mission was to have four major characteristics: the bombers would fly in at low level, five thousand to six thousand feet; they would carry nothing but incendiaries; they would carry six tons of incendiaries in each bomber; and the raids would be staged every two nights. But McKelway credited LeMay for the plan, not Power. He said that Power and Montgomery were in favor of the plan while most others in the command were not, but this was Power's only mention in McKelway's article about the raid he published.[131] Perhaps because of McKelway's reporting, history portrays this plan as the LeMay plan, and Power was simply the man who flew it. Richard Frank writes that "the outstanding feature in the plan incubating in LeMay's mind was the attack altitude . . . by far the most radical part of the plan."[132] Warren Kozak credits Power with developing the low-altitude idea but simultaneously suggests that Power was brought in to help plan the mission only because he was chosen to lead it: "His decision [to attack Japan with incendiaries] made, LeMay worked on the problem with Tom Power who would lead such a mission."[133]

Kozak's account is most likely precisely backward. Power had only been to Tokyo once before, on a mission that was mostly a failure, and he was the least experienced wing commander on Guam at the time. LeMay would not have chosen Power to lead the mission based solely on his record thus far or on his support for the plan. LeMay would have preferred to lead the mission himself, but "they wouldn't let me lead that one. I had to send Tommy Power instead. I was relegated to walk the floor at XXI Bomber Command headquarters."[134] It made sense to send the man most familiar with the plan, the man who had originally taken it to him, if LeMay could not himself go. The 9 March firebombing of Japan should be considered as much Power's idea as LeMay's.

With Power's and Wheless' plan developed, suitably modified by LeMay and his staff, XXI Bomber Command issued the order on 7 March 1945 to commence mission Meetinghouse Two. On 9 May LeMay went to the 314th Wing briefing area to attend Power's briefing of the experimental and dangerous mission. Meetinghouse Two was planned to put three hundred B-29s from the three wings of the XXI Bomber Command over Tokyo at low level armed with nothing but incendiary bombs. Ralph Nutter, a navigator on LeMay's staff at the time, captured the scene of the mission briefing in his outstanding memoir. Nutter remembered the crews did not know that the mission would be at low altitude until the meeting. Power told his startled crews, "I know this comes as a surprise to you, but it's going to be more of a surprise to the Japanese!"[135] Power chose low-level bombardment in part because Japan had neither antiaircraft guns with radar capable of tracking aircraft at altitudes below seven thousand feet, nor an effective night fighter capability. This meant Power could remove the machine guns and gunners on the B-29s, lessening the strain on aircraft engines and allowing more bombers to return home safely.[136]

There was near rebellion in the briefing room. LeMay sat motionless, smoking his cigar. Power, however, took command of the room and explained the mission's changes to the crews, who were very unreceptive. "I would not lead this mission and we would not be sending you if we thought it was an unreasonable risk," Power argued. He stressed that LeMay, who had the lowest losses of any air combat commander in Europe or Asia, agreed with Power's plan.[137]

Power argued the XXI Bomber Command had lost more crews from engine and mechanical failure than from Japanese opposition. Many of those losses were caused by the strain on the engines from climbing to high altitude. "With the lighter loads and in the cover of darkness, you can fly over Tokyo and get the hell out of there with the least strain on the engines," he explained. "We have to face reality. There's no advantage to be gained by continuing to bomb at high altitude and keep returning to the same targets again and again. More missions mean more losses. This is a plan to quickly defeat the Japanese."[138] Power concluded by saying this was "the most important mission of the war. Success will mean that our troops may not have to invade Japan. I know you all have the guts to make this mission a success."[139]

At the end of his appeal, Power turned to LeMay and asked, "Would you like to make any comments, sir?" LeMay shook his head—"No, you said it all much better than I could"—and left the room. Some of the crews were reassured by Power. Others were frightened. Others were angry.[140] Regardless, the 314th Bombardment Wing, Thomas Power in the lead, took off on the evening of 9 March 1945 toward Tokyo.

Despite Power's assurances, the mission was so novel that no one really knew how dangerous it would be, and that made it very risky. It sounded crazy. With flak and enemy fighters, low-flying bombers were sitting ducks. Without their machine guns, the bombers were also defenseless. Given the great physical risk to the crews and the high political risk for failure, Norstad—as Gen. Hap Arnold's agent—might have sacked LeMay on the spot if the crews sustained heavy casualties. These risks were probably why LeMay took such heavy responsibility for the decision to order this mission. LeMay remembered, "We might lose over three hundred aircraft [the mission used 325] and some three thousand veteran personnel in this attack. It might go into history as LeMay's Last Brainstorm."[141]

"LeMay's Last Brainstorm" may have been a rhetorical flourish added by LeMay's ghost writer, MacKinlay Kantor, rather than something the general himself said; Kantor was known to do this, the most famous being the "We're going to bomb them back to the Stone Age" quote.[142] "LeMay's Last Brainstorm" is certainly less bombastic than Kantor's other fabrication, but it may have assisted in writing Power's genius out of the development of the 9 March mission.

When Power's plane reached Tokyo, he radioed a terse update to LeMay: "Weather clear. Bombing visually."[143] Forty-nine of the 314th's fifty-one aircraft that reached Japan bombed Tokyo. Power's lead plane carried no bombs and was strictly used for observation before, during, and after the attack. Seven of the bombers carried 122 100-pound M-47A2 incendiary bombs fused to explode on impact and, combined, they dropped 830 on their primary target. The remaining aircraft were armed with 20 to 24 500-pound E-46 incendiary clusters each, primed to burst and scatter at 2,500 feet above the target. The 314th dropped approximately 950 of these incendiary clusters, causing an extraordinary firestorm.[144] Power's bomber was the first to arrive and the last to leave.[145] He was over the target for about an hour and fifty-five minutes total, and he and his intelligence officer, Col. Harry Besse, sketched pictures of what was happening to the city below. It only took fourteen minutes from the first dropped bomb for the firestorm to erupt. The destruction was shaped like a rectangle three miles wide and five miles long. Although the searchlights were active and there was a great deal of flak, there were few fighters. The low-level attack worked, though the Japanese were able to retaliate with heavy antiaircraft fire.[146]

Power circled the city as LeMay ordered, observing the attack as best he could. He had a hard time controlling his airplane due to the updrafts from the firestorm below. His pilots at lower altitudes were facing much worse. Capt. Gordon B. Robertson of the 29th Bombardment Group, blinded by the glare of a searchlight at 5,600 feet after he released his bombs, was hit by an updraft that rolled his plane and battered the B-29 "like a cork on water in a hurricane."[147] Some B-29s were lifted five thousand feet by the firestorm below. Eventually, Power and Besse estimated that about fifteen square miles had been burned out. A more detailed study afterward concluded that the actual total was seventeen.[148] Power claimed that "that fire raid was the most destructive single military action in the history of the world."[149] He compared his formation dropping tens of thousands of bombs to "a giant pouring out a big shovel full of white hot coals all over the ground, covering about an area of about 2,500 feet in length and some 500 feet wide—that's what each single B-29 was doing!" And there were over three hundred airplanes. The individual bombs started fires everywhere but, since Tokyo was highly flammable, the fires eventually ran together into one single hellish inferno.[150] Later, Power said of the Tokyo mission, "It was the greatest single disaster incurred by any enemy in military history. It was greater than the combined damage of Hiroshima and Nagasaki. There were more casualties than in any other military action in the history of the world."[151]

Power landed at North Field at 8:30 a.m. on 10 March. LeMay, Norstad, and Wheless were there to meet him. The general came down, unshaven, wearing aviator sunglasses, a crushed mission cap, and a ragged, sweat-soaked uniform with a .45-caliber Model 1911 pistol on a shoulder holster. "It looks good," he told LeMay.[152] Of the 325 planes launched, 14 had been lost to accident or enemy action, less than 5 percent losses. Ninety fliers died that night; six more captured were later killed. Of the losses, Power's group suffered the most: nine of his fifty-four bombers went down.[153] Japanese casualties were 84,000 killed, 40,000 injured, and 1.1 million people homeless.[154] Power's conclusion: "It was a hell of a good mission."[155] LeMay looked at the sketches. Power and his men had proved the feasibility of low-altitude incendiary raids, prosecuting immense destruction with acceptable losses to aircrew. LeMay ordered more of the incendiary missions.

For his lead role on the 9 March raid, Power was awarded the Silver Star. His citation, dated 14 March 1945, cited his "bravery, skill, efficiency, and scorn for his personal safety . . . while participating in the greatest mass flight of B-29s ever dispatched against a single target."[156] Over the next few days, the 314th launched similar incendiary raids against Nagoya (Microscope 2, 11–12 March 1945), Osaka (Peachblow 1, 13–14 March 1945), Kobe (Middleman 2, 16–17 March 1945), the Mitsubishi aircraft engine plant at Nagoya (twice—Eradicate 5, 24–25 March 1945, and Eradicate 6, 30–31 March 1945), Kanoya airfield (Fearless 1, 27 March 1945), and Omura airfield (Fearless 2, 31 March 1945).[157] The 314th was hitting Japan not only hard, but also with extraordinary efficiency. In the nineteen days of extraordinary duty by the 314th since their first combat mission, the wing's ground crews ensured that not one aircraft was grounded for parts in the entire effort, a feat of which Power was extremely proud.[158]

On 20 March 1945, after driving his wing to near exhaustion with almost two weeks of nonstop missions, Power wrote a special commendation for the wing. "We have just finished eleven days of all-out effort. The result of this effort has made history. Terrific damage has been inflicted on the enemy's vital manufacturing and shipping centers. Your effort has shortened the war and saved American lives. . . . Your tireless effort and fighting spirit have exemplified the highest traditions of our armed forces. . . . I am humbly proud to be your Commander."[159]

Thomas Stack wrote a letter to his son on 7 March 1945 praising the heights he had attained: "I am not inclined to give praise, but I want you to know I am very proud of you." Perhaps regretting his own actions years earlier, he continued, "You have climbed the mountain side strictly on your own. It was steep and rough. The only help you received was inherent in yourself. . . . You have reached the plateau at the mountain top and I am sure you will establish yourself there in a magnificent way." Concluding, Thomas Stack wished Tommy "the very best of luck and a good road to Tokyo. Write as soon as you can. Dad."[160] Thomas Stack could not have known when he was writing that Tommy had already been to Tokyo, nor that his son destroyed the city a mere seventy-two hours later.

On 12 April 1945 personal tragedy struck the Power family on Guam. Aircraft commander 1st Lt. Robert Ziegele, Kathleen Power's son and Thomas Power's nephew, was flying his B-29 back to Guam. Ziegele had been assigned to the 330th Bombardment Group in his uncle's wing. Ziegele's first mission had been a long trip in very poor weather. Consequently, the group's bombers were dangerously low on fuel. The weather had gotten worse around Guam, and Harmon Field visibility was poor. Due to the harried pace of the 314th Wing upon reaching the Pacific, many of the field's improvements were not yet completed, including adequate airstrip lighting for use during poor weather flying. On final approach, due to a combination of heavy weather, poor visibility, and his unfamiliarity with Harmon Field, Ziegele crashed. He and nine others in his crew were killed on their very first mission; a single man survived.

It is likely Power was at the airstrip waiting to congratulate his nephew on his first successful mission. Instead, Power witnessed his nephew's tragic death. Clearly distraught, Power tried to contact his sister Kathleen to tell her personally but was unable to connect via telephone. Lauris Norstad agreed to reach Kathleen as soon as he got back to the states. Norstad passed a message from Power to Lieutenant Ziegele's young wife in Colorado Springs, personally sent a letter to Kathleen, and was able to talk to her husband over the phone.[161]

Right after Ziegele's crash, Power ordered a complete suite of all-weather landing lights to be installed on the North Field immediately. It was a flight safety lesson Power learned painfully through the loss of kindred blood.

Power continued to lead his wing until he was relieved of his command on 23 July 1945 and assigned as director of operations on Gen. Carl Spaatz's staff at United States Strategic Air Forces in the Pacific on 1 August. LeMay later called Power "the best wing commander I had on Guam," though at the time he described Power as a "truly outstanding officer" and ranked him his number two of six general officers.[162] Upon learning Power would be transferred to Spaatz's staff, LeMay wrote Power a personal letter of commendation, which ended prophetically, "It is my earnest hope that there will be other opportunities in the future to serve in the same command."[163]

Reflecting on his experience with the 314th Bombardment Wing in the introduction to Gene Gurney's book about the B-29, *Journey of the Giants,* in 1961, Power stated the Strategic Air Command was born in the Pacific:

> Just as the B-17s and B-24s in the World War II European Theater helped develop the original concepts of strategic air warfare as we know them today, B-29 operations in the Pacific led to the development of many of the basic techniques and tactics which are reflected

in the evolution of modern strategic aerospace power. . . . the invaluable lessons learned with the B-29s . . . in attacks from very high to very low levels, radar-bombing, massive fire raids, and atom-bomb drops, to name but a few—are still put to good use in maintaining the free world's most powerful deterrent to aggression.[164]

Power was in charge of operations within Spaatz's staff during the planning and execution of the atomic bomb missions against Hiroshima and Nagasaki.[165] Power did not take any direct role in these attacks, but he would soon come to know nuclear weapons quite well. His sixteen days of wartime service with Spaatz were short but extremely eventful. As operations officer, he would have known of Olympic, the planned amphibious invasion of Japan with a target date of 1 November.[166] However, on 6 August Hiroshima was destroyed in the first wartime use of atomic weapons, followed three days later by a second atomic attack on Nagasaki. On 15 August 1945 the Japanese surrendered, and the war was over. Overall, from 5 June 1944 to 14 August 1945, B-29s dropped a total of 169,421 tons of bombs and mines on Japan in 32,612 sorties.[167]

Power was not allowed leave between his time in Italy and the Pacific, and he was excited to get home and finally see his wife Mae. Before he could depart for the United States in December 1945, his leave was abruptly canceled. He was instead ordered to Washington, D.C., where he again met Curtis LeMay, by then chief of research and development on the air staff. LeMay told Power that he was now the assistant deputy task force commander for air of Joint Task Force One under Adm. William H. Blandy.[168] Power's first day back in the United States was spent sitting in a meeting regarding Operation Crossroads, a series of atomic bomb tests to be held at Bikini Atoll. A few days later—with Mae still wondering when he would be home—Power joined the rest of Joint Task Force One on Kwajalein. Even though the war had been over for almost six months, Power still had not seen his wife.

As assistant deputy task force commander for air, Power was the airborne commander for the small air flotilla assembled for the atomic bomb tests, coordinating all of the seventy airplanes supporting the tests.

"There was a great deal of instrumentation, on ships and on shore and in the air, and the cloud cover had to be just right," he recalled.[169]

The Able shot, the first atomic explosion since Nagasaki, was dropped from the B-29 *Dave's Dream* on 1 July 1946. The underwater Baker shot, which produced the eponymous photograph of Operation Crossroads, was detonated on 25 July. Viewing both explosions in person was deeply moving for Power. He described his awe in an understated way, but the bomb's impact on him was unmistakable, and the explosions "made an even greater impression on me, compared with the previous bombings I had seen."[170]

Power was released from Crossroads in August and, after some much-needed and well-deserved leave, he was assigned on 14 September 1946 to the air staff working for chief of staff for operations, Gen. Earle E. Partridge, Power's former tactical school instructor, as his assistant for operations. On 27 May 1948 the commander of United States Air Forces Europe, Curtis LeMay, convinced the secretary of the Air Force to order Power to report to Frankfurt, Germany, two days later for temporary duty of approximately thirty days "in connection with USAF matters."[171] While in Frankfurt, on 15 June 1948 Power was assigned as the first ever USAF air attaché to the U.S. Embassy in London, England.[172] On 9 July 1948 General and Mrs. Power were on board the *Queen Mary* bound for Southampton, England. The Powers arrived on 14 July.[173] The job started with a bang. "I was actually on a special mission. . . . This was about the time when the Berlin Airlift started, and we brought in B-29s. It was actually a fighting force that we set up on British bases, a SAC force. I handled all the arrangements in connection with that," Power explained.[174] Power's Frankfurt duty was probably LeMay's way to gear up Power for his British assignment, which also ended abruptly. On 19 October, less than four months into Power's assignment, LeMay sent for Power once again—this time to be the SAC deputy commander.

After he arrived at SAC headquarters in Offutt Air Force Base in Omaha, Nebraska, Power got his former secretary in London a pay raise and sent the family of his former chief of staff Col. John Ackerman a Smithfield ham, which Mrs. Ackerman said the family missed most about not being home.[175] Power also indicated that he may have understood he had a poor reputation and lamented it when writing to Colonel Ackerman. "Thanks . . . for passing on the nice things people said about me. There is no sense in being coy about it—one does enjoy hearing a kind word. People have a nasty habit of keeping them quiet and just telling the nasty things people say about you," he wrote to his friend.[176]

By 28 October 1948 Power was deputy commander of SAC. This is where his reputation of being cold, mean, and potentially unbalanced really began. Thomas Coffey perhaps best summarizes the traditional view of Power's role in SAC as LeMay's deputy commander: "As his deputy commander he chose Tom Power, a man so cold, hard, and demanding that several of his colleagues and subordinates have flatly described him as sadistic. LeMay himself, when asked if Power was actually a sadist, said, 'He was. He was sort of an aristocratic bastard,' but 'He got things done.'"[177]

Hewitt Wheless, SAC deputy director of operations under Power, offered a different interpretation of Power at SAC. Wheless described Power as "the guy that saw black and white. There were very few gray areas where he was concerned." More interestingly, Wheless recalled, "LeMay had the reputation, but Power was the toughest guy I ever knew because when he said something be done a certain way once a decision was made, he made sure you did it." Power, to Wheless, was not hardheaded: "If [someone] disagreed 100 percent with the boss he could speak his piece." However, once LeMay or Power made a decision, any disagreement thereafter "fails as far as Power was concerned." After a decision was made, "that was an order, there was no compromise. . . . He was that tough a guy."[178]

Wheless stressed that Power was responsible for watching wing commanders very closely and making sure that they were following policy, and that he became a hatchet man only when needed. When changes needed to be made, "Power carried them out and he saw that all these correctives were carried out in detail. . . . Many Wing Commanders were fired because they didn't carry it out the way it was supposed to be, and that was Power." However, Wheless had nothing but respect and admiration for his friend and commander. "Power was a great man," Wheless concluded, "Wonderful."[179]

As strong as Power's reputation as LeMay's "hatchet man" at SAC is, much evidence exists that running across Power was not always as dangerous as some feared. On 2 December 1953 Power wrote a character reference letter to the disciplinary board for a SAC wing commander who had lost a folder of classified documents in Germany. Power's comments may have been worth a great deal, since no adverse action made it into the commander's personnel file.[180]

In addition to his administrative role observing commanders, Power was also responsible for overall SAC crew health. Power helped bring judo to the United States by making it the centerpiece of the SAC fitness regime. Power sent SAC enlisted men to Japan to become judo instructors to keep combat crews in shape. Power also personally studied judo under Emilio "Mel" Bruno, a founder of judo in the United States and the first non-Asian fifth-degree judo black belt, eventually earning the rank of fourth-degree black belt. Judo helped Power in uniform. He sometimes intimidated visitors by offering to work out with them on the judo mat.

Power was promoted to major general in December 1948, and for two years he helped LeMay transform SAC into a legendary military force. However, in early August 1950 Power was sent to Guam on a quick three-day trip to gain "a better insight" into airpower problems in the Korean War.[181] Power's visit was noted in Gen. George Stratemeyer's diary on 6 August 1950.[182] In fact, Power had been sent as the SAC X-Ray commander, in charge of SAC atomic forces in the Far East.[183] His job on this trip was to oversee the deployment of the 9th Bombardment Wing on a "training mission" to Guam and perhaps Okinawa. The 9th Wing carried enough nuclear cores to complete nine bombs, for use if the North Koreans began to advance too quickly into South Korea for conventional forces to handle. Power's trip was so sensitive that when the Air Staff noticed that a congressional delegation would be at Guam at the same time, they gave direct orders to Power to "be missing."[184]

Power's own full command came soon. By early 1954 SAC had become the world-class strike force LeMay and Power had envisioned. Aiming to groom his trusted deputy for further command, LeMay positioned Power to be promoted to lieutenant general and given command of the Air Research and Development Command, an important organization in the technologically intensive Cold War. After serving as LeMay's deputy for almost a decade from Guam to Nebraska, Power was about to take major command himself.

Exploring Power's life and career before he became a caricature helps illuminate him as he really was. The standard narrative of Power being uneducated and mean-spirited is not based on lies. He was the last general officer without a college degree; there is no evidence he even graduated high school; he had an ordinary, perhaps modest, career before becoming LeMay's deputy at SAC; and he could be very demanding of subordinates.

However, this is not Power's complete story. What the caricature leaves out is that Power, through pure perseverance, taught himself the equivalent of two years of college through studying alone, at night, for a handful of weeks, and excelled on the Air Corps entrance exam that most candidates failed. Though his early career focused on flying, Power also displayed a keen and experienced technical mind. Power was an insightful and innovative tactician, both as a lieutenant who had developed a concept of operations for an air-to-air missile using chemical rockets, and as a heavy bomb wing commander who developed most of the low-altitude incendiary tactics that brought Japan to its knees. Although often taciturn, he was not always the merciless hatchet man detractors claim. Power's human portrayal offers a different view of the man beyond a Cold War cartoon villain. Considering Power as a complex man—with positive and negative traits, as all people have—alone makes his extraordinarily important contributions to the Air Force much more believable.

CHAPTER 3

Constructing the Aerospace Force

————— •••• —————

Air Research and Development Command, 1954–57

When Lt. Gen. Thomas S. Power gained his third star and his own command, he had been SAC deputy commander for six years. On 15 April 1954 he took command of Air Research and Development Command (ARDC) in Baltimore, Maryland. Although he had been indispensable in SAC as LeMay's deputy, Power had not commanded a unit since his time with the 314th Bombardment Wing on Guam. The ARDC mission was to "attain and maintain qualitative superiority of material and to conduct or supervise scientific and technical studies required for the accomplishment of the Air Force missions." This included seeking "new basic knowledge from which improved aeronautical equipment, materiel, weapons, and techniques can be developed." Finally, the command developed "complete weapon systems, techniques, and procedures applicable to Air Force purposes."[1]

Power was no stranger to the importance of new technology. In addition to personnel matters, as SAC deputy commander, Power also had responsibilities for SAC requirements. One of these requirements was to prepare for a long-range strategic bomber follow-on to the B-52. Development of the intercontinental ballistic missile and the hydrogen bomb led some defense planners to believe the manned bomber had ceased to be a cost-effective or militarily effective platform. SAC disagreed, but no bomber besides the aircraft nuclear power experiment was yet planned or in development.[2] On 30 March 1953 Power wrote to the director of requirements, Headquarters USAF, that "regardless of the missile program, it is the opinion of this headquarters that the continued advance in the art of manned flight to high altitudes and long ranges should be at all times a priority objective of the Air Force's development programs."[3] Power's letter began the B-70 Valkyrie Mach 3 bomber program, which he would manage as ARDC commander.

Power assumed command of ARDC at a critical time that was highly advantageous to SAC. By 1954 the ballistic missile question—a technology that seemingly both threatened the manned strategic bomber and promised to open the space frontier—became the paramount defense concern in the nation. ARDC's work would heavily influence the Air Force of the future, including SAC, and Power knew this. Ten days prior to Power assuming command, the Air Staff had delineated the responsibilities of Air Materiel Command (AMC) and ARDC. ARDC would hold "executive authority" of more than forty major system development projects, many of which became famous in their later Air Force service, including the B-58 Hustler, the C-130 Hercules, the KC-135 Stratotanker, and many of the famed "century series" fighters such as the F-101 Voodoo, F-104 Starfighter, and F-105 Thunderchief. Further, ARDC developed a number of the Air Force's first missiles, including the Snark and Navajo cruise missiles, Bomarc surface-to-air missile, and XB-65 Atlas ICBM.[4]

Although he had executive authority over all of these projects and the ability to execute most of these authorities with only minor interference, Power certainly did not have overall authority of one of the most important projects—the XB-65 Atlas ICBM project. ICBM development was a high priority in Washington, and civilians quickly asserted control. One of the most important early civilian decisions was to establish an organization dedicated solely to ICBM development.

On 26 February 1954 special assistant for research and development Trevor Gardner, fresh from the Teapot committee that had reviewed the U.S. Air Force's strategic missile programs, argued the Air Force could not field the Atlas ICBM by 1960 under current management conditions. Gardner insisted the Atlas program be given top priority and be managed by a streamlined organization dedicated solely to the ICBM. The chief of missile development would have to be a major general dual-hatted as vice commander of ARDC.[5]

Air Force chief of staff Gen. Nathan F. Twining agreed with Gardner's recommendations. On 21 June 1954 Lt. Gen. Donald Putt, deputy chief of staff for development, ordered Power to speed Atlas "to the maximum extent that technological development will permit" and to "establish a field office on the west coast with a general officer in command having authority and control over all aspects of the program, including all engineering matters." On 1 July Power ordered the establishment of the Western Development Division (WDD) as an ARDC field office charged with developing and fielding the Atlas ICBM, in Inglewood, California.[6]

Gardner originally wanted Maj. Gen. James McCormack, the serving ARDC vice commander, to become chief of missile development with Brig. Gen. Bernard Schriever his deputy and industrial contractor coordinator.[7] However, McCormack suffered a heart attack and retired from the Air Force. In his stead, Schriever became ARDC deputy commander and chief of missile development as commander of WDD.

From the beginning, Power was unhappy with this arrangement. Power knew Schriever from prior interaction at SAC headquarters. Years earlier, Colonel Schriever had squared off with LeMay over support of the aircraft nuclear propulsion (ANP) program. Schriever was against continuing the development of ANP because his technical advisers believed the power plant would melt down in flight. However, ANP was LeMay's favorite research and development (R&D) program at the time. LeMay thought Schriever insubordinate and in one rather tense meeting, Power (as LeMay's deputy) asked Schriever if he would like to practice judo with him.[8]

A lingering distrust of Schriever aside, Power found the practical problems of the WDD far more troubling. The Teapot committee had encouraged not only the development of the WDD, but also the creation of a unique systems engineering management process that overturned the traditional Air Force approach of prime contractor acquisition. ARDC had begun the Atlas project in January 1951, and up to that time Convair had been the program's prime contractor. Gardner and Schriever were convinced that Convair lacked the engineering design skills to manage the complex ICBM project and instead chose the Ramo-Wooldridge Corporation (later TRW) to manage the development of the entire system. Convair would focus on manufacturing. This decision was met with furious objections from the aerospace industry in general, and Convair in particular. Power, who had personally seen aviation mature from canvas biplanes to aluminum superbombers, did not agree that the ICBM provided such a significant challenge that the aviation industry could not tackle it. Worse than the TRW decision, however, was the fact General Putt's 21 June order gave Schriever command over all ICBM decisions but left Power with overall responsibility for the project's success. Power carried out the order but was not happy about it.

Power and Schriever met to discuss the WDD on 17 July at ARDC headquarters in Baltimore. This initial meeting was very tense. Schriever had assumed that Power would support his decision to abandon Convair in favor of Ramo-Wooldridge. Power instead disagreed with almost every decision that had been made on the Atlas program over the last few months and with Schriever's actions in particular.[9] Worse for Schriever, Power "let Bernie know it in direct and brutal fashion."[10] After the meeting, Schriever wrote that Power thought "we were attempting to tie [a] can to Convair and R&W [Ramo-Wooldridge] would grab off the prize." Power was further concerned that he would not be able to supervise Schriever adequately from Baltimore if Schriever was in Los Angeles. As a young brigadier general, Schriever would be "a country boy among the wolves" of California's aircraft industry.[11] Power wanted WDD in Maryland. Schriever explained that only California had the engineering talent necessary to field the ICBM. Schriever was persuasive, but only barely.

Schriever had told Gardner earlier that in order to deliver the ICBM on time, he had to be free to make decisions "without any interference from those nitpicking sons-of-bitches in the Pentagon." According to Schriever, Power took that sentiment poorly, making "a point that he was senior to me and had much more at stake than I. . . . By his several allusions to my making big decisions on my own . . . he must feel that I am motivated by a personal desire for power. . . . He obviously does not trust me nor have confidence in me—very important factors when undertaking a job of this magnitude." Schriever left the 17 July meeting shaken but insistent that he would "win over Tommy Power."[12]

As commander of WDD, Schriever reported to Power weekly on WDD progress, phoned or sent a teletype message to him whenever a significant event occurred, invited him to all significant meetings, and personally traveled to Baltimore to brief him as often as possible. By far the most important olive branch Schriever offered Power was arranging for rounds of golf for the two men whenever he could; both were highly skilled aficionados of the game. The personal connection developed between the two men on the links assuredly was vitally important to their improving relationship.[13]

Schriever's overtures to Power worked, aided immeasurably by Schriever's bureaucratic successes at WDD. Power listened to Schriever allies such as John von Neumann regarding the ICBM and its importance. He also began to accept that the Ramo-Wooldridge systems management organization paid off and was impressed that Schriever had prevailed over Convair's objections. Power eventually realized "how badly he had misjudged [Schriever] in assessing him as a naïve amateur."[14] In his April 1955 fitness report on Schriever, Power wrote Schriever has "excellent staying qualities when the going gets rough. Professionally, he is characterized by his thoroughness. He has a brilliant mind and can be depended upon for outstanding work."[15]

Less than a year after their first acrimonious meeting in Baltimore, Power and Schriever were working with a mutual professional respect and personal trust. After a T-33 trainer crashed, killing the pilot and an ARDC brigadier general, Power immediately worried that "Schriever is flying coast to coast in that T-33, and he has all that [Atlas] program in his head!"[16] Power immediately replaced Schriever's aide and pilot with the most experienced jet pilot he had, Bryce Poe (who himself would become a general officer).

Even if their relationship improved dramatically, Power remained a stern and sometimes irascible boss when the occasion—at least to Power—called for it. Poe recalled that during a meeting with a colonel on Schriever's staff, "General Power was upset about another aircraft accident; kept interrupting the briefing by asking what the weather was at the accident, this, that, and the other. It was a fatal accident. We lost a flight surgeon in a T-33." The worry about the accident, coupled with his frustration over the quality of the briefing, apparently had drained any patience Power had for the colonel. After hurrying the colonel through his presentation, Power barked, "Hold your horizontal!" Surprised and puzzled, the colonel asked, "Sir?" Power yelled, "Parallel to the goddamn floor!" at which point the colonel held his pointer out horizontally over his slide projection. Power said, "Now put it up higher, higher, higher," until nothing appeared above the pointer except "Commander, Western Development Division." Power said, "There! I approve everything above the pointer. Do the rest of it over!"[17] When Poe told Schriever about the colonel's performance and Power's rejection of the plan, Schriever said, "I'll go in tomorrow and talk to him about it." Poe recalled that Schriever got the presentation approved as originally proposed during a private meeting the following day.[18]

It was critical for Power and Schriever to develop a good working relationship because of both changing priorities in the Air Force and emerging opportunities driving the need to confront new organizational decisions almost immediately. The establishment of the WDD and a new emphasis on developing an ICBM also meant that there might soon be a rocket capable of placing a satellite into orbit. Many Air Force officers began to believe that space-age weapons would shortly be operational and that the Air Force would need to develop an operational space capability. As one historian wrote, "To a great many Air Force planners it seemed obvious that only a military space capability could provide an effective counterweight to an intercontinental ballistic missile force."[19]

In May 1954 Air Force headquarters directed ARDC to study the potential implications of a satellite program based on RAND's Project Feedback, which looked at potential reconnaissance capabilities of spacecraft. ARDC released System Requirement 5 on 27 November 1954 to request industrial support to develop a reconnaissance satellite. RAND Project Feedback contributors presented multiple briefings to defense officials over the next few months. General LeMay became an enthusiastic early supporter. He wanted the reconnaissance satellite for pre- and post-strike intelligence on the interior of the Soviet Union, even though his SAC staff was much more interested in manned bombers and refueling requirements.[20] Power understood LeMay's support; the satellite was critical to strategic warfare.

In October 1954 Gardner asked the ICBM scientific advisory committee to explore the ramifications of the satellite program, eventually named Weapon System (WS)-117L, and other rocket programs within the Atlas ICBM effort. The group concluded that the review should be conducted by the Air Force, and an internal WDD staff recommendation on 15 October 1954 said that WDD should take responsibility for the management of the satellite, ICBM, and intermediate-range ballistic missile (IRBM) programs.[21] However, the von Neumann committee—a group that shared many members with Gardner's ICBM scientific advisory committee—argued in January 1955 that placing the WS-117L under WDD would put the rapid introduction of the Atlas missile into the Air Force inventory at unacceptable risk. Power acquiesced to the von Neumann recommendations.[22] In March 1955 Power placed WS-117L under the management of the Wright Air Development Center in Dayton, Ohio, the center in charge of managing Air Force air vehicle development. Schriever and Gardner both wanted WDD to stay away from the satellite business.

However, pressure began to build from ARDC, and perhaps Power himself, to place both the WS-117L satellite and the Thor theater ballistic missile (TBM) under WDD's control. In June 1955 Gardner again called the ICBM scientific advisory committee to discuss the issue. The committee unanimously agreed that "any Satellite program, Scientific or Reconnaissance, which is dependent on components being developed under the ICBM program, would interfere with the earliest attainment of an ICBM operational capability" and asked the chairman to write a letter to the secretary of the Air Force advising that such interference could inflict grave damage on the ICBM program.[23] Historian Robert Perry criticized the findings of Gardner's group, saying, "There was no question of lack of foresight in such a decision. The group was overwhelmingly concerned with keeping the infant ballistic missile program alive and satisfying the critical need for an operational ballistic missile."[24] To Gardner and his men, space took a back seat to the ICBM.

Nonetheless, on 10 October 1955 Power resolved the question of who was to manage WS-117L "in Gordian-knot fashion" by placing the satellite program squarely in WDD's jurisdiction.[25] Power notified Schriever of this change officially on 17 October.[26] Power did not appear to have left any significant documentation on why he made the decision to place these two space missions together at WDD (adding a third, the Thor TBM, on 9 December 1955), against Schriever and Gardner's recommendations.[27] However, Schriever's arguments were well documented in two memoranda sent to Power in November and December 1954.

After the October meeting of the ICBM scientific advisory committee, Power requested Schriever study the potential relationship among the ICBM, TBM, and WS-117L programs. In a November memorandum, Schriever reported WDD's findings.[28] Schriever noted that many of the technical problems shared by the ICBM and TBM "are virtually identical from 1,000 to 5,000 miles range" and argued that ICBM research could help TBM system development but that "the opposite is not necessarily true."[29] Schriever explained that the ICBM needed to push the state of the art in materials and aerodynamics research, while the TBM, a much simpler weapon, did not.[30]

Schriever made a quite forceful argument that the TBM program could be satisfied through the use of alternative approaches to the ICBM that WDD contemplated for Atlas. Schriever contended that the ICBM needed to be explored in two configurations: a single-tank one-stage system with detachable rocket engines (which would become the Atlas), and a different two-stage system. The TBM could be a modification of the two-stage model.[31] Instead of seeing the TBM as a legitimate program in and of itself, Schriever saw it as a potential pathway to secure a much-desired second approach to fielding his ICBM.

Schriever was just as protective of the ICBM when he discussed the satellite. He made an early distinction between the ICBM and what he called the satellite missile, or launch vehicle. He agreed that the two systems were very similar but warned that "it would also be erroneous to conclude that the success of the Satellite missile is easily and directly assured by the success of the ICBM, for there are formidable technical problems associated with the Satellite vehicle that have no counterpart in the ICBM."[32] Among these many problems were satellite power, terrain scanning, data storage, processing, and transmission, and launch vehicle trajectory control.[33] Schriever also noted that overlapping ICBM and space programs could overwhelm America's limited number of missile launch ranges, damaging both programs.[34]

Schriever noted that a space launch vehicle was a more difficult project than an ICBM and implied that his mission as he saw it was to provide an ICBM and not a general space capability. There was overlap between the two, to be sure, but developing the ICBM first would help the space program itself, because the "major problems of propulsion, launching, structure, and guidance along the powered trajectory, by being solved in the ICBM program will save much time for the Satellite vehicle because of the great similarity of these problems."[35] But Schriever remained clear that his priority was the ICBM.

Schriever concluded against merging the ICBM, TBM, and satellite systems into a unified Air Force space effort. "The Satellite program is similar to ICBMs in only certain aspects of the total or initial vehicle," Schriever wrote, and "that it is not necessary to center control of both programs in one part of ARDC," obviously referring to WDD.[36] Schriever was, however, insistent that if the satellite or TBM program began to endanger the ICBM program with delays, then the ICBM program must immediately take over their management in order to keep ICBM delay to a minimum.[37]

The apparent contradictions in this document indicate that Schriever was of two minds regarding WDD involvement in both the satellite and the TBM programs. The earliest fielding of the ICBM was foremost on Schriever's mind, and he thought that both the satellite and TBM programs were dangerous distractions. But he also acknowledged that close coordination among all of these activities under one office might be the only way to mitigate the space program's danger to the

ICBM. Ultimately, it seems as if Schriever preferred to focus exclusively on the ICBM but, if necessary, was prepared to take on both the TBM and satellite programs to ensure that he could minimize their hindrance to his main objective.

Schriever's reluctance to add the TBM program to WDD was justifiable. His mission was to develop an operational ICBM as quickly as possible. However, the Thor TBM was fielded a few months before the Atlas and became a critical component of the early U.S. space program, and Thor's descendant, the Delta II medium lift vehicle, remained in service as one of the world's most successful launch vehicles until 2018. Schriever's primary focus on the ICBM could have significantly impeded the space program if not for Power's decision to overrule him.

In mid-1955 Schriever sensed he would lose, and WDD would eventually assume both the TBM and WS-117L programs. In a memorandum to Col. Charles Terhune on 15 April 1955, Schriever wrote that the "Satellite Development Plan, if implemented beyond the study stage . . . is certain to interfere with the ICBM program. I feel quite certain that management of the satellite vehicle program, when it reaches the hardware development phase, must be under WDD in order to control the coordination which will be required among the several large rocket vehicle programs."[38] Schriever had seen the writing on the wall, and while he was still opposed to the satellite program for endangering the ICBM program, his management of it was the best choice available among bad options.

There are many possible explanations why Power overruled Schriever's objections to these transfers. From a purely bureaucratic standpoint, Power might have thought that the merging of the three programs, however detrimental to the timely deployment of the ICBM, was inevitable. All three programs were critically dependent upon advanced rocket propulsion and guidance technology. Indeed, the RAND report *Preliminary Design of an Experimental World-Circling Spaceship* saw "little difference in design and performance between an intercontinental rocket missile and a satellite" and envisioned the satellite vehicle as the rocket itself, not necessarily the payload of a launch vehicle as we know it today.[39] The spaceship *was* the launch vehicle, and the majority of the RAND report was on rocket engineering. The intellectual underpinnings of the ICBM, TBM, and satellite all sprang from the same source without distinction between a satellite and a missile. Perhaps Power understood that intellectual inertia was simply too great to attempt to artificially isolate the ICBM from the push to develop space capability.

Schriever himself was of two minds regarding the merger. He did not want the TBM and satellite to interfere with the ICBM, but he also felt that under WDD, both inferior projects would pose the least risk to the ICBM should the Air Force pursue them. Thus, Schriever's resistance against taking those two projects may have been rhetorically intense but practically very low. Schriever likely understood that, while he did not *want* the TBM or satellite, he *should* have responsibility for them.

Another reason why Power may have overruled Schriever to widen the scope of the WDD was because he knew Schriever could handle it. Power was originally skeptical of Schriever's managerial skill but concluded by 1955 that he was highly capable. Even if the TBM and satellite would put the ICBM at risk, Power may have concluded that only Schriever could accomplish all three of them.

A final possibility is that Power valued a holistic space program above early accomplishment of the ICBM in order to develop a true aerospace force—an Air Force that owned a seamless combination of military power through both the air and space domains. Schriever was singly enamored with the ballistic missile as a technology, and his association with Trevor Gardner and John von Neumann attests to this deep—possibly myopic—view. Power, by contrast, was primarily an aviator and one of the leaders of the "bomber mafia," but he also had a keen interest in technology in general. As deputy SAC commander, Power defended the manned bomber from claims of obsolescence by the ballistic missile and was not convinced that the ICBM was the "ultimate weapon." Further, Power realized how important a reconnaissance satellite would be to SAC for operational reasons. While Schriever may have seen the potential for space, he was primarily interested in the ICBM, whereas Power thought that the ICBM was important, but the real payoff of the technology was in opening up space to the Air Force—a natural extension of its "higher, farther, faster" mantra.

In 1954 Power approached industry to study problems regarding space, including manned craft and lunar probes, without Pentagon direction. Power saw space's potential as the next great Air Force frontier, and he saw the ICBM as the initial gateway to that future. He believed the Air Force needed a dedicated space organization, that such an organization was bureaucratically inevitable, and that Schriever could accomplish all of these tasks in a reasonable time. Therefore, Power made the decision to turn WDD into a space organization. By doing so, on 10 October 1955, Power put the United States and the Air Force on the path to space power.

Schriever quickly integrated the satellite as well as the rocket into a unified Air Force space effort through his "concurrency approach" whereby he developed both the satellite and the missile in parallel, including site construction, installation and checkout, flight testing, and crew training following overlapping and accelerated schedules.[40] This approach dramatically increased risk and cost but was "revolutionary for the R&D community" and saved an enormous amount of time, which allowed the Air Force to obtain many operational space capabilities in the 1960s.[41] Schriever eventually adopted a version of Power's space vision. As early as January 1955, Schriever boasted that the ultimate goal of the ICBM was not war but conquering outer space.[42]

Schriever, however, did not totally convert to Power's vision of aerospace. Schriever accepted the WS-117L and IRBM into WDD but rejected adding the Wright Air Development Center's BOMI (Bomber-Missile) space flight project to the WDD portfolio in November 1955.[43] BOMI was an early design of a "boost glide" spacecraft designed by the renowned German aerospace engineer Walter Dornberger. Meant to travel into space on a rocket (boost) and use aerodynamics (glide) to maneuver to a landing site, BOMI was a precursor to the space shuttle and the direct antecedent of the Dyna-Soar (later X-20) Air Force manned spaceplane program. Schriever's flat rejection of BOMI in 1955 presaged his later lukewarm attitude toward human spaceflight as commander of the Ballistic Missile Division and, ultimately, Air Force Systems

Command. With the BOMI decision, Schriever hinted that under his leadership, the Air Force space program would focus on space applications of missile technology, not birthing an expansive, operationally focused manned space program, which Power would eventually strongly support. Although Power made WDD into a space organization, he did not force Schriever to accept BOMI and make it a truly aerospace one, perhaps to the ultimate detriment of Power's space vision.

Air Force history has tended to neglect the debate over adding WS-117L and the IRBM to WDD. In his detailed history *Beyond Horizons*, David Spires claims Schriever gained WS-117L for WDD over Power's implied objections (based on Power's initial support of keeping WDD focused on the ICBM following the von Neumann committee recommendations) and declared Schriever the father of the Air Force space program.[44] This is a complete inversion of reality. In actuality, it was Power who established the Air Force's first organization dedicated to collecting, investigating, and managing the development of U.S. space power. "The late fall of 1955 arguably [marked] the beginning of what would evolve into a space subculture within the Air Force,"[45] but contrary to popular belief, this was not due to Schriever's actions. Thomas Power was the man that founded the Air Force space effort.

Once Power created an organization for space, he began to establish doctrine to guide it. One prominent scholar, I. B. Holley, explained that "doctrine is what is officially approved to be taught."[46] Ideally, military doctrine is derived from past experience such as actual combat operations (the best case), or tests, exercises, and maneuvers (acceptable methods). However, in some instances, often when dealing with new technology, doctrine can be developed from reasoned extrapolation.[47] Military space activity in the mid-1950s qualified as such because there was precious little actual experience with spaceflight at the time, yet doctrine capable of employing this new technology was necessary to remain competitive in the Cold War.

Effective doctrine has two purposes: to provide guidance to decisionmakers, planners, and policymakers, and to provide common bases of thought and handling problems.[48] Holley concluded in *Ideas and*

Weapons that in the end, doctrine, or the accepted concept of the mission to be performed by a weapon, determined the direction of development for the weapon.[49] Holley posited the "Doctrine Continuum" where an action motivates an observer to create a concept that would eventually be developed into and accepted as doctrine that, if durable, could mature into a principle.[50] To Holley, a concept was a speculative and tentative mental construct or theory—an unproven idea that springs from a creative imagination.[51] Doctrines, on the other hand, are "precepts, suggested methods for solving problems or attaining desired results" based upon reflection on accumulated experience and promulgated by competent authority.[52] Thus, concepts are not doctrines, yet they can be considered doctrines in larval form. In the search for an appropriate doctrine for Air Force space power, collection and study of concepts with which to build that doctrine were essential. Power was very quick to place ARDC to work toward developing the concepts necessary to germinate doctrine that would intellectually arm the Air Force to dominate space. He did so by dramatically increasing basic research at ARDC, which eventually became a large portion of the command's portfolio.

Throughout his tour as its commander, Power stressed that ARDC's main responsibility was to retain and expand qualitative U.S. superiority in weapons relative to adversaries, especially the Soviet Union. Speaking about ARDC's role in the Cold War, Power said, "In their determined quest for world domination, the Soviets have unscrupulously resorted to a seemingly inexhaustible variety of hot and cold war techniques. Since the end of World War II, they have placed increasing emphasis on a third type of warfare—the slide-rule war. As a result, the United States has been forced into an all-out struggle with the Soviet Union for technological supremacy."[53] To win the slide-rule war—the technological war—ARDC stood ready to play its part.

Power argued, "We *can* remain ahead of the Soviets in the development and production of new weapons. I am confident that continually advancing the state-of-the-art; by an aggressive development program, utilizing the latest findings of basic research; and by applying principles of management which are possible only in a free economy such as ours and which are far superior to any advantages the Soviets might derive from their system of dictatorship, we can maintain our qualitative supremacy for as long as is needed and can do so within the limits of our economic capability."[54] Nowhere did Power apply this method with more enthusiasm than in determining the role of space in the future Air Force.

In May 1955 ARDC proposed a feasibility study of a manned ballistic rocket research system. Major aircraft companies and other interested organizations were briefed on the study and urged to conduct independent investigations of the problem—because ARDC had no money to support a study on its own. One defense contractor, Avco, studied a manned satellite, and RAND, a strong proponent of reconnaissance satellite systems since 1947, reported on space vehicles for purposes other than reconnaissance. In May 1956 a RAND proposal for a lunar instrument carrier circulated through ARDC and the Air Force.[55]

Cold War competition helped this nascent activity. The July 1955 Moscow air show deeply shocked the nation, the Air Force, and Thomas Power. The clever Soviet deception of flying ten Bison bombers in formation twice, the second time with their last eight bombers, to convince the viewing public that the Soviet Union had twenty-eight at the show scared the Western alliance, and also jarred the United States into closing a perceived bomber gap at lightning speed.

At the same time, Power began to shift ARDC's focus from what he saw as an inordinate focus on near-term, incremental improvements toward basic research and long-range technological breakthroughs that could catapult the United States into newer classes of revolutionary technology—technology that could provide such a qualitative superiority over the Soviet Union that recovery would be effectively impossible. On 9 May 1955 Power wrote to Roger Lewis, the assistant secretary of the Air Force for materiel, arguing, "I am profoundly concerned about the possibility of this country falling behind in the technological race due to our inability, or failure, to support an adequate basic research and exploratory development program. By this, I mean an aggressive, imaginative effort to push for new ideas, new techniques, advanced components, and new applications of the basic sciences, rather than our timid attempts to squeeze another 10% improvement out of materiel in the inventory."[56] In this, the last non–college graduate to become a general officer presaged the innovation guru Clayton Christensen by more than a half-century.[57]

Accordingly, Power presented Lewis with a proposal to end ARDC funding to any development plan that had been awarded to a contractor for production and thus was no longer concerned with basic research. Power argued weapons systems in the development stage should be paid for through Air Materiel Command, and he needed $100 million in ARDC money currently going to incremental developments to be freed so he could fund the basic, long-range breakthrough research "which provides our real payoff." He knew ARDC could deliver.[58]

When Lewis demurred, Power took his concerns directly to Air Force chief of staff Gen. Nathan Twining in a 2 August 1955 letter. Power noted that the fiscal year (FY) 1956 research and development requirements placed on ARDC totaled $720 million, but the Air Force had only funded ARDC to $356 million. This state of affairs, Power argued, "will operate inexorably to sacrifice our longer-range research and development to accommodate the shorter-range, time-oriented production for the inventory. Consequently, those areas of research and development characterized by aggressive imagination and novelty, and by the new, radical approaches and designs which represent our future technological advantage will be seriously impaired if not nullified." Power concluded, "I plan to keep you informed of specific projects in the R&D program which are delayed due to lack of funds."[59]

On 29 May 1956 General Twining was invited to Moscow to attend the official Soviet air show on 24 June. Although the invitation caused some controversy in Washington, President Dwight Eisenhower approved Twining's attendance a day later, with a message that a reciprocal invitation for Soviet air force officials to attend an American air show would probably not be forthcoming.[60] On 13 June 1956 the government announced that nine Air Force officers, all "technical or tactical specialists," would accompany Twining. Power was among them.[61] On 21 June the ten men left for Moscow for a ten-day trip. Twining told the press that his team would "see and listen" and that the generals with him were "the very best men in the Air Force for a trip of this nature," adding that all were able to fly Soviet planes.[62]

The first national reports on the results of Twining's Russian visit hit the wires on 1 July as the Air Force contingent was heading back. The first report was of the amiable farewell dinner for the foreign delegations to the Soviet aviation day ceremonies hosted by marshal of aviation Pavel F. Zhigarev, where the Chinese People's Liberation Army Air Force commander general Liu Yia-lo deliberately sat next to Twining because he had not drunk a toast with an American general since the Korean War.[63] Not all social events went as smoothly. At another vodka party immediately following the 24 June air show, Soviet communist party leader Nikita Khrushchev "poured out a string of derogatory remarks" about the United States—and other big nations, and little nations, and Soviet satellite states, eventually encompassing "the whole world." Twining reported to the Senate that it was a rough party, but everyone took it in good humor.[64] During the trip, marshal of the Soviet Union G. K. Zhukov presented Power with some perfume and a lacquered box; Power wrote to Zhukov after the trip, "I thoroughly enjoyed my visit and I wish to take this opportunity to thank you for your excellent hospitality."[65]

Brig. Gen. William Blanchard, deputy director of operations at SAC and also on the trip, recalled the Americans and their Soviet hosts boarded five Il-14 twin-engine transports to fly from Moscow to Stalingrad. The transports were "elaborately equipped with Persian rugs, ornate china, heavy drapes, plush chairs and divans" but no seat belts. The officers passed the flight trying their best to maintain a "dignified position on the divan without a belt and rescuing the sliding china." However, on the return trip to Moscow, the weather became very poor as the caravan of aircraft took off at twilight. The U.S. generals were then introduced to Russian flight safety as the transport planes took off just before dark at five-minute intervals and flew the entire trip at only four hundred to five hundred feet altitude in what passed as Russian visual flight rules. Blanchard wrote, "The first thing I know I'm looking out the window at the tree tops going by—close. . . . We seemed to be the only ones worried.

The crew and our Russian counterparts weren't the least bit concerned over making this trip at night, usually on instruments, in and out of the soup, and right on the deck. We didn't have them a bit scared." Twining reported to Eisenhower that the "trip back was made at an uncomfortably low altitude," which the SAC aviation safety magazine *Combat Crew* called the understatement of 1956.[66]

Twining's report to Congress indicated that he was impressed with the technological and production strides of the Soviet air force. In addition to seeing a few Soviet aircraft at two air bases and the actual air show, the U.S. team had tours of aircraft production facilities, air training academies, the Monino Air Academy, and the Zhukovskii Air Engineering Academy. However, nothing Twining saw justified "any hasty action to write down or, for that matter, write up our previous assessments of Soviet airpower," though he also noted the Soviets revealed nothing about their guided missile program. Twining did stress that he was convinced that Air Force R&D spending was "not only fully justified, but that increases in this area are warranted."[67] Twining also issued a dire warning: "We must in prudence reckon on the possibility of their achieving a scientific breakthrough and consequential technical surprise in new weapons."[68]

Power was quick to second Twining's opinions. What most impressed, and disturbed, Power in his own recollections of the trip were the sheer number and quality of Soviet technicians and scientists. In a statement to the House Un-American Activities Committee meeting on 23 September 1956, Power testified that the Soviets

> possess the tools for enforcing security to the point where the free world knows only as much about their technological progress as they permit to be known—and that is very little indeed. . . . While the rate at which we graduate engineers and scientists in this country has been declining steadily, the opposite is true in Soviet Russia. Steadily increasing numbers of Soviet youth are attracted to the engineering professions and allied sciences through compulsion, if necessary, but mainly through early indoctrination and such incentives as liberal stipends, awards, and bonuses as well as professional prestige and social position.[69]

Power was specifically impressed with Moscow's Zhukovskii Air Engineering Academy, which had "some 2,500 students—all Air Force officers ranking from first lieutenant to major—who undergo a 5-year course of considerable breadth and depth. It is significant that the Soviets can spare so many Air Force officers for such a long period of time."[70]

"The outlook is grave but not hopeless," Power concluded. "As long as we recognize and face the facts and act accordingly; as long as we work together as a team in maintaining technological superiority; and as long as we can and are willing to pay the price for 'security by deterrent force,' we have nothing to fear" from the Soviets.[71]

Seeing the Soviet Union first-hand reinforced Power's desire to crush the Soviets in the technological war as ARDC commander. "There is no person in this country who is not directly or indirectly concerned with the race for qualitative supremacy in the air—the keystone to our survival as a free and prosperous people," Power wrote in August 1956. ARDC provided that qualitative supremacy. Power lauded the ARDC as "the greatest team ever assembled for one single purpose—qualitative superiority for the Air Force-in-being as well as the Air Force-to-be."[72]

To continue to develop this team meant that many long-standing barriers between the military and industry had to be broken down. To achieve and maintain qualitative superiority required shortening the development cycle of new weapons, necessitating the quick development of new weapons systems, and transmitting military requirements to industry as quickly as possible. ARDC began to expedite this process, based on a number of contributing factors. First, contractors often complained about the lack of guidance the Air Force traditionally gave to them for their internal preliminary studies. Second, ARDC desired to channel contractor research and development efforts along promising lines and prevent misdirected effort. Third, ARDC wanted to encourage "independent proprietary" work by contractors. Finally, ARDC wanted to decrease the time of the development cycle by gaining contractor interest and effort at the earliest possible date while conserving "valuable engineering and technical manpower."[73]

On 7 October 1955 Power requested that his newly established board of officers on guided missile development "be bold and imaginative in its concept of the scope and importance of future space vehicle development programs."[74] The Air Force commissioned a variety of studies—exploratory, feasibility, analytical, and design—to assist in planning during the technological revolutions that took place in the 1950s and beyond, but money for such studies was lacking. An ARDC review for FY 56 indicated the fifty-five studies ARDC contemplated would require $13.7 million, but only $4.4 million existed in the current budget authorization. To bridge the gap, Power established a weapons system requirements release program in late 1955 to communicate "future weapon system requirements to industry sooner than heretofore" and encourage contractors "to conduct voluntary, unfunded studies which will be used for planning purposes."[75] Rather than keep industry at arm's length until a contract was awarded, ARDC would instead "let industry in on what used to be ARDC secrets."[76] Power said this effort planned "to invite industry to review our study areas with the objective of enlisting interest and stimulating work on the basis of no cost to the government."[77]

An opportunity to test the philosophy of the requirements release program occurred in summer 1955, with an urgent need for design information to "satisfy Air Rescue, Resupply, and Assault requirements."[78] ARDC conducted informal conversations with "appropriate members of industry in an effort to discover those members who would have both a capability and a desire to undertake studies in these particular areas."[79] The command stuck with well-known contractors Convair, Douglas, Grumman, Fairchild, Lockheed, Martin, and Stroukoff. As Air Force regulations prohibited the release of general operational requirements documents outside of the government, ARDC quickly generated a new document called "Performance and Characteristics Design Data Sheets" that, within legal parameters, provided the needed information to the contractor. ARDC insisted that contractors safeguard the classified information released to them as well as fully understand that participation in these studies "does not constitute a request for work, nor will any such request necessarily follow-on, and that USAF assumes no obligations of any sort by virtue of passing on this data."[80]

With those ground rules in place, industry and ARDC leaders forged ahead during a week of meetings in November 1955. Both contractors and the Air Force reacted positively to this "trial balloon" experiment. Lockheed believed that the new approach would produce "superior results."[81] George Bunker, president of the Glenn Martin Company, told Power, "All of us are familiar with the term 'technological breakthrough.' . . . It seems to me of equal import that you and your command have accomplished a comparable 'policy breakthrough' by conceiving and putting into effect your System Requirement Plan." Bunker added that this "plan should bring about a much closer relationship between the Air Force and the industry and reduce to a minimum the misconceptions and loss of time that have resulted in the past from lack of complete understanding between two groups of people intent on a single purpose."[82]

ARDC quickly codified these lessons learned into an established system; thus emerged the system requirement (SR) program. The system requirement was "a statement of an anticipated requirement for a weapon or supporting system, including a definition of the problem area or need, and all considerations having a bearing on the problem and its solution, such as background, intelligence information, present state-of-the-art, related development, etc."[83] ARDC's directorate of system plans, under Maj. Gen. Albert Boyd, oversaw the SR program. The directorate was responsible for the long-range planning and programming of ARDC weapons systems and assisted Air Force headquarters in preparing general operational requirements documents. They were the primary point of contact between the Air Force and industry during the early stages of SR studies. By conducting SR studies and other explorations, the directorate turned ARDC's interests into the "shape of things to come" for the Air Force and nation. Through the SR program, the directorate provided a great deal of information that benefitted Air Force planning in the early 1960s.[84]

Directorate Systems Plans Office Instruction No. 2 contained the SR release procedure. An SR could be initiated at the discretion of any ARDC division chief and, after coordination with ARDC headquarters, this and other proposed SRs were discussed in conference with industry representatives.[85] "At this point some company representatives face temptations like those of a boy at the candy counter," declared one writer, "but they are forced to limit themselves to the two or three areas where they have the greatest capability."[86] After the conference, the chosen SRs were published and distributed to selected contractors. The resulting document, the ARDC system requirement (study), included a statement of the problem the SR addressed, background, desired performance requirements, a list of previous work that might be pertinent, a technical brief, and a statement of desired work the SR intended to accomplish.[87] Because the SR was unfunded, the industry group retained proprietary rights to the information they provided, with the single caveat that the proprietary aspects of the study not prevent or retard the reporting of the overall study to the Air Force or ARDC. Within six months of beginning the formal SR program, ninety-five industry groups representing more than thirty contractors were working on fifty-four separate studies.

The SR system, popular with both ARDC and industry, offers a window into the intellectual life of Power's ARDC. Claude Witze argued that the SR program offered both the government and industry a distinct advantage: "At no time in history has there been closer co-operation between industry and the government. . . . The secret is that the System Requirements study program should improve industry's capability before the final weapon system requirement becomes urgent. Technical knowledge, placed on the shelf as it sometimes will be, will shorten the engineering learning curve when the project gets hot. The same holds true for the USAF: with better material upon which to base decisions, the decisions should come more quickly and have more merit."[88] Even though most SR studies were completely unfunded, many of them eventually began to be moderately funded, and others evolved into major programs.

Power, assessing the early results of the SR program, concluded, "Industry in general has indicated a willingness to expend effort toward defining possible solutions to Air Force problems." Power was inclined to give them more opportunities to do so. "It is the intent of the [SR] program to identify areas for study which will significantly improve our operational capability," Power declared, "thus permitting contractors to channel engineering efforts into the most profitable fields."[89]

The SR program could be considered a key growth avenue for the military-industrial complex that President Eisenhower warned of on 17 January 1961, only five years after the program began. However, for Power, closer cooperation between the Air Force and industry short-ened the development cycle for innovative weapons systems. The goal was qualitative superiority of weapons over the Soviet Union, and that required "big jumps" in advanced weapons technology.[90] In the late 1950s, especially after Sputnik in 1957, the "big jumps" were into the new domain of space. The SR program was ready for the transition, and the development of space doctrine began when space systems started to be studied in-depth.

Power was able to guide ARDC on the path toward space power, but he did not stay long enough to take significant part in it. He established ARDC's guided missile and space vehicle working group in December 1956 before leaving command in July 1957. It was only after Power departed ARDC that his efforts began to pay off. In December 1957 that group issued a "Special Report Concerning Space Technology" that laid out an ARDC five-year projected astronautics program. This included the manned lunar-based intelligence system, with a projected first flight in 1967. By January 1958 the Air Force initiated Program 499, a lunar base system, and by March the Air Force was formalizing plans for a manned lunar base study.[91]

In 1959 the Air Force space study program was initiated to lever-age Power's SR program to specifically study space issues. The SR stud-ies under the space study program in 1959 were SR 126, boost glide; SR 178, global surveillance system; SR 181, strategic orbital system; SR 182, strategic interplanetary system; SR 183, lunar observatory; SR 184, twenty-four-hour reconnaissance satellite; SR 187, satellite intercep-tor system; SR 192, strategic lunar system; SR 199, advanced ballistic missile weapon system; SR 79500, intercontinental glide missile; and SR 89774, recoverable booster support system.[92] These studies ranged from modest looks at approaches to new ICBMs to expansive visions of the military utility of U.S. space forces on other planets. The FY 59 program was funded at $2.9 million, but the $3.3 million requested for FY 60 was placed on the deferred list by director of defense research and engineering Harold Brown, who would often prove a thorn in Power's side, and was not released to the Air Force.[93]

The studies confronted many issues relevant to the space age, including the controversial issue of manned spaceflight. In the *Air Research and Development Command Long Range Research and Development Plan 1961–1976*, the section entitled "Strategic Offensive" noted that the role of man was still undefined in the ballistic missile strategic force of the next decade, but "[m]anned aircraft have very definite and vital capabilities which should assure them a complementary position in the SAC inventory during the entire 1961–1976 time span."[94] Manned aircraft would need the "ability to recognize targets otherwise inaccurately located or fleeting targets of opportunity" and to complement "the vastly intricate machine computers with man's inherent judgment and ability to make decisions on the spot."[95] The document considered four platforms for SAC manned requirements: a subsonic airborne military platform, a subsonic nuclear powered aircraft, the Dyna-Soar spaceplane, and an advanced recoverable booster system "space plane."[96] Of the four, two were space platforms.

Along with the strategic air offensive mission, the ARDC SAC plan included a dedicated space programs section that stressed deterrence, explaining, "Deterrence implies a mixed force with capabilities appropriate to the several missions, exploiting fully the spectrum of survival techniques." This mixed force would have to exploit space eventually to maximize survivability "in an era of ever increasing enemy offense capabilities." The plan identified Samos, Midas, Discoverer, and other Air Force space efforts with National Aeronautics and Space Administration (NASA) and Advanced Research Projects Agency (ARPA) connections. The document noted there were few current programs for offensive space systems, but ARDC studies indicated that there were many promising strategic weapons systems possible in the 1961–76 time period.[97] Results of SR 181 (strategic orbital system), initiated in 1958 before space-related SRs were consolidated into the space study program, indicated there were three "specific space systems warranting future study": a low-altitude offensive space system (SR 79821), a stationary orbit offensive space system, and a high-altitude offensive space system (SR 79822).[98]

ARDC even assessed the military utility of an "Earth orbital space force," asking key questions regarding its utility: could it provide additional security for the nuclear retaliatory force? Could warning time of an enemy attack be increased sufficiently to provide adequate time for making a responsible decision to retaliate? Could a space force draw the enemy attack away from American population centers and the Earth's surface in general? Would a space force complicate the enemy's military posture to a measurable extent?[99] Power later devoted a significant portion of his career to answering those questions.

The ARDC plan acknowledged that human crews might not enhance the military utility of space systems but concluded that "the question can be considered academic at this time because it is pretty well established that man will be included in the Nation's exploration of space for peaceful purposes." The plan also said that "we have every reason to assume that the Soviets will put man on space platforms in cislunar space and on the moon as expeditiously as possible. For both reasons, this Nation must have man in space, and man probably will be utilized eventually in space offensive weapons."[100]

Many of the SR space studies were highly visionary, to say the least. However, doctrine requires more than just vision, and regardless of their visionary contents, the SR studies would be worth little if they only collected dust on Pentagon shelves. Very little is known about most of the SR studies. However, some information regarding SR 183 and SR 192 has been declassified, and a few documents exist that shed some light on how they were received by the Air Force and the broader space community.

SR 183, lunar observatory, and SR 192, strategic lunar system, were ultimately combined by the contractors in the late 1950s to study the requirements of an Air Force lunar base. Under SR 183/192, six contractor studies were delivered, three from paid contractors (Boeing, North American Aviation, and United Aircraft) and three from voluntary participants (Douglas, Minneapolis-Honeywell, and Republic Aviation).[101] In keeping with Power's desire to leverage contractor funds as much as possible (SR space studies began to receive funding briefly with the U.S. space expansion after the Sputnik launch), the Air Force paid $800,000 for the studies with a voluntary contractor contribution of $1.2 million of corporate funds.[102] The lunar base studies concluded the total cost of the program would be $8.1 billion.[103]

Edwin P. Hartman, of NASA's western coordination office in Los Angeles, was present at the SR-183 midpoint briefing at the Air Force Ballistic Missile Division (AFBMD) in Los Angeles, which took place 24–26 March 1959. He was relatively unimpressed with what he saw. In his trip report memorandum to NASA's director of space flight development, Hartman noted that fifty to one hundred people from around the Air Force, Space Technology Laboratories (a division of Ramo-Wooldridge), and one other NASA member from the Jet Propulsion Laboratory attended the series of briefings. Over the three days, presentations from North American Aviation, Boeing, Westinghouse, Aerojet Nucleonics, Douglas Missiles Division, Republic Aviation, Systems Corporation of America, United Aircraft Corporation, and Minneapolis-Honeywell (Westinghouse, Aerojet, and Systems Corporation would later withdraw) presented their case. "There is not much of a general nature to be said about the presentations except that they all seemed a little fantastic," Hartman wrote. "All of the presentations suffered greatly from a lack of basic knowledge about the subject discussed. In them the meager knowledge that exists was over-extrapolated. Fanciful concepts were described which, aside from the intellectual stimulation they produced, are probably of little value."[104]

Hartman also questioned the "free" nature of the SR program. He wrote, "The companies that undertake SR studies for the Air Force do so largely at their own expense. However, as the income of most aircraft companies comes mainly from the government, it is obvious that the studies are paid for by the government with the costs appearing as over-head charges on military contracts."[105] Overall, Hartman preferred the modest presentations, favoring the Douglas, North American Aviation, Boeing, and Republic proposals. He chose Douglas as his favorite because the "presentation was the briefest, most pessimistic and most down to earth—if a lunar venture may be so described."[106]

Interestingly, the Air Force funded continuation of two of Hartman's top three proposals (North American and Boeing) but did not fund Hartman's favorite, the pessimistic Douglas presentation. Since the Air Force meant for the SR system to push the envelope of the possible, the Douglas presentation may have been considered excessively timid. Was Hartman conservative because he was better educated than Air Force officials, or was he simply from an overly cautious NASA culture? Ultimately, he did find some utility in the SR series. "The companies carrying out the SR studies benefit by the buildup of their technical competence in the space field," he admitted, and "the intellectual stimulation of the SR-183 studies is of definite value and if the practical limitation of the material produced is recognized, the studies may be regarded as being a worthwhile effort."[107]

The intellectual underpinnings of the two lunar studies found expression in "The Military Potential of the Moon," a 1959 *Air University Quarterly Review* essay by Lt. Col. S. E. Singer of the Air Force's Air Command and Staff College. Singer, a physicist, discussed the moon as a potential observation post as well as a deterrent base. Singer also posited some very advanced concepts that still challenge modern space thinkers. Among them was Singer's concept of "lunar autarky." Autarky is an economic term for self-sufficiency. Singer wrote the "moon is not nearly so barren as it seems. All the energy man could conceivably use is certainly available on the moon, and most if not all of the chemical elements he requires are probably there as well."[108] Singer offered, "The concept of an eventual lunar autarky cannot be excluded from consideration, and no analysis of the dollar cost of long-range lunar programs is meaningful unless this concept is included."[109] Today, the concept is known as in situ resource utilization. Indeed, SR 183 indicated that the total cost of a permanent lunar base would be $8.15 billion over ten years with annual operating costs of $631 million, or one-tenth of the U.S. farm subsidy program of the time. Singer argued, "Developing lunar resources [SR 183 does not use the term lunar autarky] could decrease the total cost of strategic lunar operations by 25%!"[110] Through SR 183, an Air Force officer identified—at the very beginning of the space age—a key economic consideration that NASA and space entrepreneurs still struggle with today.

Singer concluded that one of the most important developments a moon base could help engender was in the field of military doctrine. He opined, "Military doctrine is a product of both vision and experience. But its very essence is experience. [Billy] Mitchell's visionary views were vindicated by experience and not by the rhetoric that surrounded them." Singer, channeling Holley, declared, "Only experience will permit the evolution of a meaningful space doctrine."[111] Perhaps this is true, but the existence of the SR studies no doubt started the ball rolling to get that vital experience.

Many of the advanced space-related SR studies were made the responsibility of the Wright Air Development Division (WADD) and not WDD's successor, AFBMD. However, the dissemination of the SR studies did not appear to follow any type of clear responsibility, since some "forward-leaning" space studies, such as SR 182 (strategic interplanetary system) was an AFBMD study, while SR 181 (strategic orbital system), a similarly advanced and expansive study to which SR 182 seems like a sequel, was sent to WADD. Even with this unclear demarcation of responsibility, it makes sense that AFBMD programs would be mostly developed while WADD's forward-leaning "aerospace" systems were discarded when Schriever took over ARDC. Schriever knew the ballistic missile systems of AFBMD best, and he did not care as much for WADD man in space studies. All this suggests that while Schriever, as ARDC commander, neglected WADD space studies, Power at SAC certainly did not.

While the SR studies themselves may not have risen to the level of doctrine as strictly defined by Holley, they certainly moved the Air Force's institutional thinking on space along Holley's doctrinal continuum to at least the concept stage. Collectively, the SR studies also provided a potential opportunity to agglomerate a holistic "proto-doctrine" for the Air Force in space (exemplified by the "nested SR" characteristic in the program where many study requirements were expansions of previous studies) capable of determining the direction of Air Force space development for years to come. Unfortunately, the studies were never given the opportunity to do so.

In a 10 November 1964 letter to AFRDC on "The Air Force Space Program," Power's former World War II subordinate and now deputy chief of staff for programs and requirements, Lt. Gen. Hewitt T. Wheless, stated his deep concern that the future of manned spaceflight in the Air Force would soon be completely subsumed by NASA. Wheless vented his frustration at Robert McNamara's defense department insistence that the Air Force ground its space development to specific operational requirements for space systems at the expense of exploratory and advanced development programs that "constitute essential prerequisites to the statement of realistic and supportable requirements for operational space systems."[112] Wheless lauded the SR studies, saying, "The Air Force Space Study Program, which proved so successful in providing fresh thought and new ideas during the 1958–1961 time period, has ceased to exist. Sterility of ideas in most areas of planning has resulted. Imaginative thought can again be applied by re-instituting a well-planned study program."[113] One never came.

Wheless' lament was a reaction to a set of events that took place after Power had left ARDC, dooming the Air Force space vision generated by the SR studies. On 7 October 1957 the Soviet Union launched the Sputnik satellite. In the massive U.S. reaction to catch up with the communists in the space race, ARDC responded with the January 1958 weapons system astronautics program. The program was intended to leverage existing Air Force programs such as the X-15 and Dyna-Soar systems "to acquire sufficient knowledge of 'astronautics' so that you can speak with authority in your area of responsibility" and the pursuit of "specific programs to be accomplished within the limits of available resources."[114] Systems specifically addressed in the program were a nuclear rocket test system, an ion propulsion test system, a twenty-four-hour reconnaissance satellite program, a lunar base intelligence system, and a manned variable-trajectory spacecraft.[115] Many of these systems were assigned an SR study. However, the overall ARDC program was under threat as soon as it began, with the establishment of ARPA in February 1958. As soon as Eisenhower announced that ARPA would lead the U.S. military space effort and that space would be used for "peaceful purposes," the Air Force would never be allowed to prosecute such a large program as ARDC's weapons system astronautics program. ARDC's official history recorded that "the Air Force did not have the opportunity during the first year of ARPA's existence to develop the appropriate relationship that would have enabled all the parties concerned to exploit this storehouse of experience in military research and development that the Air Force had accumulated."[116] The SRs were deprived of all funding by Harold Brown in 1960.

The SR space studies were tantalizing glimpses of what might have been in space had ARDC been allowed to pursue space activities. However, ARDC was never given this opportunity. As the command historian wrote of the first fateful year of the space age, "Events removed from the command most of its natural mission of research and development in the space area in much the same manner and for the same reason that decisions by a commanding officer may remove suddenly the duties of a subordinate: policies made on a higher level, from which there was no appeal, changed the course of action."[117] ARDC was sidelined in space.

One wonders if a strong commander might have been able to change ARDC's fate. Power had left ARDC on 1 July 1957, only a few months before Sputnik. Would Power have been able to resist ARPA encroachments? ARDC had developed advanced space concepts that included both evolutionary subjects such as advanced ballistic missiles and revolutionary combat concepts such as warfighting formations in Earth orbit long before Sputnik. The Air Force was considering space stations as orbiting component development laboratories and lunar bases. These studies, if allowed to inform the later U.S. efforts in the space race, might have provided the concepts from which powerful space doctrine could have emerged.

Much of Power's efforts to nurture an Air Force space program remain poorly understood. This is ironic because he appreciated history. The ARDC command historian Ernest G. Schwiebert opened his official history, *History of the Air Research and Development Command 1 January—30 June 1955*, with a foreword describing Power's policy toward and relationship with his command historian's office. In 1955 Power directed the command historian to attend all top-level meetings, conferences, briefings, and other events at his own discretion, resulting in an unprecedented level of openness between the commander and historian. "General Power then expressed what, to the historian, is the best possible assignment: that once the historian had all the facts, he should tell the story exactly as it happened and 'let the chips fall where they may.'"[118] This foreshadowed and underscored Power's attitudes about open communication. He believed in openness and by nature did not appreciate secrecy outside of very slim parameters. This character trait revealed itself often in later events, including during the Cuban Missile Crisis and in some of Power's unorthodox ideas to strengthen deterrence.

Power accomplished many things as commander of ARDC. He oversaw the development of some of the most iconic equipment of the Cold War U.S. Air Force. He held overall responsibility for the Atlas ICBM and used his authority to impose a controversial merger of the Air Force's ICBM, TBM, and satellite systems to forge the WDD into a space organization against the wishes of Gen. Bernard Schriever, the "father of the Air Force space program." He brought the Air Force into the space age intellectually with his SR studies and brought the U.S. industrial base to bear on pressing space questions. He also saw national leadership stripping the Air Force of its space responsibilities through the creation of ARPA and NASA and the marginalization of the SR series of space studies he initiated. However, the space work begun by ARDC under Power's leadership did not die with the activation of ARPA. The Air Force space vision, carried on by the Air Force space study program using Power's SR system, would find a new champion. Gen. Curtis LeMay was appointed vice chief of staff of the Air Force in July 1957, and SAC was in need of a new commander. The focus of advanced Air Force space thinking would move from a defanged ARDC to one of the most powerful military organizations ever created—the Strategic Air Command and its new commander in chief, Gen. Thomas S. Power.

CHAPTER 4

Power as CINCSAC

Strategic Air Command, 1957–61

In nine years, Gen. Curtis E. LeMay had organized and developed a well-oiled machine in Strategic Air Command. He transformed a small, faltering collection of obsolete aircraft and demoralized pilots into the world's most technologically advanced nuclear strike force with a global reach. SAC had grown under LeMay by four times in personnel and three times in aircraft, and men and materiel had also increased in quality. As LeMay's deputy aside from his four years at ARDC, Thomas S. Power also shared much of the credit of building SAC. When LeMay handed him the reins on 1 July 1957, the 29,946 officers, 174,030 airmen, 2,711 tactical aircraft, 40 bombardment and strategic wings, 5 strategic reconnaissance wings, 40 refueling squadrons, 68 bases spanning the globe, and the mission of deterring Soviet aggression via nuclear retaliation became newly promoted Gen. Thomas S. Power's responsibility.[1] No longer would the technological future of the Air Force be Power's primary concern. Now he had the immediate responsibility of defending U.S. interests and ensuring the Cold War stayed cold.

The SAC Power inherited was still a work in progress. The new commander had to improve SAC's organizational structure, especially to accommodate the new weapons he had helped develop at ARDC such as the ballistic missile, the satellite, and other space programs, but his biggest challenge was to lead SAC operationally—to thwart communist aggression as the Soviets began to field capabilities that could directly threaten the United States during the darkest days of the Cold War. Although SAC was unquestionably successful in its deterrent role during LeMay's tenure, much of its success in those years can be attributed to the

Soviet Union's lack of capability.[2] When Power took command, SAC was much more vulnerable due to the Soviet Union's remarkable advances in space technology. The Soviet Union successfully launched an operational ICBM on 26 August 1957 and three months later, on 4 October 1957, proved it could hit SAC bases from Russian territory with the launch of Sputnik, the world's first artificial satellite.

The ICBM manifested a Soviet threat that had been gaining steam for over a decade. The Soviet detonation of a fission weapon in 1949 had broken the U.S. atomic monopoly much earlier than analysts had anticipated, but fission bombs still had relatively low yields. Because of their limited destructive power, fission bombs did not change the strategic warfare calculus significantly from World War II. The Soviets needed hundreds of bombers with fission weapons to launch a successful nuclear first strike on the United States. Furthermore, the limited speed, range, and vulnerability of the scant number of Soviet bombers at the time—coupled with the significant early warning time the United States could anticipate—made defending against a Soviet air attack with SAC intact a reasonable assurance.

Then, the Soviets again shocked analysts when they detonated a thermonuclear weapon in 1953. Now one Soviet bomber with one fusion weapon could destroy an American city, or an entire SAC base, all by itself. A year later, the Soviets began production of two new long-range bombers with the range to attack at least a few targets in the United States without the need for refueling: the propeller-driven Tu-95 Bear and the all-jet M-4 Bison aircraft. By 1956 many defense analysts believed the Soviet Union had produced enough of both aircraft and ordnance to have a formidable offensive capability to strike the United States, though without enough force to preclude a strong SAC counterattack.[3]

The Soviet ICBM, however, and a perceived growing "missile gap" threatened to place SAC's survivability in doubt. SAC bombers and tankers would have only a few minutes to escape destruction in the event of a Russian ICBM strike, and they would need to be armed at all times in order to retaliate. The threat to SAC, and the intense pressure on its commanders and combat crews, beyond 1957 was far worse than anything

SAC had seen before. Faced with such an altered strategic picture, within a few weeks of taking command Power became "the first CINCSAC to be faced with a credible Soviet challenge" to SAC's deterrent mission.[4]

LeMay had every confidence Power was up to the new challenge, telling SAC officers at the change of command ceremony that Power was "one of the finest combat leaders in the Air Force."[5] For his part, Power's most intense belief about SAC was that it was first and foremost a deterrent force. Perhaps unknowingly channeling the great war theorist Sun Tzu, Power believed SAC's greatest success would be to defeat the Soviet Union without fighting. Power's second fundamental belief was closely linked to the first but has often been mistaken as paradoxical by later historians. He believed that the surest way to promote peace and deterrence was to make SAC the strongest nuclear strike force possible. That meant making and keeping SAC the undisputed master of strategic nuclear warfare, which required the command to plan, remain alert, and train to the standards of fighting nuclear war—at all times. Power believed deterrence only came from possessing a war-winning capability. Thus, SAC was designed to deter general nuclear war by being ready to destroy the Soviet Union at any time, in the face of any threat, on the order of the president of the United States. Power could provide this capability because SAC developed the necessary strength to achieve its primary mission "to maintain peace through an overpowering posture of strength" against any aggressor, including the Soviet Union.[6]

Power's insistence on an overwhelming position of strength convinced some that he was a warmonger who was in favor of preventive war and wanted to strike the Soviet Union to end the Cold War with a surprise nuclear blow. Such accusations plagued him for the rest of his life. Power often had to defend himself against such charges, claiming, "I am not advocating preventive war. The mission of SAC is deterrence. . . . I think you can deter by operating from a platform of strength—unquestionable strength. If we go on the premise of trying to deter a war, I also submit that you will not deter a war unless you have the capability to start a war. . . . Any fool can get in a war. It takes a smart man to stay out of one on his terms."[7] In this, Power was a strict adherent of the Eisenhower administration's policy of massive retaliation, whereby any aggressive military action against the United States or its allies would invite a counterstrike by the full U.S. nuclear arsenal. By 1957 such an assault would completely annihilate any aggressor, including the Soviet Union.

Since massive retaliation formed the basis for Power's concept of deterrence, it is not surprising that he was a disciple of the policy. Power, who had seen the destructive power of every atomic weapon since the device's inception, was convinced that no rational adversary would seriously consider any aggression that might warrant the full nuclear wrath of the United States. In many ways, Power's belief matched historian Campbell Craig's conception of Eisenhower's own sense of the efficacy of the threat of nuclear massive retaliation. Eisenhower believed nothing less than the threat of massive retaliation would limit Soviet ambitions. In order to make Eisenhower's threat believable, the president needed generals who would carry out this threat and be convincing in public. Much of Power's belligerence may have helped convince the Soviet Union that the United States was dead serious about its dedication to massive retaliation.[8]

Power also believed national preparedness was key to deterrence. Having experienced the bitter fruits borne of unpreparedness in the air mail fiasco and the early years of World War II, Power fought doggedly against the growing trend toward embracing disarmament in the 1960s. He viewed disarmament schemes as the equally arrogant and ignorant actions of fools that would erode the nation's capability to deter the Soviet Union. In this way, these otherwise fine intentions invited general nuclear war at best and were outright sympathetic to communist goals at worst.

Second only to accomplishing SAC's mission of deterrence in peacetime or massive retaliation in wartime, the lives and well-being of the men under his command were Power's major concern. The staggering losses of aircrew (including his own nephew) under his command in World War II made Power fiercely opposed to anything he thought would put his crews in danger beyond that which was necessary to accomplish SAC's mission. Detractors sometimes accused Power of ignoring the lives of Warsaw Pact populations and disrespecting the lives of his men through schemes such as one-way missions, but those who knew Power knew better. Power himself told the House Appropriations Committee on 13 February 1959, "I get a little indignant with people who become very lofty in their thinking and do not want to kill a few of the enemy but would gladly risk additional American lives. My crews are more important to me than the enemy." Moreover, "If I can send only one airplane over and do the job of a thousand, that is what I want to do!"[9]

Power often described SAC as "charged with being prepared to conduct strategic air operations on a global basis, so that in the event of sudden aggression, SAC can mount simultaneous nuclear retaliatory attacks designed to destroy the war-making capacity of an aggressor to a point they no longer have the will nor the capability to wage war."[10] SAC deterred the Soviet Union from aggression because its capability to win a nuclear war was far greater than that of the Soviet Union, and "Mr. Khrushchev is damn well acquainted with that capability." But Power was no fan of nuclear war, often telling visitors to SAC headquarters, "If man resorts to the use of thermonuclear weapons to settle his differences or accomplish his aims, well then in my opinion, mankind will have reached his highest plateau of stupidity."[11]

When Power took command of SAC, he believed that a general nuclear war could be fought and "won" in a military sense, meaning that the Soviet Union's military forces could be destroyed so completely that they could not achieve their political or military objectives, while the United States would retain sufficient military power to continue to operate effectively in the field. But he did not think nuclear wars could be won in a political sense. The massive amount of death and destruction—millions of casualties and billions of dollars of damage to infrastructure—would never justify any political objective short of national survival in a war of self-defense against the Soviet Union. This distinction between wider political and narrower military victory, coupled with his belief that deterrence required nuclear war–winning capabilities, allowed Power to prepare for general nuclear war while believing it would be disastrous if forced to engage in one.

In addition to Power's belief in the viability of nuclear warfighting was the understanding that "nuclear weapons and their delivery systems existed on the ragged edge of [man's] technological abilities" and were consequently "less than fully reliable." Recognizing this dilemma, Power and other military planners sought to substitute "redundancy to compensate for lack of reliability" and demanded ever-increasing numbers of weapons systems, often to the exasperation of political leaders, which sometimes led to charges of SAC "overkill."[12] Power retained his beliefs on deterrence throughout his tenure as CINCSAC and kept pushing the ragged edge of technology, especially in space.

In a coincidental honor to his work in bringing the Air Force into the space age, the same day Power took command of SAC, the first operational U.S. ICBM unit, the Atlas-equipped 704th Strategic Missile Wing (Training), was activated at Cooke (later Vandenberg) Air Force Base in California.[13] With his ARDC experience, neither space nor ballistic missiles was foreign to Power. However, the technical development of missiles and their actual integration into SAC were much different things. Historians have criticized Power for his lukewarm attitude toward ICBMs, but this charge is overblown. Unlike many proponents of the time, Power saw many flaws in the ICBM. In 1956 he made his position clear: "There is no doubt that our operational missiles are effective weapons and that the missiles now under development hold much promise. . . . But no matter how ingenious, how complex, and how advanced their guidance mechanisms, guided missiles cannot cope with contingencies which have not been previously keyed into them. Only the human brain can make important decisions quickly in unexpected situations."[14]

Power's philosophy on the ICBM was simple. Where the missile could help SAC's mission, it belonged.[15] In 1958 Power argued, "In order to maintain its deterrent strength indefinitely and at a convincing level, SAC must always have, first, an adequate quantity of weapon systems that reflect the latest advances in technology, and second, a global and centrally controlled organization flexible enough to be readily adaptable to any new weapon system or technique, no matter how revolutionary."[16] All of SAC's weapons were intended to "serve but one purpose: the *strategic employment* of the most advanced weapon systems in the most effective manner."[17] Consequently, missiles would "supplement and compliment [*sic*] rather than replace the manned bomber" because "the coordinated employment of both will give us an invaluable flexibility in the choice of weapon systems best suited for each strategic mission."[18]

Power argued, "As with every other new weapon system, SAC must make optimum use of current missile capabilities by exploiting their favorable characteristics and minimizing their deficiencies."[19] The ballistic missile had great range, very high speed, and a quick-reaction capability that made ICBMs invaluable to SAC. However, Power recognized that they were not perfect: "Operational limitations and problems affecting the employment of ballistic missiles in their present state of development pertain primarily to accuracy, reliability, limited payload, maintainability, and lack of operational experience."[20]

ICBMs had a fixed flight trajectory that made them potentially vulnerable to antiballistic missile weapons. ICBMs could also not be recalled once fired or be retargeted in flight. Nor could they alter their flight path in case their initial target position information was wrong. "No matter how ingenious," Power reminded others, "the missile's 'brain' has no reasoning power to deal with unexpected situations but can only follow the instructions given it prior to launch." ICBMs were, in short, highly inflexible. To cope with these problems, Power reasoned, "it is important to assign missiles only to those missions which are within their capability at the prevailing stage of development."[21] SAC required operational flexibility, and that quality was "reflected in improved combat capability only if there is an adequate choice of advanced weapon systems to meet satisfactorily the requirements of any strategic missions SAC may be called upon to perform."[22] Power eventually concluded that the most useful role of the ICBM would be to suppress Soviet air defenses.[23] Operational flexibility required that both manned bombers and ICBMs be in SAC's quiver.

Power was also concerned by the public's tendency to regard the ballistic missile as an ultimate weapon. He offered five reasons why he believed no "ultimate strategic weapon" was possible. First, complex weapons systems have long development timelines—enough time for an adversary to develop a defensive counter. Second, monopolizing highly advanced weapons was no longer possible for "any appreciable length of time"; as an example, Power pointed to the nation's recent loss of its nuclear monopoly. Third, revolutionary weapons would not end arms races since all sides would keep searching for a "still more potent weapon."[24] Fourth, Power stressed that strategic operations entailed "a number of highly specialized missions that can best, or perhaps exclusively, be accomplished by a variety of specialized weapons or combination of weapons." Lastly, he claimed, any "tool fashioned by the mind and hand of man has weaknesses and limitations."[25]

Power also argued that Soviet ICBMs were not meant to deter war like U.S. missiles were, because the Soviets had an offensive purpose. To him, Soviet ICBMs were meant solely to spearhead a Russian first strike on the United States. Since the United States had a purely defensive motivation and the Russians were purely offensive, Power was skeptical of any near-term thawing in the Cold War. Therefore, for him the ICBM would add an important new dynamic to deterrence that SAC had to master: "As ballistic missiles will improve our deterrent posture, so will they improve the Soviets' offensive power. As a result there will continue to be a precarious balance between aggressive intent and deterrence, which is the best we can expect under existing conditions. Whether or not that balance will be maintained hinges on our ability and determination to grow with the threat and on the Soviets' continual respect for our retaliatory strength." Unfortunately, miscalculations could happen, and deterrence could fail. "For this reason," Power argued, "we must make absolutely sure that what we consider our deterrent strength is backed by our actual strength. For it is that strength which we must always be ready to apply decisively in fighting for our survival if deterrence fails."[26]

Power may have been a bomber baron, but he did not have an anti-ICBM bias. The ICBM's role in Power's SAC would not be as an ultimate weapon; it would be commensurate with its advantages and disadvantages as a weapons system. Power applied this rule to any weapons system, including, later, concepts of space weapons. He spent his early years as CINCSAC integrating ICBMs into the force.

Power could not focus solely on the ICBM for long. On 4 October 1957 the Soviets launched Sputnik I, and the race for space became real in the American imagination. The Sputnik launch eliminated from the American psyche many comforting illusions about the conduct of the Cold War. First, Sputnik demolished the faith that Soviet technology rested upon theft of American technology. The Soviet Tu-4 Bull long-range bomber was clearly a copy of a U.S. B-29, and popular sentiment was that Soviet nuclear weapons were developed through the machinations of spies Klaus Fuchs and Ethel and Julius Rosenberg and not the genius of Soviet scientists. In contrast, Sputnik was clearly a feat of technology that the United States had not yet accomplished. The communists were first, and the warm blanket of smug U.S. technological superiority no longer shielded the American people from the icy winds of the Cold War.

Recriminations were not long in coming. American Union Theological Seminary professor and avowed socialist Reinhold Neibuhr had argued for years that a totalitarian state was equal—if not superior—to capitalist democracies in exploiting advances in science. Most Americans prior to Sputnik assumed that the free exchange of ideas enjoyed in democratic countries would always produce more imaginative and productive scientists, but after Sputnik, the public was not so sure that the advantages of freedom could outweigh the seeming superhuman abilities of totalitarian states to shift their entire society's resources toward addressing a single problem. In the United States, this apprehension manifested in accusations that the government and the military had let the public down by allowing the Soviets to get ahead in space. Overseas, citizens of other modern democracies wondered if the American system was truly superior, while newly freed ex-colonial societies saw the Soviet Union, a "dismally backward theocracy in 1917," had advanced technologically beyond the world's richest country within fifty years.[27]

Power, like the military establishment, was not concerned about general U.S. technological inferiority. He was more concerned that a rocket that could lift a 184-pound satellite into an orbit hundreds of miles above Earth could also carry a Soviet thermonuclear warhead to a SAC base in the continental United States in the span of about thirty minutes, and nothing could stop it.

Power knew, however, his demeanor at this time was important. With the new Soviet technological threat, and a more bellicose and aggressive Khrushchev rhetorically threatening the United States in ways not seen since the death of Joseph Stalin, the American people looked to SAC as their primary weapon to keep them safe. Instead of portraying a commander besieged by an implacable enemy with a newfound threatening power abroad and an increasingly skeptical political class resisting necessary defense spending at home, Power expressed confidence, reassurance, and calm. He acted nonchalant about Sputnik and most probably really was. Power was well aware of the Soviet Union's capabilities and what its space launch meant. However, he also knew that SAC still possessed overwhelming nuclear superiority, and the Soviets' ICBM and Sputnik successes did not change it at all. Nonetheless, Power had plans to respond.

Power was asked in a press conference in Paris on 12 November 1957 whether SAC Boeing B-47 Stratojets currently stationed in England carried nuclear weapons. Power recalled that it was a "tricky question" because the B-47s were flying with nuclear weapons, and political leaders in the United States and Britain wanted to keep that hidden. However, Power also wanted to encourage America's European allies and to counter the demoralizing effect of Sputnik. In true Power fashion, he bluntly replied, "Well, we did not build these bombers to carry crushed rose petals!"[28]

Power later reflected that the effect of his words went far beyond what he had intended. The communist countries reacted in uproar, and many excited editorials condemned the United States for placing nuclear weapons on British soil. Khrushchev himself, when talking to international correspondents on 22 November 1957, claimed, "Such a situation serves as an illustration of the extent of the military psychosis in the United States," and he warned that a deranged SAC pilot may inadvertently start a nuclear war.[29] Khrushchev's warning became a staple in antinuclear fiction. Khrushchev did not cite Power by name, but in December a letter from Soviet premier Nikolai Bulganin to Belgian prime minister Achille Van Acker specifically addressed Power's statements, indicating the Soviet Union was paying attention to him.[30]

Many have assigned to Power an "abrasive voice" and a lack of people skills.[31] Like so much else about the man, the facts indicate otherwise. Power had been noticed by Army leadership early as having a presence that was well-suited to public relations. His deep, slightly aristocratic voice commanded any room he was in, and, later, public audiences were often spellbound by his wit and oratory skills. To counter Sputnik, Power decided that the best way to bolster American confidence in the Cold War was to take SAC's message to the public at large.

Power's public relations offensive began on 24 November 1957 when, for the first time ever, a journalist—Pat Frank of *This Week* magazine—was admitted to SAC headquarters. Frank toured, photographed, and described the facility as well as many of SAC's procedures to his American readers—in far greater detail than previously reported.[32] Frank noted that Power "believes the greatest present danger is that the Kremlin, exultant over scientific triumphs, will underestimate the ability of the United States to deliver certain and awful retaliation. Lest the Kremlin be tempted, [Power] is taking the wraps off SAC's new war plan which until now has been kept top secret. . . . The Kremlin must know that neither words nor rockets nor manned bombers can stop SAC. If war comes, nothing can save Russia."[33] Power was communicating SAC's determination to both the Soviets and the American people.

For Power, clear communication was "an important element of deterrence. One, you must *be* strong. And two, you *must* make damn sure that everybody knows it."[34] A few months into Power's media campaign, he spoke plainly to *U.S. News and World Report* and stated his final overriding belief as CINCSAC in May 1958: "It is my considered opinion that the Soviets will attack us once they are convinced that they can do so successfully and with relatively small losses to themselves."[35] Although some criticized the interview as too belligerent, Power believed, "Our enemies had learned that SAC's global alert posture was not an empty threat, and our friends were made to realize that they had to accept the existence of *our* nuclear weapons as their best safeguard against the nuclear weapons of an aggressor."[36]

The Soviet Union recharged its own propaganda thrust in response to Power's public relations campaign. In a 29 April 1958 press conference, Soviet politician Andrei Gromyko explained the new danger of accidental nuclear war through a nuclear accident or a psychotic break in a pilot, even without any "evil intent," because of SAC's airborne alert.[37]

The Soviets also hyped a report that a Russian "forensic psychologist" claimed experimental work demonstrated airmen continually subjected to changes in atmospheric pressure—such as SAC pilots—were prone to "quickly-passing" mental disorders "which ha[ve] a considerable effect on higher nervous activity" and could seriously impair judgment.[38] On 21 May the Soviet press published a completely fabricated letter from Dr. Frank Berry to Secretary of Defense Neil H. McElroy that revealed "over two-thirds" of all U.S. airmen were suffering from psychoneurosis, especially SAC pilots on nuclear alert, and that if this situation was allowed to continue, "the world would be plunged into nuclear war."[39] The Soviets broadcast this charge again on 18 June 1958 with the added claim that U.S. "Air Force personnel are so terrorized by war psychosis that the behavior of individual flyers may lead to major catastrophe." Soviet media also reported other dubious claims, such as General of the Army Omar Bradley "admitting" that "the actions of some unbalanced person in charge of operations at a given moment" may unleash nuclear war.[40]

Although Power may have dismissed this Soviet propaganda at the time, these accusations plagued him for the rest of his life and have altered the perception of SAC to this very day. The 1958 book *Red Alert* and the movies it inspired, *Fail Safe* and the SAC-defining *Dr. Strangelove*, both released in 1964, placed the scenarios pushed by the Soviet propaganda firmly in the minds of the American public. While *Fail Safe* explored nuclear war by accident, *Dr. Strangelove* introduced the world to Gen. Jack D. Ripper (a caricature of Power himself) as a mad SAC commander deliberately starting World War III.

Undeterred, Power maintained SAC's alert posture. To confront the threat that an overwhelming Soviet nuclear first strike might forever be only fifteen minutes away, Power stuck to his decree that a portion of SAC—the SAC alert force—would remain constantly on combat alert, ready to launch its attack at any time, within fifteen minutes. This meant SAC combat crews often worked seventy or more hours a week, a crushing pace. But such was the price of eternal vigilance.

Power realized "that this will entail personal inconvenience and sacrifices to you and your families," as he told his SAC alert force at the time. "But you can be sure that I will do everything possible to ease this aspect of your alert duties. The success of this system depends on you, and I count on you to insur [sic] that the alert force will always be ready to achieve its vital objectives."[41] From start to finish as CINCSAC, Power's first priority was to stare down the Soviet Union in the Cold War game of nuclear deterrence. But Power did not forget that innovation was as necessary as determination for the winning player.

Given the amount of space exposure Power received during his time in ARDC, it is unsurprising that he was among the first senior Air Force officers to develop a specific policy response to the space challenge. In a 13 August 1958 letter to Air Force chief of staff Gen. Thomas D. White, Power outlined his SAC space policy. "During the past year, public recognition that we are standing on the threshold of the space age has been amply demonstrated," Power began. "Broad national policy on space exploration, and the organizational structure to carry out this policy, have been established by both executive direction and recently enacted congressional legislation. As an operational command that will translate basic national and Air Force space policies and programs into concrete military capabilities it is deemed appropriate to state Strategic Air Command policies for the development and integration of future spacial [sic] weapon systems."[42]

Power outlined three basic objectives for the American space program. First was "Prestige through Leadership." In the Cold War, Power saw space as a race for technical and scientific leadership: "The prestige that accrues from leadership in space exploration will immeasurably strengthen the position of the Free World," and "the conquest of this vast new [space] frontier provides us the channel for unlimited U.S. initiative."[43]

Second, space provided a new medium to apply military power "through application or potential application to the enemy heartland— the source of hostile power." SAC, in particular, could use space-based deterrence weapons "to expand the airpower of today into the space power of tomorrow." Space power should be used for reconnaissance, but also for weapons systems. "We must not," Power wrote, "in the fashion of decadent nations, permit our gross potential to be bled off into purely defensive weapons, weapons that will neither further our advance into space nor achieve any significant capability until just too late to be of any real military worth. As we enter the space era the primacy of the offensive has never been more clearly defined."[44]

Third, Power stressed the economic and commercial potential of space. At some point, he reasoned, "technological progress will provide the basis for astronautics to contribute to civilization in the next century as significantly as aeronautics has in the twentieth century."[45]

In support of these three objectives, Power argued scientific and military space efforts needed to remain integrated in a national space program aimed at conquering space. "The rate at which this conquest will be achieved is a function of our national will and determination, the proper allocation and concentration of resources, and the integrated direction of a long term program."[46]

Power also stressed the importance of establishing the role of man in the space environment, but his highest priority for space was for "offensive space weapons" to "provide a dimensional extension in system capability for the accomplishment of the strategic air warfare mission." Power concluded, "Because space offers the ultimate in mobility and dispersal for weapons which can be addressed at the enemy heartland, the ultimate in deterrence may very well be in this direction." For Power, these two firm conclusions, that man in space was essential and that the future of deterrence would be in space, "form the premises for SAC policy on future space programs."[47]

Power, in an October 1958 address, was able to publicize some of SAC's new space policy. "Today," Power began, "space is no longer an exclusively scientific medium whose primary strategic significance lies in its effect on communications, navigation, weather, and other terrestrial factors." Tomorrow's space vehicles were "expected to carry instruments designed to obtain vital strategic information and to accomplish other strategic missions not even dreamed of a few years ago. Hence, our first efforts in utilizing space will not only usher in the kind of space age man has been dreaming about for untold centuries, but will also initiate a new era in warfare—the era of strategic space operations."[48]

Even though Power admitted that military astronautics was at roughly the same level as military aeronautics in the day of the nineteenth-century hot air balloon, Power claimed the promise of the ballistic missile was still so great that it would be able to compress the time to apply firepower to a military target from hours with jet bombers to mere minutes. "Therein, I believe, lies the real significance of strategic space operations of the future—the compression of time for both action and reaction to the point where the dramatic role of the time factor will, in effect, assume the significance of a new dimension in military strategy."[49] Ballistic missiles and space weapons will spur "four dimensional warfare," a "new regime of strategic operations in which utilization of the space medium will place a fantastic premium on action and reaction times."[50]

Speculating on what the future might hold, Power argued the "evolution of the 'manned missile' [manned spacecraft] would, of necessity, be gradual and in measured steps. The forerunner of such a missile could well be the B-70 'chemical' bomber [the B-70 was originally meant to use advanced beryllium fuel], which is presently under development as a successor to the most advanced bomber in SAC's present inventory, the B-52." The B-70 was the vital aerospace link between the Boeing B-52 Stratofortress and the strategic "manned missile" because "the B-70 will operate at speeds and altitudes that approach missile performance although still considerably below the performance of a ballistic missile flashing into and out of space."[51] Power argued the Dyna-Soar space plane under development would exceed the utility of a ballistic missile. "Indeed," Power maintained, "such a vehicle would represent the first true manned strategic spacecraft."[52] Power's search for a manned strategic spacecraft became an important part of his space vision.

Power's vision for space in SAC guided him for the rest of his career, and the 1958 SAC space policy is among the most visionary of Air Force space documents. Power identified that the immediate U.S. concern in space was to earn prestige over the communist powers, but his conception of spacepower as an evolutionary step in order to better perform classical airpower missions such as strategic warfare was most important. Power's thoughts were codified into Air Force policy through General White's "Aerospace Concept," which White coined only a few months after Power published SAC's space policy. Power's emphasis on manned spacecraft also shaped Air Force space policy through the mid-1960s. Unfortunately, historians of the space age, such as Walter McDougall, have ignored Power's contributions in their classic treatments, probably because space systems were not Power's foremost concern.[53]

Power had very good reasons for wanting to keep all options open regarding weapons systems. He thought the aerospace concept provided a mix of weapons systems with different operational modes that would be less prone to defeat and more capable of keeping an adversary guessing as to whether they could successfully strike the United States first. Power was worried about the vulnerability of ICBMs to an anti-ICBM technology, so he resisted excessive reliance on them. Operational flexibility required manned bombers and missiles—the most modern available. Speaking to visitors to SAC headquarters, Power argued, "I think we owe it to our military men to give them machines that are at least comparable to the machines of the people that they are going to have to fight against. And there's a rule of thumb, an old rule of thumb, of seven years to obsolescence and ten years to obsolete for first-line inventory." Obsolete technology did not offer flexibility, and if deterrence failed and SAC had to go to war, "you must have flexibility because we're fighting the toughest battle to fight. We're fighting in the retaliatory role. We give the initiative to the other man."[54]

Power kept relatively silent publicly through most of 1958 in order to begin writing a book to bring to the public his thoughts on deterrence and SAC in detail. Enlisting Col. Albert Alexander Arnhym, an aide from ARDC that Power brought to SAC, as a coauthor, both men went to work converting Power's speeches. The men received approval to begin from the Air Force director of information services on 11 June 1958. The title, *Design for Survival*, was Arnhym's idea. Power did not like it and favored *The Problem—Survival*, because "I don't think anyone can truthfully say that we have an actual design for survival."[55] Over the next few months, both men developed an initial manuscript. On 17 September 1958 Power accepted an offer from Random House to publish the work.

When processing the book through Defense Department security and policy review in early 1959, Secretary of Defense Neil H. McElroy reviewed the draft manuscript and refused permission to publish it. Power was not officially told and learned of McElroy's decision only after reading about it in the local Omaha newspaper. McElroy argued it was inappropriate for such a highly placed commander to write a book while on active duty, but the press quickly accused McElroy of censorship. The secretary's statement and Power's stony silence served to fuel rumors that Power's book was a scathing rebuke of current administration policy. Fueling this speculation further, soon after McElroy's decision was announced, Power began speaking publicly again and started to make serious waves.

On 29 April 1959 W. Barton Leach, a Harvard law professor and Air Force Reserve brigadier general, launched a broadside against the secretary of defense's arguments to suppress *Design for Survival*. Leach pointed out that, contrary to McElroy's argument that it was unprecedented for a senior active-duty officer to write a book, there were many books published since World War II by officers on active duty, including ones by Omar Bradley, George Kenney, and Mark Clark. Leach added that, in the current world of rapid technological and military innovation, if the Department of Defense objected to everything that was "unprecedented," then "we are in serious trouble."[56] Power himself was disappointed that McElroy was holding up the book because "I do not believe that we, in the Government, can solve today's problems unless we have the full understanding and support of the American people. It was with this in mind that I wrote the book."[57]

Many editorials around the country excoriated McElroy's decision. The *Greenville News* concluded that McElroy's excuse to suppress the book because Power was on active duty was "nonsense" and that the Pentagon simply did not like the book.[58] The *Denver Post* argued that the public needed to know about defense, claiming, "We can't tell whether we agree with the *military* opinions expressed by General Power in this book. How could we, since we aren't allowed to read it?"[59]

Leach vented to Power privately, writing that a subordinate of McElroy had said the secretary was right to ban the book because if Power's "book was published it would just produce other books by people like [General] Max Taylor and [Admiral] Arleigh Burke—as if this were an objection!" Leach expressed the opinions of many military men, lamenting, "It is all very well for people like Henry Kissinger to write about military policy in the nuclear age, but he doesn't know the facts of life. You professionals do know them, and if these ideas are placed before the informed leaders in comprehensive form, sooner or later the truth will emerge. If you're right, this will appear; if you're wrong, ditto."[60]

Regardless of the criticism, McElroy stayed firm. On 24 September 1959 Random House informed Power that "we think the action by the Secretary inexcusable" and that they had waited "in the obviously foolish hope that Mr. McElroy would change his mind." Unfortunately, they were forced to honor Power's request to cancel the contract to publish *Design for Survival*.[61]

Power had other avenues for getting SAC's message out. He testified on his assessment of the nation's strategic readiness before both houses of Congress in early 1959. After the Atlas ICBM had been declared operational and the Soviet Union built up its own ICBM force, Power began to request accelerated spending on strategic forces. By early spring, *Aviation Week* began echoing Power's calls. In the 13 April 1959 edition, the magazine's editor, Robert Hotz, wrote a scathing editorial detailing Power's testimony. Hotz warned his audience about the alarming problem of SAC's supposedly decreasing combat readiness, claiming the 1960 defense budget was "risking the future of the United States by imposing fiscal limitations on the technical, industrial and military capability of this country to modernize its strategic deterrent forces fast enough to maintain a continuous margin of significant superiority over Soviet strength." Hotz argued that Power was "probably better qualified in modern military technology and the fast-changing factors of the strategic deterrent equation than any other general, active or retired, in this country today. And he is the man who now has the ultimate responsibility to make good in searing thermonuclear combat the promises and boasts made to the American people by political generals and general-politicians."[62] There is little doubt that Hotz was referring to Eisenhower and the joint chiefs with phrases such as "political generals" and "general-politicians." Whether fair or not, such attention did not endear Power to either.

Concerns over obsolescence pervaded Power's congressional testimony. He also expressed great concern over the "fantastic compression of time" in warfare in the modern age. This compression threatened strategic forces' ability to survive a thermonuclear ICBM attack. This lack of warning time had led, in Power's testimony, to his "one-third airborne alert" whereby one out of three of the command's bombers—primarily B-52s—would be armed and airborne at any given time. Operation Chrome Dome had tested a very small airborne alert, but more was required. Power emphasized that an expanded airborne alert was a strictly short-term solution. The permanent solution was the activation of the ballistic missile early warning system radar stations in the north then under construction, which would provide fifteen minutes of warning of an impending Soviet ICBM strike.[63]

Power continued that the current mainstays of the SAC fleet, the B-47 medium bomber and the KC-97 tanker, were becoming obsolete and needed to be replaced. Power's first acquisition priorities were the B-52G heavy bomber, along with its Hound Dog air-launched nuclear missile, and the KC-135A tanker. Secondly, the solid-fueled and much more stable and reactive Minuteman ICBM was necessary to place the ICBM as a reliable leg of the deterrent. True to his sympathy for crews, he also stressed alert crew pay, continuation of the LeMay system of spot promotions, and better on-base housing.[64]

Eventually, his testimony turned to the concept of the "minimum deterrent." What was an adequate deterrent? Some budget-conscious politicians and even military members such as Chief of Naval Operations Adm. Arleigh Burke argued that a minimum deterrent sufficient to dissuading the Russians from attacking was adequate. Power saved a great deal of wrath for these men, claiming, "If anybody tells you they know what the minimum deterrent is, tell them for me that they are liars. The closest to one man who would know what the minimum deterrent is would be Mr. Khrushchev, and frankly I don't think he knows from one week to another. He might be willing to absorb more punishment next week than he wants to absorb today. Therefore, deterrence is not a concrete or finite amount."[65]

Some have argued that, instead of a "minimum deterrent," Power wanted a "maximum deterrent."[66] In his testimony, it certainly sounds true. When Rep. George H. Mahon (a Democrat from Texas) questioned Power's request for more B-52s, B-58s, and Atlas ICBMs by asking, "Is it sufficiently important that we do something about this?" Power testily replied, "I think you are just risking the whole country. That is how important I feel it is. If you do not deter this man [Khrushchev or his chief planner], as I said before, nobody is going to win a thermonuclear war. . . . The force which is now programmed—which I am told by the Pentagon is now programmed—is not adequate because it is not coming fast enough."[67]

Power often explained his concept of deterrence—and the flaw of minimum deterrence—by comparing it to shingling the roof of a house or buying insurance. Power argued that both minimum and maximum deterrents were equally foolish. Too small a deterrent would invite war. Too large a deterrent would "destroy economically what you're trying to protect militarily."[68] Although duplication of effort and equipment in nuclear deterrence was not necessarily efficient, it was certainly not wasteful. In a "sensible margin," Power argued, "there is duplication and waste to the same extent that there's duplication and waste when you shingle a roof. Now do you put the shingles end-to-end? No, you don't put the shingles end-to-end! You overlap them, and the more confidence you want to have that you're building a good roof that won't leak, the more you overlap your shingles." The principle that guided Power, the sensible margin, was the same principle for insurance. "If you knew exactly how much you were going to be sued for . . . you'd be a fool to take out a penny's worth of insurance more than that. But you don't know. So, depending on who you are you take a varying amount. It depends on what you're trying to protect. What price you put on the peace of mind for security." The fundamental question to the American people was how much they were prepared to spend to prevent nuclear war and attain a measure of peace of mind.[69]

Considerable disagreement over what constituted an adequate deterrent had already arisen between the armed services' senior staffs. The dispute took on a very acrimonious edge during the John F. Kennedy administration, but the final Eisenhower years set the stage for the conflict. Power's testimony was an early example of that debate as he chastised the Army and Navy for preparing for the last war at the expense of preventing the next one. Power insisted that modern war would not allow any time for mobilization as was possible during World War II. The military that was left after a first strike by the Soviets would be all that the United States would ever be able to field. He implied that the U.S. Army and U.S. Navy were preparing for a general war like World War II and that the other services' "minimum deterrent" ideas, of which Admiral Burke was a vocal champion, were predicated on post-attack expansion. When a subcommittee member brought up the "minimum deterrent" viewpoints of Army Gen. Maxwell Taylor and "others in the Navy," Power replied that "General Taylor has a lot more confidence in our overall ability than I do under the condition where they attack us."[70]

Power also discussed his views of "small wars," with increasingly worrisome news from Vietnam hanging over the discussion. Power's philosophy was quite simple: the difference between small wars and large wars was only the number of nuclear weapons you would have to use to finish it. "I do not want to see us use conventional bombs, because I have a deep moral sense as it applies to Americans," Power explained.[71] If nuclear weapons could save American lives, Power felt, the United States was obligated to use them.

Power continued to hammer his points in Congressional testimony whenever he could. The day after Power again testified to the House on strategic readiness on 2 February 1960, President Eisenhower responded to a question about airborne alert: "Too many of these general[s] have all sorts of ideas. . . . I have been long enough in the military service that I assure you that I cannot be particularly disturbed because everybody with a parochial viewpoint all over the place comes along and says that the bosses know nothing about it." Eisenhower told the reporters that he placed his trust in the judgment of his secretary of defense and the joint chiefs of staff, adding that he was "not trying to impugn the patriotism and earnestness" of these generals. They were, after all, "the ablest people we could get. That's the reason they were selected."[72]

Trevor Gardner was among the first to congratulate Power on his position before Congress on airborne alert, writing, "You are now a member of a rather small but exclusive group of people serving under General Eisenhower who have put the country's needs ahead of their own interests. . . . I believe the President will regret his comments on your views as much as he must regret his comments on the success of Sputnik I, which were, if you remember, 'It doesn't bother me one iota.'"[73] Air Force legends Ira Eaker and Carl "Tooey" Spaatz sent letters of congratulations. Not everyone was as supportive. One man sent Power a handwritten note: "Here is hoping you get into one of those bomers [sic] and stay up there. Then perhaps we would not have to read about your silly ideas."[74]

Although Power's testimony to the House became the most well-known because of Hotz' *Aviation Week* articles, his similar testimony a week earlier to the Senate military preparedness subcommittee proved to be just as consequential politically. The Senate subcommittee was chaired by Sen. Lyndon B. Johnson, with Senators John F. Kennedy and Stuart Symington, a former Air Force secretary, in attendance. All three men were considered as potential 1960 Democratic presidential candidates, and all would eventually charge the Eisenhower administration with allowing the Russians to become stronger than the United States through the so-called "missile gap."

Power's testimony ignited a vicious public debate over the nation's strategic preparedness. Eisenhower, in an effort to calm American fears, made a speech that some interpreted as an advocacy of a "first-strike" policy, though it probably was not. Admiral Burke told a Phoenix, Arizona, audience that "the world well knows that it is a firm United States policy that we will not initiate the destruction of a large part of the world by launching a general nuclear war."[75]

Newspaper columnist Jack Anderson, who had read a bootleg copy of *Design for Survival*, wrote that U.S. "military policy is essentially defensive. This does not preclude the possibility that we may have to strike the first blow. But while preemption [striking an enemy preparing for an imminent strike, such as arming planes and fueling missiles before they are launched] on our part might initiate open warfare, it would still not represent offensive strategy because it would have been undertaken only in self-defense."[76]

It was not a flawed morality but rather the "fantastic compression of time" that had given foundation to ideas of preemption. Advocates of a defensive "preemptive" first-strike posture believed the Soviet missile force could destroy virtually the entire U.S. retaliatory force by 1964. This probably was not quite so, but the widespread perception mattered. As a result, even opponents of a first-strike policy were forced to concede that Power's demand for more modern strategic weapons, with far greater survivability than manned bombers and first-generation liquid-fueled Atlas missiles, could not simply be ignored. SAC's weapons needed to become less vulnerable than they were in 1957. In the *Bulletin of Atomic Scientists*, physicist Eugene Rabinowitz argued that, while he was against the airborne alert and other measures to increase SAC's alert posture, he accepted that the drive for what he called "preventive war," which, in actuality, was preemptive war, could only be met through the development of more advanced, survivable, and hardened weapons systems. "The Strategic Air Command . . . has long entertained the idea that it is not going to wait for enemy missiles or bombers to rain destruction on its bases," Rabinowitz explained; "Only when the United States acquires an arsenal of solid fuel rockets . . . will the arguments for pre-emptive attack lose their persuasiveness."[77]

The explosive rhetoric in the U.S. debate over preventive and pre-emptive war was not lost on the Soviets, especially Russian officers who knew that the Soviet ICBM fleet was nowhere near as formidable as the Americans feared. Soviet propagandists attempted to turn this weakness into public relations victories by claiming that U.S. leaders, like Power, were simply trying to scare the American people into feeding their war machine and using the peaceful Russians as scapegoats. The Soviet military journal *Red Star* insisted that "the American military command is now endeavoring to frighten the broad masses, placing before them the question: Either we attack the Soviet Union or they will destroy us first."[78]

Most of the confusion over the size of the Soviet ICBM threat stemmed from the contradictory reports provided by the intelligence community. *National Intelligence Estimate (NIE) 1958*, the initial document that projected the buildup of the Soviet missile program, was based on the Soviets' estimated maximum ability to produce missiles. Those figures were revised downward drastically in 1959 and again in 1960 because information from the newly available Lockheed U-2 reconnaissance aircraft overflights of Russian airspace provided increasingly better raw data. Even after the publication of the revised NIEs, many in the Department of Defense chose to continue basing their own projections on NIE 1958. Thus, at least two official government estimates of projected Soviet missile strength emerged: the low estimate based on an "orderly" Soviet program derived from observed deployed missiles, and a high estimate based on a "crash" program derived from Soviet missile production capability. Air Force planners—especially those at SAC—used the high estimate. The Army and Navy both used the smaller estimate to better conform to their minimum deterrence assumptions. Historian Desmond Ball estimates that there were at least a half-dozen distinctive—and conflicting—estimates of the Soviet ICBM force strength with a government imprimatur in early 1960.[79]

The debate over near-term Soviet missile capability polarized along both partisan political lines and service lines. Although he tried to be neutral and steer a middle course, Eisenhower by 1960 found himself most aligned with the minimum deterrence advocates, whose great military champion and apologist was Admiral Burke. Power, alternatively, championed the high-end estimates to support his quest to maintain a sizeable nuclear superiority against the Soviets.

It was within this context that Power delivered a highly controversial speech before the New York Economic Club on 19 January 1960. The inflammatory speech given in an election year was bound to draw attention from the Democrats controlling Congress, who were searching for issues with which to discredit the Republicans. Furthermore, syndicated columnist Joseph Alsop was in attendance and, on 25 January, reprinted major portions of the general's speech in his column. Power lectured to the attentive audience, "If [the Soviets] could effectively threaten us from a position of such military superiority that we would feel unable to defend ourselves, our capability to resist would be greatly reduced, if not nullified." This nightmare would not need much to become reality. This "would not take very many missiles under present conditions," Power warned, because the roughly one hundred SAC bases were "soft" targets, easily targeted by Soviet missiles. "It would take an average of three missiles, in their current stage of development, to give an aggressor a mathematical probability of ninety-five percent that he can destroy one given soft target. . . . This means that, with only three hundred ballistic missiles, the Soviets could virtually wipe out our entire nuclear strike capability within a span of 30 minutes."[80] The audience was horrified. However, Power finished his speech claiming that nuclear superiority was still in reach of the American people. All they needed to do was demand it.

Power's original speech had been significantly altered by Department of Defense policy review. Still, the speech was remarkably controversial.[81] Former world heavyweight boxing champion Gene Tunney called it "the best explanation of military matters that I have heard since the end of the war."[82] Lewis Shea, president of the Connecticut National

Bank, said the speech has "given me a little more optimism than I had, having listened so much to the Press. It is good to know that the professional and military people are not really ignoring the defense of our country," and he came away from Power's speech "feeling much better."[83]

Alsop interpreted the speech as Power claiming the Eisenhower administration was jeopardizing the future of Western civilization and that the United States needed to reverse course back to strategic superiority right away. He ended his column with a few ominous questions: "[Nathan] Twining and [Secretary of Defense Thomas] Gates have derived comforting conviction from the National Intelligence Estimates. But are these national estimates correct? And is it permissible to gamble the whole national future on mere estimates?"[84]

Eisenhower was incensed by "parochial general" Power's speech and Alsop's muckraking. Gates immediately stated publicly that there was no deterrent gap, and, eventually the president was forced to say the same thing at a press conference. Eisenhower pointed out his own long military experience and claimed, "I've spent my life in this and I know more about it than almost anybody . . . because I have given my life to it. . . . I believe that the matter of defense has been handled well . . . and I think those people that are trying to make defense a partisan matter are doing a disservice to the United States."[85]

Eisenhower's efforts to defuse the deterrence debate did not work. A *Newsweek* article summed up the situation: "A growing sense of national uneasiness could be detected last week—and the politicians seized upon it eagerly. In a presidential election year, national defense was far too good an issue for the Democrats to pass up."[86]

Power and Alsop kept up the heat as well. Power criticized Eisenhower's position on the airborne alert, cuts to the B-70 bomber, the resistance to the military use of space, and the Polaris submarine-launched ballistic missile. Alsop continued "unmasking" the supposed pitfalls of Eisenhower's national defense policy. He accused the administration of "literally playing a gigantic game of Russian roulette with the national future." He quoted Power extensively to support his own convictions, demanding better early warning systems and an airborne alert.[87]

Not to be outdone, and furious with the cuts made to the B-70 program specifically, was *Aviation Week* editor Robert Hotz. Also quoting Power, Hotz lambasted Eisenhower as a "misinformed, tired old man who will not be contradicted." Perhaps the worst criticism of the Eisenhower administration came from Senator Symington. On 27 January he flatly stated that "the American people are being enticed down the trail of insecurity by the issuance of misinformation about our deterrent power and especially about the missile gap." Eisenhower voiced his anger and frustration over the situation in an emotional response to Symington's charges on 17 February: "If anybody—anybody—believes that I have deliberately misled the American people, I'd like to tell him to his face what I think about him. This is a charge that I think is despicable, and I have never made it against anyone in the world."[88]

Power also kept up the heat on the Soviet Union. He worked again with Hotz to develop the special report "SAC in Transition." On 27 June 1960 Hotz, "recalling [Power's] interest in having Mr. Khrushchev adequately briefed on SAC," informed the general that the Soviet air attaché had just visited his office to pick up three copies of the report.[89] Power replied that he was "gratified" and added, "As you know, I have always maintained that SAC's strength cannot serve as an effective deterrent to war—our primary mission—unless that strength is known and respected throughout the world. It is good to know that your special report is contributing toward that objective."[90]

While Power was fighting for SAC's philosophical survival with skill and acumen, he continued to lead the men of SAC. Regardless of LeMay's assessment that Power was an aristocratic bastard, not all who served with Power saw him as sadistic or without people skills. Lt. Gen. Paul K. Carlton Jr., a former surgeon general of the Air Force, tells the story of how Power intervened to save the career of his father, Paul K. Carlton Sr., when he was a brigadier general in SAC, from an overbearing commander who wanted to fire Carlton for delivering a politically damaging accident report. The junior Carlton, who fondly remembered hunting with Power as a boy, recalled that Power was a man with integrity and stated firmly that it was "not my understanding or observation" that Power was sadistic or acted in any way other than as a gentleman.[91]

Later scholars charged SAC, and specifically Power, with a disdain for education and used SAC's reluctance to send officers to the Air War College and other advanced education as evidence.[92] Power may have explained part of his reluctance in a letter to Air Force chief of staff Gen. Thomas White on 15 October 1960: "Your staff has advised me that SAC's disproportionately high losses to the 1961 Senior Service Schools result from the disproportionately high number of outstanding colonels in this command. Thirty-one per cent of the selectees are from SAC, although we have only fifteen per cent of the USAF colonels. I am bringing this to your attention with the hope that in the next General Officer list this per cent of outstanding colonels will be reflected in promotions to general."[93]

Power received a letter from the concerned wife of a staff sergeant who complained that her husband was mocked by many officers and, as a result, morale in his unit was at an all-time low. She closed her letter worried that her husband's career might come to harm from her writing the letter directly to Power. Power responded within days, telling her that he talked directly to the vice commander of her husband's wing (the commander was away) and personally directed him to investigate her allegations and report the results directly to Power. He concluded by telling her, "I appreciate your frank letter and want to assure you that you need not feel any concern about sending it to me. The welfare of our combat crews and their families is uppermost in my mind," and he assured her that if any of her complaints were found justified, they would be corrected immediately.[94]

Even with all the political, operational, and personal turmoil Power dealt with as CINCSAC, he still insisted on telling the SAC and Air Force story through film. Power supported his old friend Beirne Lay's attempt to develop a weekly television drama about SAC starring Jimmy Stewart, but the project never materialized. Next, Power gave producer Sy Bartlett and his team unprecedented access to film their movie *A Gathering of*

Eagles starring Rock Hudson at SAC headquarters and Offutt Air Force Base. Power assisted with the script as early as 1961 when it was called "A Man's Castle."

On 9 December 1961 Power met with Bartlett to discuss the production. Power was most interested that "the SAC image of deterrence is logically and dramatically presented to the public."[95] Bartlett adjusted the attention of the movie to focus on three points: "the reason for SAC and why its mission transcends consideration of individuals," the mixed force bomber/missile concept, and the SAC background of Rock Hudson's wing commander character. Also, Bartlett stressed that the missile crews in the picture would have very high morale, accentuating "the fact that these men have been selected because of their scientific and technical backgrounds." Bartlett also assured Power there would be no mention of the Air Force in the film and that it would "establish SAC as a complete entity," though whether Power wanted the Air Force removed because he wanted to stress SAC's combatant command role as a specified command or for reasons of personal pride is unknown (perhaps both).[96] Bartlett also assured Power that "I bitterly resent the TV shows and movies that play fast and loose with SAC and its mission." After all, "I am also under 'contract' to you as an M-Day Designee [part-time Reserve officer] assigned to the 15th [Air Force]." The producer of *A Gathering of Eagles* was SAC, too! Power asked that Bartlett not use his name as an adviser to the movie, a request to which Bartlett grudgingly agreed.[97]

The filmmakers were allowed access to B-52 and KC-135 aircraft operations and Titan I missile sites at Beale Air Force Base, California, to accurately portray the operations of a blended Strategic Aerospace Wing. Power often went to the set to advise on the production, even discussing SAC operations with Rock Hudson on occasion, in accordance with Power's desire to both tell the SAC story and be a showman himself. The fictional CINCSAC was played by Leif Erickson. *A Gathering of Eagles* was released in 1963 to poor reviews and box office tallies. The movie may have suffered, at least in part, due to overexposure of SAC in the public mind between the film's production and its eventual release.

Interestingly, Sy Bartlett and director Delbert Mann noticed that SAC personnel were unusually tense as they wrapped filming at SAC headquarters in October 1962. Only after President John Kennedy's public address a few days later did they find out why. SAC had discovered Soviet nuclear ballistic missiles being deployed in Cuba.

Beginning in 1962, even though he fought for SAC as hard as he could, Power could not help but feel as if some official walls had begun to close in on him. On 12 December 1961 Power received a draft chapter on the history of the Air Research and Development Command, from historian Samuel Milner of the AF office of aerospace research, for review. In it, Milner significantly diminished Power's role at ARDC and greatly expanded his successor's role in ARDC's space research and development program. To rectify the problem, Power passed the draft chapter to his former ARDC historian, Ernest Schwiebert. He explained to Milner that the "entire study reveals a complete misunderstanding and evaluation of General Power and General Anderson [Samuel E. Anderson, Power's successor] as ARDC commanders. In fact, one knowledgeable officer remarked to this reviewer that the treatment accorded to the two men should be just reversed."[98] Milner later assured Power that he would revise the chapter using the new information he was given. However, Milner's final history did not favor Power's outlook or activities.

This historical revision gave merely a glimpse of what was to come. Not only was Power being written out of the history he helped create, but government censors also began to delay and degrade his ability to publish. Power and Arnhym had written an article to appear in the winter-spring 1961–62 issue of Air University Quarterly Review titled "The Price of Survival." It and three other articles published were held up by the Department of State for so long that the issue was published without any of the articles going to press. Only in January 1962 did Power learn that the State Department had concluded in November "that it would not be desirable for the article to be published at this time." The U.S. Arms Control and Disarmament Agency had, characteristically, taken issue with Power's dim view of both Soviet truthfulness and any potential benefits of disarmament as well as his usual recourse to rhetorical absolutism, especially the assertion that "all disarmament efforts have encouraged war."[99] Maj. Gen. Arno H. Luehman, Air Force director of information, asked if Power would consider incorporating the State Department's suggestions into a revised article.[100] Power flatly refused: "Full compliance with the State Department comments not only would require a major rewriting job and change in the basic premise of the paper but also would place me in the awkward position of supporting views which are decidedly contrary to my own convictions and personal experiences."[101]

Air Force support of Power's efforts at SAC can be split between the "bomber barons," who maintained faith with classic airpower theory and strategic bombing, and the "fighter pragmatists" who eventually sided with Secretary of Defense Robert McNamara's views on limited war.[102] Tooey Spaatz wrote on 30 March 1961 that, naturally, "all of us over-age former Air Force officers have followed your career with great interest. I have been very much inspired by your leadership of our Strategic Air Command which, as we all know, is the real military force in the world today."[103] On 26 October 1961 Ira Eaker wrote to Power, saying, "I have long admired your ideas on our military posture, and particularly the courageous and clear way in which you present these ideas to the public and Congressional Committees" and asking to visit Power at SAC to get his thoughts on a series of articles Eaker planned to write for the *New York Herald Tribune*.[104] Power readily agreed to help in any way he could and said that he was looking forward to hosting Eaker at SAC.[105]

Alternatively, retired Lt. Gen. Lloyd "Dick" Leavitt, a fighter pilot who later transferred to SAC flying U-2 and B-52 aircraft, remembers a classified briefing Power sent to all his bomber aircrews on alert. The heart of the presentation was a chart with two lines that represented the number of Soviet and SAC ICBMs on alert and projected within the next few months. Power wanted the bomber crews to know that "a Soviet nuclear attack was likely when the Soviets had more ICBMs than the United States" and that the B-52 bomber crews had to be ready to immediately retaliate. Although Leavitt had earlier "been impressed by the eloquence of General Power" and Power had inspired Leavitt to read nuclear theorists Herman Kahn and Albert Wohlstetter, Leavitt recalled that the "briefing destroyed the confidence I had in General Power." He believed that the briefing may have been Power's way to motivate his aircrews by "exaggerating the probability of a near-term Soviet attack," but he feared that Power may have been preparing crews to launch a preemptive attack before the lines of the chart crossed into the Soviet Union's favor. Leavitt explained his own beliefs regarding Power's briefing and nuclear war: "It seemed irrational to me that the USSR would initiate an attack against the United States because its ICBM force was only marginally larger than our ICBM force in 1962" and that successful "deterrence meant the Soviet Union would not attack the United States with nuclear weapons because its leaders knew our *retaliatory* response would cause unacceptable damage to their own country."[106]

For friend and foe alike, and on both the domestic and international stages, Thomas Power had arrived as a polarizing Cold War leader by the early 1960s. As the Cold War increased in intensity, that polarization only grew.

CHAPTER 5

Planning for Armageddon

The Single Integrated Operational Plan, 1960

Strategic Air Command fundamentally changed when Secretary of Defense Thomas Gates directed the establishment of a joint staff at SAC headquarters specifically dedicated to integrating all U.S., and eventually allied, strategic nuclear capability into one operational plan— the Single Integrated Operational Plan (SIOP)—on 16 August 1960. That day, he ended a nuclear planning debate that had been ongoing since 1952. Gates considered the decision to create the SIOP to be the most important decision he made in his seven years at the Pentagon. Power, who had been part of the debate from the beginning, led the team that brought Gates' vision to fruition.

The problem of nuclear planning had its roots as early as the end of World War II. From almost the day after the Nagasaki strike to the beginning of the Korean War, the nation's Air Force was the only service that possessed the ability to deliver an atomic weapon. Only heavy bombers could carry those massive early weapons to target in 1945, and only the Army Air Force had them. However, attempting to apply the lessons learned from World War II, the defense establishment pressed to organize future warfighting tasks jointly by theater. The services would work together in joint organizations (composed of two or more services) under a single flag officer assigned responsibility for a specific geographic area, in organizations with names such as United States Pacific Command, European Command, and Atlantic Command.

At the same time, the Army Air Force argued that a Strategic Air Command led by an Air Force officer with a global perspective be established to wage war with atomic weapons in the nuclear age. Starting a pattern that would frustrate SAC for its entire existence, the Air Force plan was resisted by the Navy, which argued SAC should not control any forces normally based in other theater-focused commands. The Navy's argument won the day, and in 1946 SAC was named a specified command (consisting only of Air Force elements) rather than a unified command comprised of forces from all services.[1]

This arrangement worked so long as only Air Force aircraft assigned to SAC could carry nuclear weapons. Since only SAC could fight a nuclear war, there was no real need for coordinating strategic nuclear plans with theater commanders. As part of the compromise to make SAC a specified command, the president ensured SAC's commander reported directly to the Joint Chiefs of Staff (JCS) in 1946. On occasion, theater commanders attempted to chip away SAC's responsibilities by asserting more authority. In response, the JCS often strengthened the fraying bonds between it and SAC.

By the early 1950s, as weapons became lighter and smaller, and in response to Eisenhower's "New Look" defense policies, all the services began to develop nuclear delivery–capable weapons systems. The Navy announced in 1952 that all future attack planes would be capable of carrying tactical nuclear weapons. The Army started arming units in Europe and the Far East with tactical nuclear weapons as well. Air Force tactical aircraft were modified to carry nuclear weapons. When these tactical systems became operational, theater commanders gained access to a wide variety of nuclear weapons. With these developments, nuclear planning and execution faced increased requirements for coordination.

Unfortunately, nuclear proliferation was not limited to the U.S. military services. The Soviet Union detonated an atomic bomb in 1949, and its airpower was growing so quickly that by 1952 the Soviet air force could strike anywhere in the United States. To respond to the increased threat of the Soviet Union and growing encroachment of theater commanders into nuclear matters, the JCS formed an ad hoc committee in March 1952 to study the existing procedures for the control and coordination of atomic operations across the military. The committee recommended coordinating all nuclear operations to maximize combat effectiveness.

The JCS accepted the committee's recommendations and established two joint coordination centers (JCCs)—one in Buckinghamshire, United Kingdom, and another in Tokyo, Japan. However, these JCCs were meant to coordinate operations during combat and had no authority to coordinate nuclear planning prior to hostilities.[2]

Unsurprisingly, JCC exercises made clear that coordination of atomic plans had to occur before hostilities began in order to be effective. Consequently, the JCS directed that each theater commander submit an atomic annex for all theater war plans for coordination among the theater commanders and SAC. SAC hosted the first conference of theater commanders in 1954. Originally chaired by Power himself, SAC conducted worldwide coordination conferences annually from 1955 to 1958, but the conferences agreed on little other than the date for the following year's meeting. The plans the conferences generated were placed in the JCCs, but they were generally considered coordination failures.

War planning within one organization is difficult. Effectively coordinating targeting among competing commanders with equal authorities is nearly impossible. Choreographing sortie generation, launch, refueling, and other support is even more so. New complexities arose not only out of many factors, including lack of a clear single authority, but also because the concepts, doctrines, techniques, procedures, and cultures of the separate commands were different and in many ways irreconcilable without a single commander to break impasses.

The coordinating conferences may have provided little effective coordination, but they did allow theater commanders and SAC to better appreciate each others' concerns, tasks, and objectives. Target lists, nuclear forces, and timing among the commands were compared, and some agreement was found. Yet SAC found these conferences severely lacking.

Soon, a serious problem endemic in nuclear war plans emerged called duplications and triplifications, when two or more commands planned to attack the same target. However, the 1957 and 1958 coordination conferences did not significantly reduce either phenomenon. Additionally, "coordinated" plans approved during the conferences identified "time over target" conflicts (when two or more aircraft would engage a target at times that could damage or destroy one or both of the sorties) but did not deconflict them. Globally, such conflicts ran into the hundreds. During ideal exercise conditions, the JCCs could conduct sufficient post-hostilities coordination to mitigate most dangers. However, under real-time war conditions, if communication was lost during combat for any reason, these time over target conflicts could cost hundreds of American lives.

After four years of coordinating conferences, a comparison of target lists and some minor conflict resolution were the only positive outcomes. Air Force Gen. Nathan Twining, then serving as chairman of the JCS, remarked that the coordinating committees only had one truly positive outcome—proving that "atomic operations must be pre-planned for automatic execution to the maximum extent possible and with a minimum reliance" on post-hostility communications.[3]

An opportunity to correct these problems in coordination emerged when Congress passed the Defense Reorganization Act of 1958 on 23 July 1958. Eisenhower emphasized that reorganization had to achieve "complete unity in [American] strategic planning and basic operational direction." Both the secretary of defense and the joint chiefs needed additional authority to mandate unification of strategic planning. The Air Force traditionally favored functional integration, disliking geographical integration, and supported the president's reorganization efforts. This time, the Army sided with the Air Force. The Navy was not enthusiastic.

The Navy was about to enter the realm of strategic nuclear warfare with its Polaris fleet ballistic missile program, which promised to break the Air Force monopoly on strategic nuclear warfare. The commissioning of USS *George Washington* on 30 December 1959 gave the Navy a seat at the strategic nuclear war planning table. But before that happened, Secretary of Defense Neil McElroy in December 1958 asked the joint chiefs for their views on the future employment of the Polaris missile.

Air Force chief of staff Gen. Thomas D. White immediately argued for a unified U.S. Strategic Command to plan and conduct all strategic nuclear missions, incorporating both SAC and the Navy. White recommended Power develop the new command immediately so it would be ready to accept control of the Polaris as soon as the program became operational. Navy and other personnel could be added to the infrastructure of SAC to form the core of the new command quickly. White believed complete unification was the best way to create the most effective atomic offensive plans possible. Power was extremely skeptical of the Strategic Command plan at first. Power preferred SAC be given operational control of the Polaris force directly, but having seen the failures of the coordinating conferences firsthand and realizing that the Navy would never give SAC its submarines, he begrudgingly accepted White's reasoning.[4]

Almost everyone else was adamantly opposed to the Strategic Command plan. Chief of Naval Operations Adm. Arleigh Burke led the opposition to Strategic Command in the Pentagon. Burke specifically objected to integrating all strategic weapons systems into any single command. The Navy's position was that Polaris submarines should be operationally controlled by theater commanders that traditionally went to admirals, the commanders in chief of the Pacific and Atlantic. Burke argued that the coordination committees had worked well, there was no need for changes to the current nuclear command structure, and that Polaris targeting would pose no significant problems. The joint chiefs already had the authority to prevent undesirable duplication in targeting, Burke argued, and to place all strategic nuclear weapons systems into a single command "would disrupt and alter the U.S. defense organization" in very negative ways. Burke liked the status quo.

Most, if not all, of Burke's vehement objections stemmed from two sources. First was simple interservice rivalry. Burke was against any bureaucratic changes that gave more power to the Air Force, especially at the Navy's expense. Giving the Polaris to Strategic Command would rob the Navy's Atlantic and Pacific Commands of the only major seaborne weapons system of value in nuclear warfighting and would limit the Navy's voice during budget debates.

Second, there was a real strategic debate between "massive retaliation" deterrence and "minimum" deterrence. Perhaps somewhat paradoxically, "massive retaliation" deterrence focused on defeating enemy installations, bases, and combat capability (known as counterforce) rather than specifically targeting cities. The Air Force preferred "massive retaliation" counterforce deterrence because it was theoretically (though not practically) not targeted specifically at civilians. It also demanded large and accurate nuclear arsenals. The "minimum deterrence" doctrine, alternatively, was a countervalue strategy that held that targeting Soviet cities and population centers instead of military forces would be cheaper and more effective. Also, targeting cities required far less accuracy than targeting military forces. Polaris missiles were too inaccurate for massive retaliation counterforce but were adequate for the city-busting countervalue strategy. Burke believed that the creation of Strategic Command would commit the United States to the massive retaliation strategy, thus eliminating the primary utility of the only strategic nuclear system the Navy owned. This was unacceptable. Burke's vehemence against Strategic Command and, later, the SIOP, poisoned his relationship with Power, and Burke sometimes questioned Power's honor and integrity.[5]

The Army sided with the Navy and argued that making any nuclear planning decisions was premature since the Polaris missile had not yet been operationally tested. They argued it would be best to assign Polaris missiles to the fleet and transfer them to an operational command only after the system had been proven. The Marine Corps favored making the joint chiefs responsible for nuclear targeting and then delegating targets to the theater commanders. The Marines feared that assignment of targets to a unified organization would build a "monolithic" structure that would provide the Soviet Union an irresistible target that could, if destroyed, cause a fatal paralysis of strategic forces. Regardless of the official reasons, however, it was clear that the other services saw the Strategic Command plan as a naked attempt by the Air Force to make concrete their already implied dominance of the nuclear warfighting mission— which, at least in part, it was.[6]

Because they could not reach agreement on the subject, the joint chiefs presented a split decision paper to Secretary Neil McElroy. Convinced that there was not an immediate need for a decision, McElroy tabled the discussion. However, he was still interested in improving coordination of atomic war plans. In July 1959 Power briefed McElroy and the joint chiefs on the status of the emergency war order at SAC headquarters, and McElroy requested General Twining's opinion on the matter.

After reviewing the history of nuclear coordination, Twining responded, "Not much more progress can be achieved under the present arrangements." He argued that modifications to the existing procedures would not work and advocated for what he called "fundamental changes" in targeting policy, development of targeting plans, and control of nuclear strike forces. Twining's preferred solution to targeting policy was to commit to a counterforce targeting strategy focused on Soviet nuclear forces, government and military control centers, and war industry, with population centers targeted only as a last resort. Twining also believed that after this policy was approved, a national strategic targeting list (NSTL) should be developed and reviewed by the joint chiefs' J-2 intelligence section.

Twining preferred Power at SAC to be charged with developing the SIOP to engage all targets identified in the NSTL using, at the moment, only SAC forces. Twining reasoned that Polaris was not yet operational, and Navy carrier-borne aircraft were constantly moving and could not be assigned specific targets. Polaris could be added after it had become fully operational. The development of both an NSTL and a SIOP would, to Twining, "provide a sound basis for necessary coordination of operational plans of local commanders with CINCSAC's plans" from which future questions of operational control and deconfliction would be greatly simplified.[7]

General Twining wanted to better clarify the positions of the services regarding nuclear target coordination and requested answers to a list of questions his staff generated. Initially, a multiservice ad hoc committee prepared answers to Twining's questions, but eventually each service provided its own set of answers. What Twining found was that the services had wildly divergent opinions on the command and control question for Polaris. With this finding, Twining and McElroy tabled the matter entirely.

When Thomas S. Gates succeeded McElroy as secretary of defense in December 1959, he took immediate action. On 20 January Secretary Gates informed the JCS that he wanted to discuss the "split paper" on

Polaris provided to McElroy. Gates' interest was timely. More evidence was mounting that the decision on Polaris needed to be made sooner rather than later. The participants of the spring 1960 coordination conference in Europe issued a unanimous declaration that efficient nuclear targeting was "far beyond the capability of coordination conferences." Power as CINCSAC and the commander in chief, Europe, Gen. Lauris Norstad, wrote to the joint chiefs, "With the increased number of weapons and their diversified utilization, it appears that an efficient application of the force can only be accomplished by a single authority."[8]

Regardless of the converging views of these (admittedly same-service) combatant commanders, the service chiefs continued to disagree on nuclear command and control. On 6 May Twining told Gates that the JCS could not agree on the questions Twining had asked earlier and instead presented each service's answers to the secretary for review. In June, Gates discussed the situation with the JCS over two days and, afterward, the JCS presented a paper that expanded the thoughts of each service and explained why they differed with each other. However, the JCS did agree that the combatant commanders needed a basic targeting policy to translate new national policy into specific guidance and to develop a NSTL.

Twining was convinced that the deep divisions among the services were due not simply to bureaucratic turf wars but were steeped in fundamental conceptual and doctrinal differences. He told Gates that a "perfect" and mutually agreeable solution might not be possible and that Gates simply needed to break the impasse. Twining thought issuing a national strategic targeting policy might be a useful start. On 20 July 1960 the service chiefs presented their individual positions to Gates so he could make his decision. Secretary Gates did not confine himself to discussing this matter with the JCS alone. Through his entire deliberation, Gates consulted Power.[9]

After a year of consideration by the JCS and two defense secretaries, Gates finally made a decision on 16 August 1960 on the command and control of nuclear forces. Gates rejected both a unified Strategic Command and the status quo. Gates decided to create a joint strategic target planning staff (JSTPS), directly responsible to the JCS and composed of members of all services, headquartered at Offutt Air Force Base and with the CINCSAC serving as the director of strategic target planning. At Burke's insistence, Power was assigned a Navy deputy two days later, Rear Adm. Edward N. Parker, a former destroyer captain who had gained extensive nuclear experience as former head of the Defense Atomic Support Agency.

Power immediately began to stand up his new organization while remaining SAC's commander. For the first few months Power and Parker brought in the Army, Navy, and Marine personnel assigned to the JSTPS and trained them as fast as they could. The JSTPS began work quickly since SAC had many trained nuclear planners already, but only joint officers had the expertise necessary to roll Polaris submarines, carrier strike aircraft, and Army intermediate-range ballistic missiles like Jupiter into the plan. Gates wanted a target list and coordinated nuclear plan for review by December 1960, so they had to work fast.

Power was adamant that all JSTPS personnel be experts because he demanded that the staff remain very small. He also wanted to use SAC staff as much as possible due to their unique expertise, but all services would participate in all aspects of planning. Representatives from the theater commands involved in the JSTPS, which included almost all of them, were sent to a meeting on 24 August to discuss the organization and manning of the JSTPS. Three days later, the meeting produced a draft organizational structure to prepare both a nuclear target list and an operational plan, the NSTL and the SIOP. The joint chiefs quickly approved the organizational structure and directed work to begin immediately.[10]

Power's new mandate as director of strategic target planning was to organize the JSTPS and staff it with personnel from all the services with the required skills to perform the targeting and planning functions; develop and maintain the NSTL and a SIOP for the attack of NSTL targets; and submit both the NSTL and SIOP to the joint chiefs for review and approval, highlighting the points of difference that the director (Power) had to resolve during the preparation of the NSTL and the SIOP.

The last mission was particularly important to Power. The major innovation of the JSTPS was that the director could resolve planning conflicts that doomed earlier attempts at nuclear coordination. However, the director had to inform the JCS and secretary of defense of all his decisions, and he could be overruled. Power, who had not originally supported a JSTPS, later thought that this aspect was a stroke of genius by Secretary Gates.[11]

In addition to deputy director Parker, there was also one senior representative from the Army, Navy, Marine Corps, and Air Force. These service representatives acted as a personal staff for the two directors, represented the services in JSTPS deliberations, and performed as service liaisons. Finally, there were representatives from each of the theater commanders on the director's staff. The theater representatives worked directly with JSTPS personnel on the NSTL and the SIOP. However, they were not integrated into the staff directly because they were responsible to the theater commanders and not Power himself. A JCS liaison group also assisted the JSTPS in interpreting guidance from the joint chiefs and kept them informed of the progress and actions to the JSTPS. Power kept the JSTPS small, originally only 269 billets: 140 officers, 57 airmen, and 22 civilians were to come from SAC itself, making up a majority of the staff; 29 Navy officers, 10 Army officers, 8 non-SAC Air Force officers, and 3 Marine Corps officers rounded out the group.[12] An attempt by Burke to add almost forty more Navy officers was killed by the JCS.[13] The JSTPS was, from the beginning, a rushed organization because the first NSTL and SIOP were due to the secretary of defense by 14 December 1960. However, the JSTPS delivered the initial NSTL and SIOP on time.

The JSTPS was guided by the National Strategic Targeting and Attack Policy (NSTAP), a joint staff document that established the core concepts behind the nation's strategic nuclear targeting philosophy. The policy's specific objectives were to "destroy or neutralize Sino-Soviet Bloc strategic [nuclear] strike forces and major military and government control centers, and to strike urban-industrial centers to achieve the level of destruction indicated in Study 2009."[14] Study 2009 advised the targeting of both military and industrial targets with enough weapons to achieve a 75 to 90 percent assurance of striking each target with at least one weapon, an important issue when dealing with later charges of "overkill." Eisenhower approved Study 2009 in February 1960, with 75 percent assurance directed.[15]

The JSTPS first had to determine the NSTL, the targets the United States would attack to satisfy the NSTAP. On 18 August Power directed JSTPS intelligence to prepare a preliminary target list. Six days later, the directorate presented a draft list of approximately four thousand targets—essentially a compilation of strategically significant targets inside Russia, China, and the Warsaw Pact countries that represented the combined knowledge of all U.S. intelligence sources. Their destruction would complete SAC's mission as Power saw it, to eliminate both the communist bloc's will and capability to wage war. The final NSTL was derived from this first cut. The steering committee, chaired by Admiral Parker, ensured that the targeting needs of all the theater commanders were reflected in the NSTL. Power directed that the NSTL would only have positively identified and located targets—targets that could be attacked with currently known intelligence.[16]

The NSTL began to crystallize as the JSTPS continually refined the National Strategic Target Database through identification of the highest priority targets and comparing them with available intelligence on them. Planners assigned relative worth to all targets on the list through a target weighting system developed by SAC and modified with input from the theater commanders. Once the most important targets were identified, the planners moved to developing the desired ground zeros (DGZs, or bomb delivery coordinates) for each target. Multiple installations were grouped into "target islands" or "complexes," groups of installations close enough together that they feasibly could be struck successfully with one weapon. Computers then calculated an optimum number and location of DGZs within these islands that, if successfully struck, would achieve the desired level of destruction. Computer results were always verified manually. Once analysis was completed, the final targets comprised the NSTL. After the number of weapons and probabilities of success per weapon were obtained from the computerized DGZ list, the list was compared with available weapons, and planners would then determine which targets would accomplish the objectives of the NSTAP. The final list that included the DGZs and weapons needed to engage the NSTL formed the basis of the SIOP.

While working on the NSTL, the JSTPS SIOP division and the theater commander liaisons began to analyze the capabilities of the forces available to prosecute the SIOP and compare them to the list. SAC, U.S. Atlantic Command, and U.S. Pacific Command all committed forces to the SIOP directly. NATO Allied Command Europe, however, contained both U.S. and allied forces and thus could only be included on a coordination basis. The JSTPS only considered forces currently existing in December 1960 when developing the SIOP (although future SIOPs would begin to anticipate future weapons, which presented problems later, particularly during the Cuban Missile Crisis).[17]

With sufficient work completed on the DGZs for the NSTL and forces gathered by the SIOP division, by mid-September 1960 work began on applying the weapons systems available to the required DGZs to accomplish national objectives. Planners studied communist air defenses, selected infiltration tactics, determined survivability and attrition probabilities, studied weapons effects, and identified constraints in policy—all necessary information for developing a viable plan. With the information in hand, extensive weaponeering began. Planners matched each target with a definite aircraft or missile type suitable to engage the target with an adequate probability of success. The highest priority targets on the NSTL were assigned to alert forces, those forces capable of responding with only tactical warning—usually launching within fifteen minutes of an attack warning. At the time, alert forces available to the SIOP consisted of 874 delivery systems with 1,447 weapons. Non-alert follow-on forces totaling 1,464 additional aircraft and missiles with 1,976 weapons were then assigned "to take advantage of the disruption caused by the alert strike, to increase probability of destruction of high priority targets, and to expand the NSTL coverage."[18]

Despite resolving the problem of authority that made coordination of the multiple nuclear strike plans impossible, the unified JSTPS still found coordination to be extraordinarily difficult. The remaining difficulties arose because of many physical problems. Forces available to the SIOP were very diverse in terms of weapons and delivery systems. The B-52 heavy bomber needed to be planned to operate in conjunction with the F-100 interceptor and the Atlas ICBM. The reliability factors calculated for the different forces also varied wildly among types of nuclear weapons as well as their delivery systems. The circular error probable (a measure of accuracy) for the weapons and the requirements of the targets also needed to be reconciled and matched for effectiveness.

To develop a complete SIOP, detailed source data sheets for each sortie containing available intelligence on the number of targets for the sortie as well as suitable weapons and vehicles were required. After detailed flight planning, a sophisticated SAC IBM 704 computer resolved final planning requirements. Resultant strike data sheets became SIOP Annex F, which was delivered to all unified and theater commands. Annex F included strike timing for aircraft and missiles, aircraft and missile accounting line numbers, and aircraft and missile accounting by target number and assigned DGZ. SIOP Annex F became a precursor to the modern air tasking order. However, theater commands only received Annex F strike data sheets that were directly related to the theater command's mission. Theater commands were responsible for providing strike timing and other data to their own tactical units through individual combat mission folders.[19]

Once the assignment of forces to targets was complete, expected damage assessed, and a rough analysis with as much additional data as possible developed, the final iteration of the NSTL was ready to be produced. The final NSTL was the list of targets the SIOP would attack. Power's JSTPS binned the targets into three general groupings. First, there was the "minimum NSTL," a list of the minimum number of targets whose "timely and assured destruction" would accomplish the objectives of the NSTAP. Second, there was a list of defensive systems the JSTPS believed would have to be struck in order to successfully infiltrate the Sino-Soviet bloc interior and strike the strategic targets of the minimum NSTL. Finally, there were "other targets" that the JSTPS and theater commanders agreed should also be attacked to accomplish theater objectives, as well as adversary installations that could be significantly damaged due to collocation with targets on the minimum NSTL.[20]

Burke continued in his campaign against the JSTPS by noting to Eisenhower that the emerging SIOP made no distinction between the Soviet Union and the other communist nations and other issues. Eisenhower responded by sending his science adviser, George Kistiakowsky, to Offutt in November. Quickly, Kistiakowsky concluded that the JSTPS methods for war planning were wildly excessive, arguing, "I believe the alert force is probably all right, but not the follow-on forces which carry megatons to kill 4 and 5 times over somebody who is already dead." Thus, Kistiakowsky charged that Power's "damage criteria and the directives to the planners are such as to lead to an unnecessary and undesirable overkill."[21] Power would later question the patriotism of the Ukrainian-born Kistiakowsky in a meeting.[22] Kistiakowsky advised Eisenhower that SAC was only using the SIOP to justify larger force requirements and that the president should use the Polaris submarines as reserve forces but allow SAC "to have just one whack—not ten whacks" at every target. Kistiakowsky wanted "to get this thing right down to the deterrence."[23]

Kistiakowsky's and Power's personal animosity aside, their quarrel was based on radically different ideas of deterrence. To Kistiakowsky, a "minimum deterrent" was enough. Polaris would be able to "clean up what isn't done" if the new satellites found anything to strike after the initial exchange in the event of war.[24] Kistiakowsky believed one strike was enough for SAC, either because he assumed every sortie would be successful or he did not consider mission success important. Kistiakowsky would not be the last to claim the SIOP was overkill.

While Power and the JSTPS were hard at work in Offutt, Air Force leaders at the Pentagon were worried that the ad hoc JSTPS would not be approved as a permanent organization and its SIOP rejected. The Air Force deputy chief of staff for plans and programs, Gen. John K. Gerhart, approached Col. Glenn A. Kent, who had been an early champion of abandoning the Strategic Command idea in favor of a joint planning staff, to develop a plan to ensure both became permanent.

The Air Force had earlier submitted a memorandum to the Joint Chiefs of Staff proposing that Gates and the JCS review the draft SIOP in Omaha in early December. The Army and Navy quickly opposed this suggestion. However, Gates, intending to conclude the issue, changed the agenda from a simple review of the plan to a meeting to approve the plan. Enraged, Burke went directly to Eisenhower to protest, but Eisenhower approved Gates' decision.

Attempting to find an argument for Gates to compel the JCS to accept the JSTPS and the SIOP, Kent argued that the SIOP should be presented as an operational plan that was a means for making best use of all the forces available "with not a hint as to any requirement to meet a set of objectives." He thought that questions about the likely effects and adequacy of the nuclear strikes were separate issues that could lead to refinement of the plan later.[25]

Kent proposed Power hold a meeting of the ad hoc staff in Omaha, which would include a two-star Navy admiral and a two-star Army general, to address any issues the services had with the SIOP. The meeting would no doubt be filled with controversy, but Power would end the meeting by inquiring whether anyone had any recommendations with regard to the assignment of weapons to specific targets, especially the senior representatives. Power would then immediately approve the recommendations. At the planned 18 December review, Power would state that he had asked for recommendations from the Army and Navy. Therefore, he would declare that the plan itself was not in contest. The likely effects of these nuclear strikes were a topic for continued debate.[26]

Gerhart liked Kent's plan and immediately called Air Force chief of staff Gen. Thomas White to brief him on it. White ordered Kent to Offutt to brief Power the same day. Kent explained to Power that the central issue was that the Air Force had to convince Gates that there was no protest about the plan itself, only a few particulars. Power liked Kent's plan immediately: "It will work. How many others know of this gambit?"

When Kent replied that only Gerhart and White knew, Power replied, "Then keep it that way."[27]

On 18 December 1960 Power invited thirty-two senior defense officials to SAC headquarters, including Gates, the joint chiefs, the commanders of the unified and specified commands with forces committed to the SIOP, and other high-ranking military officers and civilians, for briefings on the work of the JSTPS. There, Power presented the NSTL, operational concepts for the plans, intelligence on enemy defenses, force application, sortie success assessments, damage and casualty assessments, and potential weaknesses of the plan identified by the JSTPS itself for discussion.

SIOP-62 was a detailed plan for a strategic nuclear offensive that contained information on which targets were to be attacked, which forces would attack each target, and how the forces would attack them for the initial strategic offensive into the Sino-Soviet bloc. Power briefed that SIOP-62, upon approval from the joint chiefs and the secretary of defense, would supersede earlier joint plans in the event of any conflicting guidance. Power stressed that the SIOP was an essential tool of deterrence because it honed the complete nuclear retaliatory strength of the United States into a sword that could be applied immediately—it was a plan that made optimal use of all current forces. With the SIOP, the United States had a fearsome weapon to keep the peace, but now knew exactly how to use it to inflict unacceptable damage on the Soviet Union as well.

SIOP-62's mission was to "destroy or neutralize the Sino-Soviet strategic nuclear capability and primary military and government controls of major importance" as well as to attack "the major urban-industrial centers of the Sino-Soviet Bloc to the extent necessary to paralyze the economy and render the Sino-Soviet Bloc incapable of continuing war." The plan was a quintessential counterforce document with seven annexes that represented its heart: intelligence, command and control relationships and responsibilities, atomic information, concept of operations, coordinating instructions, strike timing (Annex F), and administrative procedures.[28]

SIOP-62, which is still classified, planned many factors in minute detail, but it also added as much flexibility as the targeting staff felt they could include in such a complex plan. Options for executing SIOP-62 existed depending on how much warning was available of a Soviet strike. SAC alert aircraft could be launched on order of the SAC commander while still waiting for the president's decision to strike (positive control). SIOP-62 was a worldwide plan for global nuclear warfare that was timed in many ways to the second. Realistically, Power knew there was no way to train for a plan demanding action in less than fifteen minutes that was so flexible that no crew could possibly know all the roles that might be assigned to it.

Secretary Gates had granted the director of the JSTPS decision authority to rule on disagreements and conflicts during coordination of nuclear plans. However, every decision had to be reported to and could be reviewed by the secretary of defense. Rear Adm. John J. Hyland, a naval aviator and U.S. Atlantic Command's senior representative to the joint chiefs, briefed to the reviewing officials the disagreements his commander had with the decisions Power made in SIOP-62 so that the secretary and joint chiefs could review them.

First, Hyland asserted that the JSTPS appeared to be justifying a maximum rather than a minimum target list for the SIOP, echoing the Navy's preference for minimum or finite deterrence and contempt for counterforce as a thinly veiled excuse for the Air Force to buy more bombers and missiles. Hyland expressed another Navy concern: SIOP forces were rigidly assigned to the SIOP as their first priority. He asserted that the SIOP as written gave theater commanders little flexibility in attacking targets not on the SIOP that were nonetheless important to theater concerns. The SIOP simply stole the theater commanders' authority to control their own forces.

Second, Hyland disagreed with how the JSTPS handled weather factors in the SIOP. In his opinion, the SIOP used aircraft with only visual weapons delivery capabilities to attack at random times, even at night. To accommodate the differences, the JSTPS had averaged the "good daylight capability" of the aircraft with their "poor night capability" for SIOP calculations. Hyland maintained that this process resulted in artificially low strike success reliability factors that gave JSTPS planners an excuse to assign additional sorties to the SIOP and increase the number of aircraft and weapons that were needed to execute the plan.[29]

Regarding Hyland's first objection, Power simply responded that as director of the JSTPS, he believed that the forces assigned to the SIOP should be programmed and that excess forces should be used in the plan to add flexibility. The president could then order the minimum SIOP or order a more robust strike depending on the situation. It is likely that Power stayed mostly silent on this point because he was aware that the Navy was objecting to the counterforce concept, not the SIOP itself, and that the joint chiefs and the secretary of defense would not want to reopen the debate.

Power did offer an in-depth explanation for his decisions about weather factors, which were very important to the JSTPS in their actions preparing the SIOP. A significant problem regarding weather was that the SIOP could be ordered at literally any time, during any season, day or night, with only minutes to execute. The JSTPS needed to estimate the probability that a non–all-weather mission would be capable of performing its mission successfully during any time of the year. Missions delayed due to weather could be rescheduled later and successfully conducted, but using the planned strike and target destruction times in the SIOP as the metric for success, the mission would be a failure.

For planning purposes, Power directed the use of success probabilities to represent the JSTPS's best estimates that for any randomly selected mission, weather and visibility conditions in each area would permit target identification and a successful strike by non–all-weather aircraft. The JSTPS used estimates ranging from 38 to 54 percent. Power included in SIOP-62 instructions that if weather was favorable, the non–all-weather aircraft missions would proceed without delay. Missions in poor weather were left to theater commander discretion, but additional missions were placed in the SIOP to cover aborted missions.

Hyland's final objection concerned the assurance factor Power used in SIOP-62. The admiral thought that the effort necessary to reach 90 percent destruction assurance rates for each individual target in the SIOP was too expensive and required delivering too many nuclear weapons. Hyland suggested the expense and collateral damage were simply too great for the results obtained. Power responded that the SIOP's maximum destruction assurance achieved for any individual target was 97 percent assurance and that many SIOP targets were below that level, but no lower than Study 2009's presidentially mandated 75 percent assurance.[30]

Much of the Navy and civilian criticism of SIOP-62 seems to have been about the plan's "overkill." John Rubel, later known as one of Secretary of Defense Robert McNamara's Whiz Kids, recalled that the plan dropped forty megatons on Moscow alone. "In retrospect," Rubel later wrote, "considering that SIOP called for dropping 7,847 megatons on the Sino-Soviet bloc and some eastern European targets . . . forty megatons seems like far too small a number for such a coveted 'target.'" However, Rubel was confident that forty megatons was more than enough for Moscow.[31] David Rosenberg carried Kistiakowsky's and Rubel's charges into scholarship with his classic article "The Origins of Overkill" in 1982, and the charges have stuck to the present day.

But the questions that Rubel begged were not how much megatonnage was enough to destroy Moscow, but how much would have successfully deterred Russia and, if deterrence failed, how much would have arrived to destroy Moscow. Campbell Craig argued that Eisenhower thought thermonuclear war absurd and ordered U.S. nuclear strategy to be equally absurd to drive all major conflict between the United States and the Soviet Union to compromise.[32] Thus, Eisenhower may have welcomed the most aggressive SIOP possible. Power, by contrast, wanted to provide the United States the greatest possible chance of surviving a nuclear war by eliminating Soviet nuclear arms, regardless of cost. Both views may have had different origins, but both were satisfied by the same means. By Study 2009, Eisenhower mandated a minimum of 75 percent assurance that all Soviet targets would be destroyed by the SIOP in the event of nuclear war. Even though Eisenhower accepted that 25 percent of Soviet nuclear forces might survive the SIOP to attack the United States, his order still necessitated multiple sorties per target. Unfortunately, mathematics of reliability are multiplicative, not additive. Achieving a 75 percent success rate required many more weapons than achieving a 50 percent success rate. As Power himself wrote in 1963, sending more than one nuclear weapon to a target was not "wasteful 'overkill' . . . planning destruction where there is nothing left to destroy. . . . Using the same logic, one might say that it is wasteful to put more than one pellet in a shotgun shell because, after all, one pellet in the heart of a duck or pheasant is enough to kill it and there is no sense in trying to kill it more than once." Power then acknowledged that it might happen that more than one nuclear weapon would reach its target, but the thing that counted was that at least one must, because the consequences of no hits were far greater than those of multiple hits. Power then accused the peddlers of overkill of not understanding "the vital difference between a 'planned' weapon and a 'delivered' weapon." However, Power was resigned that the overkill myth "will persist for as long as there are people who accept statistics at face value without troubling to examine the reasons behind them."[33]

Power and the JSTPS may have planned for forty megatons to target Moscow, but not for purposes of bouncing rubble or justifying massive expenditure building SAC. Rather, they did so to ensure that at least one weapon would successfully deliver its payload to Moscow with a confidence factor the president wanted and rational defense, as Power saw it, demanded. However, instead of responding with mathematics and logic, Whiz Kid memoirs have never confronted this rational assurance factor directly, preferring to use loaded terms like horrific, mad, and crazy, and blaming SIOP-62 as a moral failing of Power.[34]

Others have argued that SIOP-62 should have differentiated between the Soviet Union and the People's Republic of China in planning. Rubel recalled a question to Power at the briefing: "What if this isn't China's war? What if this is just a war with the Soviets? Can you change the plan?"

"Well, yeah," admitted Power, "we can, but I hope nobody thinks of it, because it would really screw up the plan." Marine Corps commandant Gen. David M. Shoup replied, "All I can say is any plan that murders three hundred million Chinese when it might not even be their war is not a good plan. That is not the American way." Rubel recalls that he "shrank within, horrified," after Power's statement.[35] Moral grandstanding aside, the simple fact was that the planning order mandated that the SIOP target the Sino-Soviet bloc. The decision to target both the Soviet Union and China was not a moral failing of Power, but a decision by higher authorities.

Rubel also charged that the SIOP "was nothing less than a capabilities plan calling for dropping every bomb and launching every missile in our possession at the 'Sino-Soviet bloc.' The 'plan,' by its very nature, reflected the conviction (usually unacknowledged) that by wiping out most of China and the Soviet Union, especially the Russian part, America would, to cite the Air Force mantra, 'prevail.' . . . Needless to say, the SIOP only described how the USSR and China would be targeted, not how the U.S. would be struck in return."[36] Overall, the Whiz Kids characterized SIOP-62 as a "spasm" war plan—which it was, since it was a plan to use all nuclear forces available in the most optimal manner, as Kent described. Again, Rubel's criticisms emerge from a lack of understanding of the military position, not from Power's moral failing. The Air Force, as Kent argued, viewed the SIOP as a plan to use all forces available in the event of nuclear war to make the U.S. deterrent as credible as possible. Power and the JSTPS wanted the plan to use U.S. forces to ensure that everything could be used immediately in order not to have to use them at all. Power's deterrence doctrine was to have overwhelming superiority so that the Soviet Union would never take aggressive action to start a general nuclear war. Rubel and the Whiz Kids never got that.

The Whiz Kids also believed the SIOP was weak and useless since it was not flexible, discounting entirely that SAC and other nuclear forces had to be always ready to enact the plan at literally a moment's notice. General nuclear war by its very nature limited the availability of options. The technology to make the U.S. nuclear arsenal survivable after being struck by Soviet nuclear forces was simply not available in 1960, and SIOP-62 had to account for that. Political flexibility would have to wait for new technology, which SAC was working to incorporate. The SIOP spasm characteristics and the lack of flexibility were operational necessities, not a moral failure.

Rubel identified two other issues in the meeting he thought relevant to Power's character. Power mentioned in the briefing, "I just hope none of you have any relatives in Albania, because they have a radar station there that is right on our flight path, and we take it out." With that comment, which was met with utter silence, Power turned to the person who had been speaking and, with a wave of the hand, told him to "go ahead."[37] Rubel attributes this to Power's depravity, though it is more likely, given Power's sardonic wit, to be a thinly veiled needle to the Whiz Kids crowd.

Rubel was struck by a final remark from Power. After a briefer reported to the group that approximately one hundred million people from the Soviet Union could be killed by radioactive fallout alone from the SIOP attack, Power interrupted the speaker and noted, "I just want to say that this assumes that Ivan just stands there in the open and stares up at the fallout. It assumes Ivan doesn't even try to take cover. He just stands there letting the fallout come down without taking cover. I just want to make that clear." Rubel was again shocked by this apparently callous remark,[38] but it appears that Power was making a very important point about the JSTPS assumptions. The casualty figure did not account for Soviet civil defense or other actions to mitigate the effect of fallout, making one hundred million a maximum estimate, of which the secretary and the JCS needed to be aware.

After listening to the objections from some in the crowd, Power stood in the front of the group and spoke directly to Gates. Power explained the difference between factors that affected the potential success of the strikes and the allocation of weapons to targets, the DGZs. Power also said that the objections presented dealt mostly with the planning factors, but that there was no debate from the JCS regarding allocation of weapons to the DGZs. Power also explained that he had accepted all changes that the Army and Navy had earlier proposed for the allocation of weapons to the DGZs.

Gates, impressed with Power's argument, replied, "General Power, if what you say is true, then this casts quite a different light on this matter." Gates asked the Army and Navy representatives on the JSTPS if their changes had been approved, and the men both grudgingly admitted that they had. Gates then said that, since there were no disagreements regarding the allocation of weapons to the DGZs, the discussion was closed and moved that the plan should be approved without further delay.

Burke objected, stating that the SIOP had not yet been officially submitted to the JCS for consideration, a stalling move that Kent had anticipated. Power responded as Kent advised, that the JCS had a copy of the plan and been briefed on it three times already. Gates, knowing that all of the senior leaders would separate after this meeting and a new meeting would take weeks to convene, deflected this stalling move, declaring, "Admiral Burke, you have a point to which I must react. You will have all night to consider it. I now amend my earlier statement. The joint chiefs will report to me in the morning at nine o'clock as to which members approve the plan and which members do not. If one member approves, I expect the matter to be presented to me for adjudication. I will surely find in favor of the member who has voted for approval."

Gates then asked Power if the audience could stay one more night in Offutt. Power beamed, "Of course! There will be a reception in the Officer's Club beginning at 1830 hours." At the reception, Power introduced Kent to General White, saying, "This is the man who made this happen!" Afterward Power ensured Kent was promoted to brigadier general in 1963 and continued to be a protégé until Power retired.[39]

Despite the Navy's and the Whiz Kids' objections, the joint chiefs, the secretary of defense, and the president approved SIOP-62 with only minor changes on 19 December 1960 and charged that it be placed in immediate effect by 1 April 1962.[40]

After delivering the NSTL and the SIOP, Power began to evolve the JSTPS into a leaner organization optimized for keeping the documents current. Again favoring lean organizations over bureaucracies, Power recommended the JSTPS be reduced: cutting the number of non-SAC personnel from 83 to 75 and reducing the SAC staff from 219 to 111. He also requested that the theater commander representatives be held to a minimum.

The Navy and Army immediately objected to Power's plan. Burke, ever suspicious of SAC organizationally and Power personally, thought the plan would gut the Army's and Navy's voices on a staff already dominated by the Air Force. Since the NSTL division was responsible for target selection and intelligence, Burke suggested that all services should be equally represented. Additionally, Burke objected to decreasing the number of theater commander representatives. Echoing his belief that the theater commanders were most important, Burke suggested that the number of representatives on the JSTPS should be at the sole discretion of the theater commanders themselves.

Further, Burke recommended an intelligence panel be created for the JSTPS "to provide the broadest and most expert intelligence base which can be achieved to support the SIOP," in which he wanted to include members from the theater commanders, the joint staff, and the Central Intelligence Agency. No doubt he wanted them to counter what he thought were inflated SAC numbers regarding Soviet missile and bomber strength in order to justify the missile and bomber increases that SAC wanted and the Navy especially feared.[41]

The Army, alternatively, did not think Power's plan supported a sufficiently balanced personnel roster to qualify as a joint staff. Furthermore, the Army rejected the idea of making SAC officers "dual-hatted" with responsibilities to SAC and the JSTPS, with the exception of the commander in chief of SAC himself. The Army agreed with the Navy. The NSTL division required equal representation among the services, and the SIOP division required proportional representation, based on the relative amount of forces each service provided to the SIOP.

Power argued that the joint chiefs' guidance did not provide precedent for the establishment of joint staffs by specified commands, and that his personnel request represented his interpretation of what the joint chiefs wanted him to do. Power's plan was simply the most economical method in both men and matériel by which the JSTPS could develop an adequate and coordinated nuclear target list and execution plan. Power maintained that his JSTPS staffing plan actually favored the Navy and Marines. Fully fourteen of the thirty-four key positions identified in the JSTPS were staffed by Navy or Marine officers. By way of compromise, Power welcomed one additional intelligence officer from each theater command to monitor that their theater was being adequately considered in SIOP intelligence plus ten more billets for theater command liaisons to establish "confidence" in coordination.[42]

By January 1961 it was time for Gates to move on. Before leaving his post as secretary of defense, Gates wrote to Power expressing "how greatly I appreciated your efforts with the solution to our problem of national strategic targeting. Your personal leadership in our strategic planning has done much to overcome some of our ill-founded prejudices which have existed within the Department."[43]

Thomas Gates was succeeded by Robert S. McNamara as secretary of defense. Considering Power's proposal as well as the other services' positions, McNamara notified Power that he had "complied fully" with Gates' directives and that he should realign JSTPS personnel along new guidelines. The new secretary directed that key personnel in the NSTL division would have no additional duties and that positions would be staffed by the best qualified officers regardless of service affiliation, that key personnel in the SIOP division would be filled by service personnel in proportion to the forces assigned by their service to the SIOP, and that no joint intelligence review panel was necessary. Nevertheless, the JSTPS should be organized to evaluate intelligence from all available resources.[44]

Power submitted his revised personnel plan to McNamara on 27 April 1961. It was only slightly different than his original proposal in January: the JSTPS would have 34 key positions and a total of 186 personnel. However, in accordance with McNamara's direction, sixteen positions in the NSTL division were not assigned to a specific service. The most qualified officer would be given the assignment. Power drafted JSTPS personnel on the philosophy of "service representation proportional to the service forces involved." The joint chiefs approved the personnel plan on 14 June 1961.[45]

The first Single Integrated Operational Plan accomplished by General Power and his Joint Strategic Target Planning Staff in late 1961 represented a revolution in war planning. Prior to the SIOP, atomic targeting was only to be coordinated during hostilities with no single commander responsible for the overall war plan or having authority to mandate cooperation. After multiple failures during exercises and years of debate, the joint chiefs could not come to an agreement on a solution to this crippling problem. The Air Force advocated creation of a unified strategic command that would be responsible for all nuclear targeting and operations. The rest of the services, led by the Navy and Chief of Naval Operations Adm. Arleigh Burke, preferred the status quo to protect the autonomy of the theater combatant commanders.

To break the impasse, chairman of the joint chiefs of staff Air Force Gen. Nathan Twining proposed to Secretary of Defense McElroy a national strategic targeting policy. Ultimately, a different secretary, Thomas Gates, decided that neither the status quo nor a strategic command was the correct choice. On 16 August 1960 Gates created the Joint Strategic Target Planning Staff responsible directly to the joint chiefs but located alongside the headquarters of Strategic Air Command. The JSTPS replaced the flawed worldwide coordination conferences and was given new authority to coordinate all nuclear plans prior to any hostilities and granted authority to the director to make decisions on any coordination problems that arose.

Working with a near impossible deadline, Power collected a number of SAC and joint officers and established a new planning organization that produced the first National Strategic Target List and Single Integrated Operational Plan in less than four months. Debates in the military establishment between the Air Force and SAC's preference for a counterforce nuclear targeting strategy and the Navy's countervalue, finite deterrence strategy continued in the Pentagon and beyond, but under Power's leadership, the JSTPS was able to present the first unified strategic nuclear offensive plan in United States history. SIOP-62 was not perfect, the SIOP evolved dramatically through the rest of the Cold War, and the JSTPS did not solve all the problems of nuclear strike coordination. However, it was a start, and the United States finally had an immediately executable, coordinated, efficient, and effective plan with which to operate its nuclear retaliatory forces at a moment's notice to fight against Soviet aggression. Power later considered the Joint Strategic Target Planning Staff one of the three highlights of his military career.[46] The JSTPS and the SIOP it created so quickly were incredible accomplishments.

But SIOP-62 was also a work in progress, and even Power admitted so. Especially under McNamara, the Whiz Kids—including George Kistiakowsky, John Rubel, and Daniel Ellsberg—went back to the Pentagon to challenge the JSTPS to account for the survivability of new weapons coming into the U.S. nuclear arsenal, including the solid-fueled Minuteman ICBM, which finally yielded the technology needed to expand the flexibility of the SIOP to better align with presidential needs. Power, as director of the JSTPS until his retirement in 1964, led the drafting of new SIOPs that were both more responsible and more flexible. When Secretary McNamara began retooling U.S. defense to deter through "assured destruction"—the ability for the United States to absorb a Soviet first strike and still have enough second-strike capability to impose "unacceptable" losses on the attacker—Power incorporated these strategic changes into future SIOPs like the loyal soldier he was.[47]

Today, the SIOP is known not as a triumph of military planning and the lynchpin of credibility of the U.S. nuclear deterrent in the Cold War. It is instead synonymous with military mendacity, SAC zealotry, and Air Force extravagance. This assessment is wrong, but it stems from the same well as Power's degraded reputation. Like McNamara, his Whiz Kids may have been quick reads, but they were also poor students. They rejected the SIOP as military brutishness and parochial politicking rather than as a plan derived from serious strategic study. Dismissing sophisticated efforts to achieve high confidence factors as simple "overkill," both severely misinterpreted and unfairly maligned the heroic efforts of the JSTPS.

The Joint Strategic Target Planning Staff was a singular victory in joint planning at a time when interservice rivalry was at its apogee. General Kent, reflecting on the JSTPS, concluded:

> In this episode, the Air Force gained its point. The result was beneficial not only for the Air Force but also for the country. Had the other services prevailed, the United States would have gone on planning

Armageddon in a disjointed way. At best, planning by the individual services would have caused inefficiencies, invited redundancies, and made the nuclear deterrent less credible. At worst, such planning might have caused uncertainty and ragged decisionmaking in a time of crisis. Whatever parochial concerns may have motivated the Air Force to advocate a single integrated plan, it was clearly in the national interest. Finally, one might argue that the SIOP set a standard for jointness that eventually expanded to conventional operations, especially through the Goldwater-Nichols reform.[48]

The SIOP and the JSTPS were watershed events that improved U.S. military planning. They were just more ways General Power helped keep America strong.

CHAPTER 6

SAC's Finest Hour

••

The Cuban Missile Crisis, 1962

S trategic Air Command played a critical role in the military operations conducted during the Cuban Missile Crisis of October and
November 1962. Visions of nuclear-laden bombers in the air and
ballistic missiles on the ground waiting for the call to begin World War
III dominate the public view of Air Force operations during the crisis, but
that is not all SAC accomplished during those tense months. SAC's operational activities during the crisis highlight both Power's organizational and
operational acumen. His skill leading the command's combined reconnaissance, bomber, and missile team as its operational commander during one of the most dangerous periods of the Cold War allowed SAC to
complete its ultimate mission—to help deter Soviet aggression—when the
world came closest to nuclear war and when the country most needed it.

SAC's participation in the Cuban Missile Crisis started with reconnaissance. Fidel Castro's Cuba had been under photographic surveillance
by the Central Intelligence Agency's (CIA) covert U-2 spy plane operations for seven months prior to October 1962. The CIA operations had
detected the buildup of Soviet defensive weaponry on the island. That
buildup suggested the Soviets may have been planning to bring forces
significant enough to defend Cuba, but the CIA had not found any con-
clusive sign of offensive forces.

SAC remained vigilant. On 14 September SAC crews in R-47H aircraft, the reconnaissance variant of the B-47 bomber, from the 55th
Strategic Reconnaissance Wing at Forbes Air Force Base (AFB), Kansas,
began weekly electronic intelligence (ELINT) flights to the edge of Cuban
airspace and flew four more missions before the crisis began in earnest on

14 October, when SAC immediately pressed for two flights per day. These flights were considered reasonably dangerous because the R-47Hs flew with their identification transponders off to confuse Cuban defenders.

Not only could Cuban or Soviet fighters hound the crews of the R-47Hs, even U.S. fighters posed a threat. It was standard procedure for a fighter to intercept any unidentified aircraft flying near Cuban airspace, lock on it with its fire control system, and positively identify it. However, the R-47Hs were equipped to fire automatically at aircraft in such a circumstance. One R-47H got intercepted at night by a U.S. fighter, and it was only because the R-47 pilot turned off his defensive systems for fear of firing on a friendly aircraft that his plane did not fire at the interceptor, thus saving both aircraft from potentially being destroyed in a firefight. Eventually, the reconnaissance planes flew with their standard identification transponders on at all times, even though the act betrayed their purpose to Soviet and Cuban air defenders. Eventually, 116 Operation Common Cause ELINT flights were flown during the crisis, all without significant incident.[1]

However successful and necessary SAC ELINT flights were, it was the SAC U-2 that provided the most important reconnaissance of the crisis. On 10 September Secretary of State Dean Rusk, Secretary of Defense Robert McNamara, National Security Advisor McGeorge Bundy, General Power, and others considered some problems in the national U-2 effort. Almost two weeks earlier, a SAC U-2 accidentally flew over the Sakhalin Islands off the Soviet east coast. The Soviets did not try to shoot it down, but they did protest to the United Nations, forcing the embarrassed United States to apologize. However, the Chinese did not mind firing at U-2s. Less than forty-eight hours prior to the 10 September meeting, the People's Republic of China shot down Republic of China air force Major Chan Huai in his Taiwanese U-2 with a Soviet SA-2 missile, the same system that had shot down Gary Powers' U-2 flying over the Soviet Union two years earlier. Major Chan was killed.[2]

With two high-profile failures, Rusk and Bundy wanted to shut the whole program down—at least temporarily. The Corona spy satellites were already producing amazing photos and promised far more. The

National Reconnaissance Office, they argued, could provide the strategic intelligence the United States needed without the political danger and difficulty of manned aircraft. Power disagreed, arguing that the satellites were useful but limited. SAC needed more intelligence, with better fidelity, than satellites could offer, and Power needed the U-2s flying to keep him appraised of many different theaters, including Cuba. Eventually, McNamara decided that the U-2s would keep flying, but to limit the political damage of another mishap, the military would fly missions over Cuba because they would be easier to justify.

SAC had developed a plan to conduct the Cuban U-2 operations by 4 October under the codename Brass Knob. However, SAC pilots needed to qualify in the latest U-2 model, so two of the best U-2 pilots from the 4028th Strategic Reconnaissance Weather Squadron, Maj. Richard Heyser and Maj. Rudolf Anderson Jr., were flown to Edwards AFB, California. The newest U-2, the F model, could refuel in flight and had higher thrust and a maximum altitude of 75,000 feet, 5,000 feet higher than previous versions. In preparation, the majors started training in takeoffs and landings on 12 October.[3]

The same day, Power arrived in Washington, D.C., after an overseas inspection tour. During lunch with Secretary of the Air Force Eugene Zuckert, they discussed U-2 overflights of Cuba to better understand the increased Soviet activity on the island. Zuckert asked Power if SAC was capable of flying U-2 missions over Cuba. Power said SAC would be ready to fly by Sunday 14 October. Zuckert approved SAC to begin flying as soon as they were ready.[4]

However, Power sensed the U-2 flights might find something serious and decided to take broader action even before the full crisis began. On 13 October Power increased SAC's alert posture to 50 percent and addressed his combat crews: "There is no need to impress on you the seriousness of the present situation and the gravity of the threat we face. . . . I realize that this entails added efforts and sacrifices on your part, and I want to assure you that I have done and will continue to do everything in my power to prevent undue hardships." The hardships included an average duty week of seventy-four hours—longer if the crisis got worse. Power exhorted his men, "You have been carefully selected for your demanding duties because you have met the exacting requirements placed on SAC crewmen. I know that yours is a hard way to live, and there is no magic formula to make things easy for you. But millions of people everywhere look to you as the principal guardians of their security and freedom."[5]

Major Heyser took off from California on the first SAC U-2F overflight of Cuba on 14 October at 11:30 p.m. local time. His flight took him over the Gulf of Mexico, and he photographed Cuba's northern coastal plain. Upon landing at McCoy AFB in Florida, Major Heyser's camera film was sent immediately to Washington, D.C. Major Anderson had to be transferred to McCoy without flying his mission after his U-2 snapped its tail strut. Both Anderson and Heyser flew U-2 missions from McCoy on the morning of 15 October. Flying five hours each, both men were able to photograph almost the entire length of the island thanks to extraordinarily clear weather during what was normally Cuba's rainy season.

Heyser's and Anderson's three flights on 14–15 October detected the first evidence of "the missiles of October." Photos captured three medium-range ballistic missile (MRBM) sites near San Cristobal, and two IRBM sites at Guanajay with warheads considered to be in the three- to six-megaton range. Cruise missile sites were also discovered, as well as the first positive identification made of Il-28 Beagle bombers (though crated for shipping) at the San Julian airfield.[6]

With proof of Soviet nuclear weapons in Cuba, SAC's alert force took center stage. On 16 October Power met with the Joint Chiefs of Staff in Washington, where he recommended an immediate increase in SAC's readiness to respond to the crisis. First, he called for a declaration of defense condition (DEFCON) 2 in order to generate all SAC forces for immediate operations. Second, he wanted to initiate SAC's B-47 dispersal plan to increase the survivability of medium bombers by moving them to civilian airports around the country, complicating Soviet nuclear targeting in a potential first strike. Finally, Power recommended expanding SAC's airborne alert. The joint chiefs quickly approved Power's suggested actions but would only allow him to place SAC on a "modified" DEFCON 3.[7]

After a day's pause to prepare for extended operations, U-2 missions resumed on 17 October. Major Heyser and Major Anderson continued flying their U-2Fs out of McCoy, joined by four U-2A flights out of Laughlin AFB, Texas, to confirm the situation on Cuba. These six flights photographed the entire length of the island flying routes forming tight parallel lines, again thanks to unusually clear weather. By 19 October SAC U-2s had identified six Soviet MRBM sites, three IRBM sites, and about twenty-two Il-28 bombers in Cuba, all offensive in nature.

Before SAC could generate forces in response, it first needed to evacuate as many of its units from Florida as possible, both to increase the survivability of SAC in the face of the Soviet missile threat and to assist the buildup of conventional forces in the southeast in case the Cuban crisis erupted into open confrontation. The air defense requirements of Florida and other considerations flooded the limited space for Tactical Air Command. SAC pulled many of its assets from three Florida bases, McCoy, Homestead, and MacDill, as fast as it could. On 17 October Power approved a hastily completed evacuation plan for all three bases and directed the plan's execution on 19 October to assist Tactical Air Command in improving the air defense of the newly created Florida military emergency zone. Eventually, the unprecedented conventional force buildup led Power to order the evacuation of all SAC aircraft, including those scheduled for alert duty, from Homestead and MacDill on 22 October and from McCoy two days later. With the extra time given the alert forces, SAC planners were able to complete the evacuations without seriously degrading SAC's emergency war orders (EWO) capability.[8]

Power also ordered SAC to begin preparations for the dramatically increased strategic posture. First, Power ordered all "adjusted and degraded" aircraft and missiles to be immediately returned to alert status. Bringing the training, test, and maintenance delivery systems back into alert service would be SAC's priority in increasing its readiness posture for the duration of the crisis. Next, Power ordered all SAC B-52 units to generate two bombers per squadron and place them on standby status. These aircraft were intended to be ready for ground alert duty if SAC was ordered to begin 1/8 airborne alert (placing one of every eight SAC bombers in the air with a full combat load of nuclear weapons). In addition, similar orders were given to SAC KC-135 tanker units to support the additional bombers. However, since President Kennedy had not yet revealed that the United States knew about the Soviet missiles in Cuba, these actions were conducted covertly, and Power insisted that these actions were not to be considered a change in the SAC DEFCON. SAC accomplished all directives by the morning of Sunday 21 October. However, SAC canceled all inspections until further notice, and its air police and other units also initiated their maximum security measures short of sabotage alert operations.[9]

On 22 October the crisis came to a head when Kennedy addressed the nation and presented the evidence of Soviet offensive weapons that SAC had collected. Consequently, he ordered a strict quarantine of Cuba to prevent the placement of more offensive weapons and demanded that Khrushchev "halt and eliminate this clandestine, reckless, and provocative threat to world peace and to stable relations between our two nations"[10] and withdraw all weapons already there.

SAC was ready for the president's order. Hours earlier, the joint chiefs had directed SAC to initiate 1/8 airborne alert and to begin dispersing SAC B-47 medium bombers. Power executed the 1/8 airborne alert order six hours ahead of Kennedy's speech, and B-47s began to disperse an hour after airborne alert had been established. By the time the president had announced the increase in alert status, SAC was already at high alert. When Kennedy promised that any hostile Soviet action would be met by "whatever action is needed," SAC bared the teeth necessary to make the president's threat both credible and terrifying. As soon as Kennedy had begun speaking, the joint chiefs placed all U.S. military forces at DEFCON 3, including SAC.[11]

By the end of Kennedy's speech, two-thirds of Power's recommendations had been adopted. The last step was the generation of the complete combat power assigned to SAC. Bringing the command to DEFCON 3 had little impact because SAC had begun taking the actions necessary for that alert status hours earlier, although DEFCON 3 did give Power the authority to reinstate the degraded aircraft and missiles to EWO status. SAC remained in DEFCON 3 for a total of thirty-nine hours, from the president's speech to the imposition of the naval quarantine of Cuba, when the joint chiefs ordered SAC to DEFCON 2. SAC was now at its highest alert ever reached.[12] Power had been arguing for an airborne alert for years prior to the crisis but had never been given the approval for a 1/8 airborne alert or a dispersal of medium bombers. SAC was ready, though, because the Chrome Dome alert indoctrination plan SAC had been flying and, fortuitously, had recently overhauled acted as nearly a full contingency plan.[13] Thanks to Power's foresight, SAC was ready to accomplish both when the president demanded it.

The original Chrome Dome indoctrination plan, officially named for the silver-skinned bombers flying overhead but known by the aircrews for the bald spots on aviators' heads from the rub burns from their flight helmets, consisted of twelve B-52 sorties a day along three specific routes centered over Spain, Alaska, and Thule Air Base, Greenland. The tanker requirements for 1/8 airborne alert were enormous. The tanker airframe requirements of the Alaskan task force grew from seven to ten, the northeastern United States more than doubled from six to thirteen, and the Spanish task force grew more than six times, from six to thirty-eight planes needed. Thanks again to proper planning, coordinating the dramatic increase of SAC activity over both Canada and Spain commenced without serious problems.[14]

Even though it was much grander in scale than the indoctrination program, the airborne alert progressed quickly and relatively smoothly because all SAC B-52 units already knew their route assignments and the specific times to launch their aircraft in the overall plan. The alert was a change in scale, not in design. The 4134th Strategic Wing launched the first sortie of the airborne alert's northern route at 1824 Zulu time (Z). Within twenty-four hours of the I-hour (Power's initiation hour), the northern route was at full strength; five hours after that, at 2222Z on 23 October, fully 1/8 of SACs bombers were in the air with a full complement of nuclear weapons aloft. Every day, fifty-six B-52s (twenty-eight on the northern route, twenty-six on the southern, and two on the Thule monitor route) would take off to maintain the alert for the duration of the crisis. The tanker support necessary for the alert responded even faster.

The tankers supporting the northern route were already substantially in place, but after Power declared the I-hour, KC-135s from the United States flew to bases in Spain to support the southern route. At 1300Z on 23 October, thirty-eight of the tankers were in place and ready to support Chrome Dome, nineteen each at Moron and Torrejon.

Chrome Dome required seventy-five B-52 sorties per day—forty-two on the southern route, thirty-one on the northern route, and two around Thule. Supporting the B-52s required 133 tanker sorties. For one full day of Chrome Dome airborne alerts, 208 SAC aircraft had to successfully fly their missions. SAC continued Chrome Dome for the duration of the crisis.[15]

The balance of importance between airborne versus ground alert was also a vital consideration. The ground alert was critical because it and other nonalert sorties were committed to the Single Integrated Operational Plan just as the airborne alert flights were. A significant problem was a shortage of weapons. SAC had a sufficient total number of nuclear weapons, but they were short of the most advanced types slowly entering the U.S. inventory. The ideal nuclear weapon for SAC bomber operations could be dropped from any altitude and also be fused for any type of detonation—air, contact, or delayed ground burst—depending on the mission and situation. However, such full fusing option bombs, although developed, were not in SAC's inventory by the time of the crisis. The weapons were programmed into SIOP-63, but operationalizing the capability had not yet occurred due to a lack of approved safety rules for the new weapons and Atomic Energy Commission production delays.[16]

Airborne alert bombers were deployed with a payload of either four Mark 28 or two Mark 15/39 nuclear bombs. Mark 28 bombs at the time were rated at 1.1 megatons each, while the larger Mark 15s (of which the Mark 39s were improvements) were rated at 3.8 megatons each. However, there were many variants of each in the inventory, demanding very different delivery methods.[17] The myriad problems associated with weapons availability emphasized SAC's requirement for the broad adoption of an operationally versatile nuclear weapon, a requirement Power often brought to the Department of Defense (DOD) and Congress.

Young Thomas Power. *Courtesy Joel Dobson*

Thomas and Mae Power before flying to Guam, 1944. *Air Force Historical Research Agency*

Keystone LB-5A bombers of the 28th Bombardment Squadron, Philippines, 1930s. *Courtesy Joel Dobson*

Col. Power (*left*) and Col. Hewitt Wheless (*second from left*) with 314th Bomb Wing officers, 1944. Note the pin-up girls across the walls. *Air Force Historical Research Agency*

Brig. Gen. Thomas Power and Col. Hewitt Wheless on Guam, 7 February 1945. Both men were instrumental in planning the Tokyo firebombing raid and, later, were supporters of the Orion nuclear pulse propulsion spacecraft. *Air Force Historical Research Agency*

(*L-R*) Gen. Lauris Norstad, Col. Hewitt Wheless, Gen. Curtis LeMay, unknown flight surgeon, and Gen. Thomas Power after firebombing Tokyo, 10 March 1945. *Air Force Historical Research Agency*

(*L-R*) Generals Barney Giles, Thomas Power, and Henry "Hap" Arnold with Staff Sergeant Giles at Guam, 1945. *Air Force Historical Research Agency*

General Power at Enewetak Atoll for the Operation Ivy thermonuclear tests, November 1952. *U.S. Strategic Command*

General Power preparing to fly a P-80 Shooting Star as SAC deputy commander. *U.S. Strategic Air Command*

General Power practicing judo with SAC instructor Ken Rea, 1951. General Power was an early supporter of judo in the United States and eventually earned the rank of 4th degree black belt (*dan*). *U.S. Strategic Air Command*

General Power as Strategic Air Command deputy commander, 1952. *U.S. Strategic Command*

General Thomas S. Power, commander-in-chief, Strategic Air Command. *U.S. Strategic Command*

General Power talks with the Air Force's top acquisitions officials, late 1950s. (*L-R*) Gen. Thomas Power; Gen. Edwin Rawlings, commander, Air Materiel Command; Maj. Gen. Bernard Schriever, commander, Western Development Division; Lt. Gen. Samuel Anderson, commander, Air Research and Development Command. *U.S. Strategic Command*

General Power with SAC Commanders, 1961. (*L-R*) Lt. Gen. Archie Old, Lt. Gen. John McConnell, Gen. Thomas Power, Lt. Gen. Walter Sweeney. *U.S. Strategic Command*

General Power as CINCSAC flying a KC-135, how he normally flew on SAC business. *U.S. Strategic Command*

General Power talks with actor Rock Hudson on the set of *A Gathering of Eagles*, 1962. Power often supported movies that portrayed the Air Force and SAC in a positive light. *U.S. Strategic Command*

General Power guides President John F. Kennedy, Secretary of Defense Robert McNamara, and Dr. Harold Brown (*far left*) through a display of Air Force space equipment at Vandenberg Air Force Base, California, March 23, 1962. *John F. Kennedy Presidential Library*

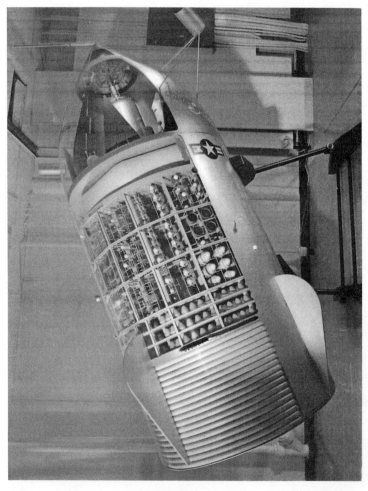

Model of the Orion nuclear pulse propulsion spacecraft General Power presented to President Kennedy, Secretary McNamara, and Dr. Harold Brown on March 23, 1962. Note the Air Force roundel and SAC blue star field. *Air Force Research Laboratory*

General Power with his sisters at Strategic Air Command headquarters, 1964. Dorothy, the Lady Brownlow, is on the left and Kathleen Miller on the right. *U.S. Strategic Air Command*

General Power is invested as a Knight Commander with the Grand Cross of the Order of St. Sylvester and Mrs. Power awarded the *Pro Ecclesia et Pontifice* medal by Archbishop Gerald T. Bergan, 14 July 1964. They both earned their honors through their work in establishing the Cardinal Spellman School for Catholic children of SAC personnel at Offutt Air Force Base. *Cardinal Spellman School*

Compounding SAC's war planning issues in addition to weapons variation was that neither of SAC's operational plans, SIOP-63 or the basic SAC Strike Plan 50–63, supported airborne alert. Despite Power's insistence on a continuous airborne alert since he took over SAC, it had never been authorized by the joint chiefs or the secretary of defense. Once SAC was authorized to prosecute Chrome Dome operations, competing and conflicting requirements emerged between SIOP-63 and Plan 50-63. Both weapons and aircraft were simply overtaxed. Supporting both plans under maximum readiness, a B-52 wing with fifteen aircraft was committed to fifteen SIOP sorties as well as two Chrome Dome sorties. The priority airborne alert reduced the number of bombers available to support Plan 50-63, and the situation also caused the substitution of weapons, and consequently bomber tactics, on many sorties that were supported.[18]

When the joint chiefs directed SAC to enact the 1/8 airborne alert, they also approved Power's second suggestion, to disperse its B-47 medium bomber force. At 1800Z on 22 October SAC ordered the deployment of the "second cycle medium force dispersal sorties" of EWO 44/50-63. A total of 183 B-47s from 17 bomb wings at 15 bases were activated and ordered to disperse. These bombers were flown in EWO configuration, with most of the bombers carrying nuclear weapons, while a minority were configured as electronic countermeasure aircraft.

The purpose of the B-47s in SAC's overall nuclear warfighting plan was to be "second cycle sorties." This meant that in a combat EWO situation, the B-47s would be refueled by tankers flying their second EWO mission—their first having refueled the B-52s for their initial "first cycle" strikes. However, SAC soon found that with their dispersal, the B-47s would be more survivable than the ground alert–only B-52s; thus, headquarters began planning for upgrading forty-one of the dispersed B-47s to first cycle status by programming eighty-seven of the obsolescent but available KC-97 tankers in SAC's inventory. The B-47s selected were all in the eastern United States, almost entirely due to the availability of the tankers. Forty-one KC-97s were deployed to Goose Bay Air Base and thirty-four to Harmon Air Force Base (both in Canada), and twelve to Lajes Field, Azores, on 29 October, along with their support personnel. The first KC-97 departed at 1800Z on 29 October, and most were ready for combat operations the next day. All tankers were in place by 1 November.[19]

Within two hours of the execution order, the first B-47 launched. Within 24 hours, all 183 bombers had arrived at their new dispersal bases. By 0600Z 24 October all of the bombers but one were ready for EWO action. Along with the 183 bombers, more than 2,000 Air Force personnel and 320,000 pounds of cargo were airlifted to the dispersal sites. Most of the dispersal locations were civilian airfields with Air National Guard or Air Force reserve units. To assess readiness, Power requested the Air Force deputy inspector general for security establish an inspection tour for all locations. By the end of October, the inspector general's team had visited twenty-six of the dispersal sites—the majority —and had rated security as satisfactory or better.[20]

An often-overlooked element of the Cuban Missile Crisis is that SAC was able to test many of its technological and organizational innovations in a real-time near–combat environment, especially its new missile force. By October 1962 the SAC bomber force had fifteen years of experience to draw upon. The SAC ballistic missile force, alternatively, was not yet even fully operational by the time of the crisis. Moreover, even though Power had been intimately connected with it for most of its history, the SAC bomber force was LeMay's force. It was LeMay, not Power, who had commanded the SAC bombers to maturity. Thus, the crisis "provided the command a singular opportunity to determine exactly how far it had progressed toward an adequate missile capability."[21] By extension, it also tested that part of SAC that was most wholly of Power's doing.

Critics have claimed that Power was part of the "bomber mafia" and did his best to limit the influence of ICBMs in the Air Force so the bomber could maintain preeminence.[22] This is manifestly untrue. Power "broke a lot of hearts" by placing "nothing but blue-ribbon people," many of whom were among SAC's best pilots, in the missile program where they were unable to maintain their flying currency.[23]

Power's decision to place only SAC's best in the missile fields paid dividends during the Cuban Missile Crisis. On 19 October SAC had 112 ICBMs on alert, including 77 Atlas missiles of the D, E, and F varieties, and 35 Titan Is. On 22 October SAC had increased the alert ICBMs to 132—91 Atlas and 41 Titan Is.[24] SAC placed all available missiles, including the operational readiness training configurations meant to train new crews, as well as all "degraded" missiles in the field (those ICBMs that were modified for a number of training and maintenance issues), on full combat alert. SAC ensured that these missiles were brought back into full operation covertly. The missiles were soon needed.

On 24 October 1962 Power ordered his crews to DEFCON 2—the first and only time SAC ever reached that level—broadcasting his order to his crews over an open channel:

> This is General Power speaking. I am addressing you for the purpose of reemphasizing the seriousness of the situation this nation faces. We are in an advanced state of readiness to meet any emergencies and I feel that we are well prepared. I expect each of you to maintain strict security and use calm judgement during this tense period. Our plans are well prepared and are being executed smoothly. If there are any questions concerning instructions which by nature of the situation deviate from the normal, use the telephone for clarification. Review your plans for further action to insure that there will be no mistakes or confusion. I expect you to cut out all non-essentials and put yourself in a maximum readiness condition. If you are not sure of what you should do in any situation, and if time permits, get in touch with us here.[25]

Able to focus on operational flying and relying on decades of experience, SAC aircrew were not completely out of their element with DEFCON 2. However, the missileers, who had to operate systems that individually were of almost unimaginable destructive power, with procedures changing on the fly, were perhaps the group that most needed Power's commanding and reassuring presence. Power's words placed many of the missileers at ease. Col. Michael Galer, commander of the

850th Strategic Missile Squadron at Ellsworth AFB, South Dakota, wrote to Power:

> [W]hen I received your message of assurance and the expression of warmth and guidance during this tense period it carried an impact to the individual that is immeasurable. . . . I can say without reservation that your comments reflected the calm assurance of a Commander who recognized the possibilities of uncertainties but opened the door wide to allow individuals in responsible field positions to make direct contact with your headquarters in event assistance was required. My missile combat crews and staff unanimously have expressed it this way: "If the big boss is this close to us when he has so many things to think of at a time like this, there is 'No Sweat.'"[26]

Critics such as Raymond Garthoff have accused Power of violating security and trying to intimidate the Soviet Union with the message.[27] However, retired Lt. Gen. Lloyd "Dick" Leavitt—no fan of Power—called these men "Monday morning quarterbacks" and argued Power's detractors ignored three significant facts that Power had to consider as commander. First, Kennedy directed DEFCON 2. Second, SAC had more than 282,000 personnel spanning 59 aircraft wings and 33 missile squadrons at more than 50 bases worldwide, and all needed to be made aware. Power's message was both easiest to distribute and minimized the threat of miscommunication. Third, modern critics downplay how essential it was for commanders who remembered Pearl Harbor to ensure that their forces did not sacrifice readiness because they were unprepared or uninformed. Leavitt also pointed out that SAC DEFCON messages were not classified until 1972. Further, Leavitt concluded, "If the Soviets were intimidated after intercepting Power's message, it probably strengthened our negotiating position" because letting the Soviet Union "know our nation was prepared and capable of retaliating with overwhelming strength" was the keystone of SAC's Cold War deterrence philosophy.[28]

After DEFCON 2 was declared, SAC missileers began working in earnest. Perhaps the most interesting missile operation during the crisis was Power invoking the SAC/Air Force Systems Command (AFSC) agreement on emergency combat capability of ballistic missile launch complexes (the ECC agreement) on 24 October. Under the agreement, SAC assumed operational control of all AFSC launch complexes in the event of "strategic warning," a time when heightened tensions suggested a nuclear exchange was possible over a specific international event. Upon declaration of DEFCON 2 or higher, or other national emergency that called for increased ballistic missile power, all AFSC launch complexes would be reconfigured for EWO status. SAC would essentially take command of the AFSC launch facilities, primarily at Vandenberg AFB, California, but also at Walker AFB, New Mexico, Dyess AFB, Texas, Malmstrom AFB, Montana, and Plattsburgh AFB, New York, for combat operations through the crisis.[29]

Showcasing the easy cooperation between Power's SAC and Schriever's AFSC, AFSC military, civilian, and contractor personnel began placing their test missiles to alert status using a plan called Golden Bull. In the span of a few days, the ECC agreement placed thirty-six more ICBMs on EWO status around the country. Most notably, however, the Golden Bull plan brought the first solid-fueled ICBM in U.S. history, the Minuteman, on alert while still in its test phase when the 341st Strategic Missile Wing at Malmstrom AFB placed two Minuteman ICBMs on alert on 27 October and two more the next day, less than a week after the Cuban crisis started. The Minuteman was a revolution in ICBM technology that could launch within thirty seconds of warning rather than the fifteen minutes of fueling time needed for the Atlas and Titan ICBMs to launch.

Col. Burton C. Andrus Jr., commander of 341st Wing, thought Power "was trying frantically to upstage LeMay's great record as CINCSAC" by trying to "kluge the system" to put the Minuteman missiles on alert so quickly, but Andrus was not about to tell his boss that it could not be done. Part of the safety procedures of the Minuteman ICBM was that any launch would have to be approved by four votes from two crews of missile launch officers in different underground launch control centers (LCCs). However, in October 1962 only one LCC was completed, with the second weeks away from completion. "Convinced that the weapons system had not yet been invented that professional airmen could not outsmart," Andrus ordered that the "critical part" of the second LCC be plugged directly into the electronics of the first LCC, thus allowing all four votes to be directed from the single operational LCC by only one crew.[30] That is how LCC Alpha-06 of the 10th Strategic Missile Squadron became the first operational Minuteman ICBM launch facility.

Echoing the vitriolic debate between safety and operational utility in which Power and many DOD civilians engaged to find the right balance for ICBM operations, what made sense under normal circumstances (such as dual verification of launch orders under normal Cold War conditions) stood in the way of combat capability under a national emergency. Whether Andrus' actions and Power's order "circumventing approved safety procedures" were irresponsible or a proper course to take under a crisis situation is debatable, but reviewed in total it is doubtful that Power was cavalier regarding safety in an effort to outshine LeMay. What is undeniable is that Kennedy was aware of the Minuteman ICBMs during the crisis. Talking to reporters after the crisis was over, Kennedy said, "I had confidence in the final outcome of our diplomacy. . . . Of course, Mr. Khrushchev knew we had an ace in the hole in our improved strategic forces."[31] Kennedy's improved strategic forces were solid-fueled ICBMs, the ace was the Minuteman, and the hole was Alpha-06 and the other LCCs of the 10th Strategic Missile Squadron, whose squadron patch still bears the motto "first ace in the hole."

Cavalier or not, a day after becoming operational, SAC reinstituted a different safety protocol to ensure against an accidental Minuteman launch. The Minuteman silos' heavy outer doors were ordered to be manually disengaged so the doors would not open if the missile accidently launched, destroying the missile in the silo. In order to launch, a maintenance crew next to the silo would need to reconnect the explosive charges that ejected the doors and opened the silo for missile firing by hand, and "run like hell" away before the missile lifted off. SAC "had sufficient safety concerns about the jerry-rigged launch procedures to insist on a jerry-rigged safety precaution."[32] The internal SAC history of the crisis was more clinical in its description of the 341st activities. SAC requested a technical evaluation of the "Flight A" Minuteman missiles to ascertain the possibility of accidental launch since the prescribed safety demonstration tests were not performed due to the crisis. After the evaluation, SAC "directed that while in DEFCONS 1, 2, and 3, SM-80 (Minuteman) lid closure ordnance would be disconnected and the safety control switch manually locked in the safety position. Only after receiving a launch execution order would silos be placed in immediate launch configuration."[33]

The 341st had to deal with bureaucratic as well as technical and operational hurdles. In the rush to bring his missiles up to EWO status, Andrus inadvertently signed for all of the squadron's missiles as operationally acceptable by the 341st without going through all the required contractor demonstrations. When Andrus attempted to implement the SAC/AFSC ECC agreement, the site activation task force (SATAF) refused the order because, even though SAC was at DEFCON 2, AFSC was still only in DEFCON 3. The only way SATAF would agree to hand over the missiles was to force the 341st to accept delivery of the A Flight missiles for operational use with signed waivers to cover all incomplete tests and demonstrations.[34] Even though airmen could outsmart the technology to get the missiles ready, nothing could prevent the bureaucracy from insisting on proper paperwork. SAC headquarters, for its part, maintained that SATAF should have released the missiles under the ECC agreement anyway.[35] For all of their technical, operational, and bureaucratic innovation, the 341st Strategic Missile Wing was declared by the 3901st Strategic Missile Evaluation Squadron to be operationally satisfactory and thus was officially on strategic alert during the Cuban Missile Crisis, although the SAC history concluded that the wing "perhaps more nearly approached an [Emergency Combat Capability] status."

The 341st was not the only missile unit to perform above and beyond the call of duty. The 556th Strategic Missile Squadron at Plattsburgh AFB, New York, had been designated an active launch squadron in 1961, but it did not get its first missile until April 1962. On 22 October the squadron had two operational missiles and twenty-two combat-ready crews already on training waivers granted during the crisis. By 28 October the squadron had seven operational missiles and twenty-three crews.[36]

Regardless of the difficulty, by 3 November SAC had a crisis high of 186 ICBMs on strategic alert, a tremendous feat of ingenuity and hard work by SAC missileers, civilians, and contractors.[37]

Even under stressful, maximum alert conditions, Air Force Systems Command did not end all test operations during the Cuban Missile Crisis. On 26 October Vandenberg AFB launched both an Atlas D ICBM and a Thor/Agena D IRBM (carrying a Corona satellite). Additional Atlas ICBM test launches occurred on 11 and 14 November and Thor launches on 5 and 24 November (again launching Corona satellites).[38] Space launch missions from Cape Canaveral, as well as multiple cosmodromes in the Soviet Union, were also carried out throughout the crisis. Only later did the idea that the AFSC test launches, which could not easily be mistaken for a missile on an attack vector and the Soviet Union undoubtedly knew of beforehand, posed an unacceptable risk of inadvertently starting nuclear war during the crisis.[39]

While the SAC alert force was building momentum, the U-2s kept flying. After a week of "routine" U-2 operations, Major Anderson was shot down on the morning of 27 October, becoming the first and only Cuban Missile Crisis combat casualty. An SA-2 Guideline surface-to-air missile stationed near Banes successfully engaged Anderson's U-2 and exploded near the aircraft, tearing it apart and puncturing Anderson's pressure suit, causing it to decompress and killing him.

Due to negotiations by the United Nations and the Swiss, the Cubans returned Major Anderson's body to the United States on 4 November. There was some worry that the Cubans may have desecrated the body upon its discovery, but Anderson was returned honorably and without incident. For his actions, Major Anderson posthumously received the Air Force Cross and the Distinguished Service Medal.[40]

Some military officials wondered why U.S. radars did not pick up the attack on Major Anderson's U-2. SAC had been assured by the commander in chief of U.S. Atlantic Command (CINCLANT) that the U-2 flights were covered by U.S. radar throughout their missions, but in reality, complete coverage was not possible. The only radars capable of tracking the aircraft were FPS-6 height-finding radars, but they could not "flight follow" the missions—both track the aircraft and provide surveillance of the surrounding area to warn of impending hostile action—and were incapable of warning a U-2 pilot of any hostile action against him. After Major Anderson's loss, the Joint Chiefs of Staff ordered all further U-2 flights canceled. Plans were developed to resume U-2 flights with many more protective measures in place, including giving CINCLANT the authority to retaliate against Cuban surface-to-air missile sites engaging future U-2 flights, but the five SAC-planned U-2 missions set to fly 1 November were not approved by the joint chiefs.[41]

Fortunately, the same day the U-2 flights were disapproved, Premier Khrushchev notified President Kennedy that the Soviet Union would cease construction of all offensive weapons on Cuba and begin to remove the weapons from Cuban soil. SAC U-2 missions changed from combat targeting to verification. Under the slowly but significantly thawing nature of the crisis, U-2 flights resumed on 5 November to verify Soviet dismantling activity. The weather in November reverted to its normal cloud and rain activity, and flights were bedeviled by thickening cloud cover throughout the month. During the seventy-one verification missions flown by the U-2s in November, SAC personnel confirmed that all MRBM and IRBM sites had been dismantled and forty-two Soviet ballistic missiles had left Cuba. The Il-28 bombers, after more negotiation, left a few weeks later. After the crisis, U-2s continued their overflights to ensure the weapons did not return to Cuba.

SAC's reconnaissance activities were not limited to ELINT and photographic coverage of Cuba. After Kennedy imposed the blockade of Cuba on 24 October, Adm. Robert L. Dennison, CINCLANT, immediately asked SAC to help locate and identify shipping in the vicinity of Cuba.[42] SAC's operations staff completed an initial plan called Operation Blue Banner for a one-day mission. The operation was given to KC-97s and B-47s stationed in the Azores. If deemed necessary, R-47s from the 55th Strategic Reconnaissance Wing were ready to fly additional missions.

Blue Banner flights began on 25 October with the tankers flying on thirteen-hour missions covering the eastern mid-Atlantic. Any sightings of ships were radioed to SAC headquarters and relayed to the Navy.

When the five camera-equipped R-47s took over the missions, they descended to five thousand feet upon sighting a ship and determined its name and registry while taking photos. On 27 October SAC R-47s found the Russian transport *Grozny*—a task specifically requested by Robert McNamara—but at the cost of four crewmen lost when one of the R-47s assigned to the task crashed shortly after takeoff.[43] Finding the Soviet tanker was the last act of SAC Operation Blue Banner, although SAC kept planes on standby until the Air Force officially relieved SAC of sea surveillance contingency requirements on 29 November.[44]

Many unforeseen situations arose during the Cuban Missile Crisis. One particular incident reveals the stakes of the crisis and Power's handling of the situations. Both the United States and the Soviet Union were testing nuclear weapons in the atmosphere even into the crisis in October. At midnight local time on 27 October 1962 SAC Capt. Charles F. Maultsby took off from Eielson AFB, Alaska, in his advanced U-2 with a mission to collect radioactive samples accumulating in the sky at high altitude over the North Pole from Soviet tests at Novaya Zemlya. Scheduled for an eight-hour flight, about halfway to the North Pole, Maultsby—a former Thunderbird demonstration pilot and considered one of the best fighter jocks in the Air Force—inadvertently started to drift off course. Maultsby had never before seen the aurora borealis, but the intense light show made it impossible to fix his location by celestial navigation.

Unfortunately, the path Maultsby thought would take him over the pole and back to Eielson instead took him directly into Soviet airspace over its eastern coast. Unknown to Maultsby, Soviet MiG fighters from Pewek and Anadyr air bases scrambled to try to shoot him down. Luckily, the U-2 flew too high for the fighters to intercept. Just before Maultsby ran out of fuel, he was able to make contact with Air Force controllers over radio (who could track his movements but for either physical or security reasons could not contact him until he was almost out of Soviet airspace) and glided his U-2, completely out of fuel, for twenty minutes until making a flawless landing at an airstrip in Kotzebue, Alaska. Only after landing did Maultsby find out he had both penetrated Soviet airspace and been pursued by MiG aircraft. The planned eight-hour flight actually took ten hours and twenty-five minutes and still holds the record for the longest U-2 mission in the aircraft's history. Maultsby was happy to be alive, but both SAC headquarters and the White House were in an uproar.[45]

Air Force Gen. David Burchinal recalled that, upon hearing of Maultsby's flight, Robert McNamara became unglued, rushing out of a meeting yelling, "This means war with the Soviet Union!" McNamara also personally ordered the recall of another U-2 pilot being sent out to fly the next air sampling mission, and he later canceled all U-2 sampling missions entirely.[46] Burchinal also claimed that McNamara tried to get Kennedy to apologize to the Soviet Union for the mistake.[47] Kennedy was somewhat less hysterical, dryly commenting that there's "always some son of a bitch that doesn't get the word."[48] However much Maultsby's flight rattled Washington, he had to answer first to SAC. Once he arrived back to Eielson, Maultsby was rushed to a KC-135 tanker ordered to fly him immediately to Offutt AFB—to brief Power about the flight.

Maultsby recalled that he was not eager to brief Power, and his KC-135 flight "wasn't long enough to suit me." Upon landing at Offutt, a staff car took him directly to SAC headquarters underground. The headquarters was a beehive of activity, and a colonel took Maultsby to a briefing room adjacent to the command post and advised that Power would arrive in a few minutes. Maultsby saw an easel with an aeronautical chart showing his flight path. Maultsby remembered, "When General Power did enter the room, eight other generals who looked as if they hadn't been out of their uniforms for days followed him. Their eyes were blood shot and some hadn't seen a razor the past 24 hours. I stood at attention while they were all seated. General Power was seated directly across the table from me. He looked extremely tired, but was clean-shaven and wore a clean uniform."[49]

Once everyone was seated, Power said, "Captain Maultsby, how about briefing us on your flight yesterday." Maultsby explained that he had been flying to the North Pole and became disoriented due to the aurora borealis. Power then asked, "Maultsby, do you know where you went after leaving the pole?" "Yes, sir," Maultsby replied. Power returned, "Show us, please." When Maultsby pointed out his flight over the Soviet

Union, he noted that the other generals became very nervous and excited, but "General Power only smiled." Power asked Maultsby how he knew where he flew, and Maultsby responded that he learned only when he saw the radar plot after he landed in Kotzebue. Upon hearing this, Power asked if any of the other generals had any questions for the captain. There were none. The generals, and Maultsby, nervously waited for Power to proclaim sentence on the pilot whose poor navigation during one of the most dangerous times of the Cold War caused near panic at the White House and could have escalated the crisis even greater and potentially sparked a nuclear war.

Finally, Power looked at Maultsby and said, "Too bad you weren't configured with a system to gather electromagnetic radiation. The Russians probably had every radar and ICBM site on maximum alert!" Power then thanked Maultsby for the briefing, told him not to speak to anyone about his flight, and dismissed the attendees. After everyone but Maultsby and the last brigadier general in Power's entourage had left, the brigadier general stopped and said to the stunned pilot, "You are a lucky little devil! I've seen General Power chew up and spit out people for doing a helluva lot less!"[50] Maultsby had survived Power with his career intact. After his tour with SAC U-2s, Maultsby returned to flying fighters in Vietnam and retired as a colonel after a full and successful Air Force career.

The Maultsby incident speaks a great deal to Power's reputation. Had Power been as unforgiving and "sadistic" as some have claimed, there is little chance Maultsby's career could have survived the incident or the meeting with the CINCSAC. LeMay once quipped that he could not afford to distinguish between the incompetent and the unlucky at SAC, and Maultsby was clearly either unlucky or incompetent on his flight. However, Power did make the distinction with Maultsby. Even under amazing pressure, Power realized that what happened to Maultsby could have happened to any other pilot, and he chose not to act against him.

From the beginning of the Cuban crisis, USAF headquarters worried that SAC could not maintain an advanced readiness posture indefinitely. On 24 October Power indicated SAC would suffer no force degradation for at least thirty days, but he admitted that SAC also had no experience upon which to base any forecasts of force degradation.[51] After two weeks of experience, Power determined that SAC could maintain its DEFCON 2 alert posture without meaningful degradation until 15 November, but he warned that combat crew proficiency and equipment inventories would begin to suffer after that date. On 9 November the joint chiefs approved Power's plan to decrease SAC's alert status to resume training sorties, and by 10 November new aircrew training priorities were established. On 15 November after the declaration of "modified" DEFCON 2, sorties began to support continued training, the combat crew training schools reopened, and commanders were again authorized to grant discretionary leave. SAC started to get back to normal.[52]

For almost thirty days, SAC continuously maintained one of every eight of its B-52 bombers fully armed in flight at all times to support President Kennedy during the most serious crisis of the Cold War. As the crisis wound down, the airborne alert was the first thing to end. At the direction of the joint chiefs, Power ordered Chrome Dome to stand down on 0600Z, 21 November. Power proposed returning SAC to DEFCON 4 within two days, but the joint chiefs disapproved his suggestion. They did authorize a return to DEFCON 3, which Power established at 2330Z that day.[53] SAC finally ended its flying participation in the Cuban Missile Crisis when, on 29 November, it was authorized to return its evacuated units to their home bases in Florida.[54]

During the month-long airborne alert, 2,088 B-52 aircraft were launched, and 47,168 airborne alert flying hours were logged. In the face of such a large and complex operation, SAC performed magnificently. Maintenance support was over 97 percent effective, and all B-52 flights were performed without incident, an outstanding safety record during the crisis. Power concluded, however, that Chrome Dome's real significance was that it provided a secure, continuous, and immediate strike capability for the United States when the country needed it most. The operation ensured that there were always sixty-five armed and airborne B-52s ready to support the president.

Power was insistent that even if the Cuban threat was removed, the recently operationally proven airborne alert should remain due to the continuing threat from Soviet submarines, missiles, and the fractional orbit bombardment systems satellite carrier vehicle to the United States and its deterrent force. SAC's hardened missile force, which required very little warning to launch, was growing, especially with the activation of the Minuteman ICBM, but Power maintained that until the missiles were completely operational, airborne alert was required due to the continuing basic instability of the international situation.[55]

On 7 December Kennedy visited SAC headquarters to present a special flying safety plaque dedicated to the men of Strategic Air Command. The plaque's official citation read that SAC received the award for "meritorious achievements in flight safety while performing a continuous airborne alert during the Cuban crisis" and that "the airborne alert provided a strategic posture under which every United States force could operate with relative freedom of action." Kennedy remarked, "This plaque pays particular attention to the contribution of the Strategic Air Command during the most intense days of the Cuban crisis. The record of SAC in mobilizing the forces of the United States was unprecedented in the long history of SAC. The number of flights made during that period of time, and the number of men that were involved, was a record unparalleled by any country in the history of airpower."[56]

SAC missileers performed no less admirably. After being placed back into DEFCON 4, SAC was able to revert to the normal 147 ICBMs on EWO status. SAC missile crews could resume their standard training and new missile acceptable regimens in addition to performing their necessary EWO alerts. SAC's missileers had completed their first national emergency.

SAC assessed that the performance of the missile crews during the Cuban crisis was "surprisingly good." A number of special problems had emerged, such as the rapid acceptance of the brand new test-phase Minuteman ICBM into the EWO inventory under emergency conditions and the crew management problems of Plattsburgh, but these were overcome and SAC had placed an unprecedented number of missiles on alert for the crisis "in a very short time and with a minimum of difficulties." The SAC/AFSC emergency combat capability agreement had worked very well, and the role of SAC's missile alert force in the crisis was "both significant and instructive."[57]

SAC's crew training program and the missile acceptance program were both delayed slightly due to the contingency operations demanded by the Cuban Missile Crisis. However, as SAC's history argues, "Cuba lent credence to the basic rationale" of the missile program. The crisis prompted no major changes to or adaptations of the program. Those procedures in place before the crisis did not require revision based on the Cuba experience, and the only real changes made were to account for accepting the test missiles early with the equipment that was on hand in October. Aside from the emergency training required to increase the proficiency of the partially trained crews that were pressed into alert service through waivers, since the missile crews were already used to twenty-four-hour alert duty, no degradation to crew proficiency among fully certified crews took place due to the crisis, unlike their flying counterparts.[58]

Also, many missile "firsts" occurred during the crisis. The first—and only—use of the ECC agreement was broadly successful, the first Minuteman solid-fueled ICBM was placed on EWO status and, notably, SAC Titan I ICBMs achieved an impressive 100 percent alert status, as all 56 Titans in the SAC inventory were on alert on 29 October, "a landmark in the SAC ICBM program."[59]

It is clear that SAC's missile crews performed as well as their flying brethren during the Cuban Missile Crisis. These missileers and their machines were the newcomers to SAC, but during the crisis they earned their place alongside their flying compatriots in the SAC alert force. They would continue to serve with quiet professionalism defending the United States from nuclear attack for the rest of the Cold War as the nation's "ace in the hole." Where SAC is often touted as LeMay's boys, the SAC missile crews were the sons of Gen. Thomas Power, and they—like he—brought to SAC a distinction all their own.

In addition to the massive generation of strategic nuclear capability to maximize SAC's deterrent power, SAC reconnaissance provided the critical intelligence requirements for the entire crisis. SAC aircraft found the missiles that alerted the United States of the crisis, then provided the president the intelligence necessary to navigate it. Reflecting upon the crisis, Kennedy said that reconnaissance pilots "contributed as much to the security of the United States as any ... group of men in our history."[60] The Air Force chief of staff listed as one of his five outstanding lessons of the crisis the need for modern long-range reconnaissance capabilities. SAC's U-2 pilots and ground crews were particularly exceptional in their ability to take over such an important mission as Cuba and, in the span of only a few days during an international crisis, to gain the critical intelligence necessary for the United States to remove the weapons from Cuba. They had justified Power's faith in them to accomplish the mission after Power promised Air Force Secretary Zuckert that they would perform as required just a few weeks before. On 24 November the 4080th Strategic Reconnaissance Wing earned its first Oak Leaf Cluster to its Air Force Outstanding Unit Award. Four days later, Power personally awarded the ten SAC U-2 pilots, including Major Anderson posthumously, the Distinguished Flying Cross at SAC headquarters for "heroism and extraordinary achievement in a duty of great responsibility from 14 October to 29 October."[61]

Despite this performance, Power never felt able to communicate SAC's incredible activities to the public. During the entire crisis Arthur Sylvester, assistant secretary of defense for public affairs, directed that no information regarding military operations be released to the public without his express permission. Power immediately appealed to Sylvester to modify the public affairs ban in order to "strengthen the nation's current and future security in dealing with incidents" of a nuclear nature. On 2 November Power sought to publicly release that SAC was conducting the airborne alert, the B-47 dispersal, Cuban reconnaissance flights, and the Atlantic sea commerce surveillance specifically due to the Cuban crisis. DOD quickly disapproved Power's request.[62]

On 7 November Power wrote a letter to McNamara specifically requesting release of the information Sylvester disapproved. Power argued that releasing information regarding SAC's activities during the crisis to the public would be beneficial for three main reasons. First, the information would lessen the partisan attacks on Kennedy's actions during the crisis that were caused in part by the DOD blackout of information. Second, being recognized for their work would increase the morale of military personnel. Lastly, the information would make sure the Soviet Union was aware of the strength of the U.S. military and the nation's resolve during the crisis. "Therefore," Power stated, "from a deterrent point of view, I believe it [is] to the national advantage that the high degree of readiness of this command be made known, within the bounds of security, to all members of the Communist Bloc, and particularly, the Soviet Union." There is no record in the SAC history that McNamara responded to Power's letter.[63]

The Cuban Missile Crisis saw the most powerful fighting force ever constructed in the history of warfare reach the peak of its readiness to go to war, and it was Gen. Thomas S. Power who commanded it. Power's Strategic Air Command emerged from the crisis victorious yet did not have to fire a single shot. Within 24 hours of the decision to act on the crisis, SAC had 1,436 bombers and 145 missiles ready to launch at a moment's notice. At SAC's peak readiness on 4 November, the command had 1,479 bombers, 182 missiles, and almost 3,000 nuclear weapons to promise the Soviet Union complete destruction should deterrence fail. While in DEFCON 2, SAC could have launched 92.5 percent of its weapons systems within one hour. The only thing preventing the rest of the weapons from launching was the lack of tankers to support them.[64]

SAC was able to succeed during the crisis because its basic command philosophy was sound. Its plans and procedures, though written for a different environment, through the Cuban crisis were able to bend and flex when necessary and to remain perfectly rigid when required. SAC's plans for deterrence, combat, and force generation did not need major rewrites in order to be effective. Everything broadly worked, and SAC proved that, with strategic warning, it was capable of being very flexible. The problems encountered by SAC during the crisis were very real, but "SAC plans consigned to the hot crucible of experience proved of good temper."[65] For SAC's activities during the Cuban Missile Crisis alone, Power should be considered one of the most remarkable combat leaders in Air Force history.

In 1984 General LeMay, in an interview on strategic air warfare and the Cuban Missile Crisis with Gen. Jack Catton, Gen. Leon Johnson, and Gen. David Burchinal, argued that the "Kennedy administration thought that being as strong as we were was provocative to the Russians and likely to start a war." The Air Force, however, did not see it that way. Catton responded that the "concept of strength was absolutely proved, and dramatically, during the Cuban Missile Crisis, when we had absolute superiority. . . . Khrushchev was looking down the largest barrel he had ever stared at, once Strategic Air Command did in fact generate its forces." This, Burchinal added, "was totally missed by the Kennedy administration, by both the executive leadership and McNamara. . . . We had, not supremacy, but complete nuclear superiority over the Soviets."[66] Burchinal concluded with words rarely heard about the Cuban Missile Crisis: "We had such total superiority at that time there was no question, no contest. As the Russians built up their capacity during the 1960s and into the early 1970s, that situation no longer obtained. It has since worried me that publications about the Cuban Missile Crisis all claim that we were so close to nuclear war; ninety-nine percent of the people who write about it don't understand the truth. . . . We were never further from nuclear war than at the time of Cuba, never further."[67]

Had Thomas Power been with the other men for the interview, there is little chance he would have disagreed. To him, and the other leaders of Strategic Air Command, the Cuban Missile Crisis was SAC's finest hour. SAC had proudly given President Kennedy not just an ace in the hole, but the nut flush against Khrushchev in the highest stakes poker game of the Cold War. But to Power, along with that pride was the frustration that the Kennedy administration was unwilling to use this unbeatable advantage to force the Soviets from Cuba completely and win a decisive victory in the Cold War.

CHAPTER 7

Destiny Derailed

———••———

Shaping the Strategic Aerospace Command, 1962–64

By the end of 1962, General Power's SAC had incorporated the ICBM into America's deterrent force, developed and employed the airborne alert, generated the Joint Strategic Target Planning Staff and the Single Integrated Operations Plan, and had "fought" SAC during the Cuban Missile Crisis, demonstrating that the United States possessed a credible "big stick."

Yet there were storm clouds on the horizon. Soviet advancements were constantly diminishing SAC's strategic superiority. More troubling to Power was the McNamara DOD, which constantly eroded SAC's plans to maintain that superiority through its focus on limited wars, and a public that was slowly turning against SAC due to an unceasing barrage of popular propaganda aimed against strategic weapons. Power's remaining years as CINCSAC found him planning for SAC's glorious future of strategic superiority while waging, and slowly losing, the fight for SAC's preeminence in the future DOD.

Given Power's deep interest in both research and space, it is unsurprising that he would see SAC's future in that new and promising domain. However, the rockets and satellites General Schriever was developing were too limited in power and capability to form the basis of a space-based future SAC. Therefore, Power kept searching for a space project that could turn SAC into a true aerospace force. He soon found what he was looking for in a small program named "Putt-Putt."

Project Putt-Putt was the Air Force designation for the Advanced Research Projects Agency program to study a nuclear pulse rocket, originally named Project Orion. Conceived by Manhattan Project alumni

Stanislaw Ulam and Fred Reines in 1947, the nuclear pulse rocket sought to use many small nuclear explosions to propel gigantic spacecraft fitted with pusher plates into orbit.[1] Dreaming of applying nuclear energy to the problem of spaceflight was not unique to these men. A year earlier, RAND, in its famous study *Preliminary Design of a World-Circling Spaceship*, had concluded, "The real white hope for the future of spaceships is, of course, atomic energy. If this intense source of energy can be harnessed for rocket propulsion, then spaceships of moderate size and high performance may become a reality."[2] However, most nuclear designs proposed were of the nuclear thermal rocket type, using a nuclear reactor to superheat a propellant gas similar to chemical rockets in action. These nuclear thermal rockets provided roughly twice the power and efficiency of chemical rockets and would open up vast new applications of space operations. However, their performance was limited by the maximum heat loads the rocket material could withstand, limiting specific impulse (a common measure of rocket efficiency in which higher is better) to about six hundred to one thousand seconds. Project Orion, alternatively, was not heat-constrained. The engine's energy production—the nuclear explosion—took place outside the engine itself, and the rocket did not need to contain all of the energy produced, just exploit it. Therefore, standard material limits did not apply, and Orion could increase performance of traditional rockets in both thrust and efficiency by an order of magnitude or more.

Ulam's original idea was taken up by legendary nuclear weapons designer Theodore "Ted" Taylor in 1957 (designer of the five-hundred-kiloton [kT] Ivy King shot, the largest pure-fission device ever tested), shortly after the Sputnik debacle humiliated American science. Under contract to ARPA through General Atomics, Taylor built an impressive team of scientists and engineers, including physicist Freeman Dyson, to study the feasibility of the nuclear pulse rocket.

The largest chemical rocket, the Apollo Program's Saturn V, could lift 155 tons of payload to low Earth orbit and 54 tons to translunar injection and had a specific impulse that ranged from 263 to 421 seconds. By 1959 Project Orion engineers estimated that even an 880-ton prototype Orion test vehicle would be able to achieve a specific impulse of 3,000 to 6,000 seconds and land 170 tons on the moon, or land 80 tons on the moon and then fly it back to Earth. Larger, interplanetary Orion craft ranging from 4,000 to 10,000 tons could achieve specific impulses of 12,000 seconds and even land 1,300 tons of payload on a moon of Saturn and return to Earth.[3]

The cost of these performance numbers would be about 800 atmospheric nuclear explosions ranging in yield from 3 tons to 0.35 kT at sea level increasing to 0.5 kT to 15 kT in space, with a cumulative total yield of 20 to 250 kT to 125,000 feet and 0.5 to 9 megatons per launch to a 300-nautical-mile circular orbit.[4] Further refinement of the Orion concept would yield higher payloads and efficiencies, as well as lower necessary yields and cleaner modes of operation. Orion was a quantum leap in space launch technology and to this day remains the most powerful space propulsion system designed. Aerospace historian Scott Lowther said the ten-thousand-ton Advanced Interplanetary Ship design "could have truly been the Starship Enterprise of the late 20th century."[5]

The Air Force was involved in Orion research almost immediately, and the officers of the Air Force Special Weapons Center were assigned to determine the military potential of Orion and develop a concept of operations for Orion spacecraft. Capt. Donald M. Mixson, a nuclear weapons officer, took up the task.

Mixson wrote *Military Implications of the Orion Vehicle* in July 1959 with the intention to "broadly survey the strategic and tactical considerations which must form the foundation of any development program."[6] To begin, Mixson comments, "Vehicle costs, measured in dollars per pound of payload in orbit, seem to be ridiculously cheap when compared to costs quoted for conventional chemical systems." Mixson noted some important facts in addition to cost that made Orion a very different model of space operations than the chemical rocketry advanced by General Schriever's Western Development Division or NASA: "First, payload capabilities for these vehicles are potentially so great that mission planning can proceed almost independently of payload mass considerations." Moreover, preliminary models indicated that the upper mass limit for an Orion vehicle could be more than one million tons, or "roughly the equivalent of twelve supercarriers."[7]

The second important fact was that the number of propulsion bombs appeared independent of payload mass, unlike conventional rockets in which high propellant mass fractions mandated that extremely large payloads required orders of magnitude more propellant. "Operationally," Mixson argued, "this suggests a space fleet with very large individual ship payloads, but a rather small number of total vehicles."[8]

Mixson was drawn to these large spaceships because he was gravely concerned that the massive retaliation deterrence policy had major drawbacks. Most important, Mixson argued, "So long as strategic retaliatory power is based on the North American continent, we run the grave risk that, should deterrence fail, our people and their culture and industrial complex would be destroyed almost incidentally as a result of the enemy's attack upon our strategic power."[9] Regardless of the way nuclear weapons were targeted, the mere fact that air bases and missile fields were in close proximity to major population centers ensured that every conceivable general nuclear war would cause catastrophic damage, even if all belligerents attempted to keep civilians from harm as much as possible. However, space—and Orion—provided a way out of this dilemma. Mixson argued that the United States had to remove its strategic power from physical proximity to the general populace, and "the only place remaining to us as a base of strategic operations is space itself. This is an overriding strategic consideration in any plan to develop a space capability and any plan that hopes to provide a defense of the population as well as the retaliatory power." Because of Orion, "For the first time in this decade, it is at least conceivable that the majority of our people will *not* die if our policies fail."[10]

To provide this assurance, Mixson argued it was necessary to remove the base of SAC strategic operations from the continental United States, eliminating any incentive for an enemy to strike the homeland for military reasons; to provide the enemy with a target of America's choice that the enemy had to be compelled to attack in any war; to provide a strategic retaliatory force that was invulnerable to attack and assured of swift and complete retaliation; and to provide a continental defense against any irrational "mad dog" attacks. A military force composed of nuclear pulse propulsion Orion spacecraft could fill all four requirements.[11]

To use Orion to answer these pressing strategic needs, Mixson developed the Strategic Space Force concept, which he estimated could be fielded by 1975. Mixson cautioned that his concept was not the result of a rigorous analysis, but rather was "intended as representative of the type of operation that one might wish to pursue and it can serve as a framework around which to build a sophisticated plan for the tactical employment of strategic space power" based on the Orion concept.[12]

Mixson's force contained twelve to fifty Orion vessels organized into three major combat elements, loosely characterized by their mission orbits: a low-altitude force (two-hour, one-thousand-mile altitude orbits); a moderate altitude force (twenty-four-hour orbits); and a deep space force (operating around the moon and beyond).

Mixson described the low-altitude force as a line of pickets possessing independent offensive striking power meant to compel the enemy to attack this force as a prerequisite to continental attack. The moderate altitude force would serve as fleet command and control, with one of its vehicles as the combat operations center. The deep space force had two major functions: "to pose a threat of total annihilation to the entire land mass occupied by the Communist Empire, and intercept and destroy any major Soviet space vehicle which penetrates the low and moderate altitude forces."[13] Mixson's description of these forces and their operations concepts should be considered a classic of military space philosophy. Other documents, especially those written by Mixson's friend and fellow Orion project officer, Capt. Fred Gorschboth, further refined his concepts.[14] Their work did not stay restricted to the Air Force Special Weapons Center for long.

On 17 September 1959 Mixson traveled from New Mexico to Omaha to brief Project Orion to the SAC command staff, including Power.[15] No records of the meeting have been found, but on 21 January 1961 Power issued a SAC Qualitative Operational Requirement (QOR) for a "Strategic Earth Orbital Base."

In this remarkable document—the only SAC space requirement letter signed by Power himself—the QOR defined "a Strategic Air Command requirement for a strategic Earth orbital platform capable of sustaining extremely heavy, composite payloads from low orbite [sic] to lunar distances and beyond." The document explained that conventional space technology afforded "only a partial solution to the long term space capability problem." SAC needed to deploy tons of payload to orbit, and conventional rockets could barely deliver pounds. SAC needed space-craft "virtually unrestricted by propulsion or payload limitations."[16]

SAC needed a number of these spacecraft "in various orbital planes at progressively distant orbital altitudes" in order to "provide integrated facilities for unlimited surveillance, depth of force, secure command and control, and a high probability of delivering weapons to any terrestrial target." These spacecraft had to be integrated with SAC's aircraft, missiles, and other vehicles to provide an optimum mixed force to provide world-wide deterrence. Each strategic Earth orbital base had to be capable of "accurate weapons delivery, with a variety of weapons" and "include the capability to attack other aerospace vehicles or bodies in the solar system occupied by an enemy."[17]

The spacecraft had to be maneuverable "in both altitude and orbital plane" to defend itself against attack and be responsive to military conditions. SAC also requested the craft have an "open ecology" that would support the crew for at least thirty days. The document further suggested an "artificial gravity system" and adequate shielding to protect crews from radiation. In addition, SAC requested "growth potential to include use as a support base for refueling space craft, planetary explorations, astronomical and astrophysical observations, nuclear weapons testing, equipment testing, and other appropriate activities."[18]

SAC desired that the base be "placed in orbit by a nuclear pulse rocket (or other propulsion system of comparable performance) capable of orbiting extremely heavy useful payloads; [i.e., on the order of five thousand tons by 1975 and fifteen thousand tons by 1985], or erected in space with components transported to orbit." Specifically stating that only Orion seemed to offer the capability of producing the strategic Earth orbital base, SAC nonetheless declared itself open to reviewing other technologies with similar performance.[19]

SAC requested that the method of meeting the requirement of the base "be met by implementation of an intensive R&D effort to include early testing of the nuclear pulse rocket [Orion] principle. Unusual means of shielding such as vehicle fuel, gaseous envelopes, and charged barriers should be explored. The feasibility of employing electron beams, focused intense electro-magnetic fields and other forms of destructive energy should be determined. A nuclear reactor as a secondary power source should be investigated."[20]

The operational requirement was a tall order by any stretch—Yuri Gagarin's first human orbital space flight was still three months in the future—but perhaps Power's most aggressive requirement was stated last. SAC wanted the first operational vehicle to be available "in the 1970–1975 time period."[21]

Mixson's mark on the strategic Earth orbital base QOR is unmistakable. In it, Power stated SAC needed the capability that Orion provided to perform the mission that Mixson described in his Strategic Space Force concept. It is interesting that this QOR describes a base rather than a ship, but with its emphasis on maneuverability, it is likely the vehicle was described as a base to match the contemporary public desire of the Air Force to develop a manned space station. In 1960 Power was arguably the third most powerful general in the Air Force, behind only the chief of staff and the vice chief of staff, and he wanted Orion so much that he put his name to a requirement document asking for nuclear pulse propulsion vehicles that only Project Orion could provide. Power brought Mixson to SAC on 17 July 1961 as a space plans officer in the space and advanced development programs systems section of the future weapons branch, plans division, Headquarters Strategic Air Command.[22] There Mixson worked a number of advanced space programs, including Orion, for SAC until he retired on 30 June 1969.[23]

Between Mixson's briefing to SAC senior leadership and SAC's issue of the QOR, Power wrote in *Air Force Magazine*, "The past year has witnessed continued and significant improvements all along the line which have added greatly to SAC's fighting capability and, hence, its deterrent strength. But these improvements were possible only because of steps taken in the past. Future improvements will depend on the steps which are taken today, and it is, therefore, none too early to prepare ourselves for the unprecedented demands of the dawning space age."[24] As he stated in the 1958 SAC space policy, Power insisted that "to achieve and maintain such supremacy for the sake of a lasting and honorable peace will demand an all-out cooperative effort which will have to draw upon all the economic, technological, and military assets at our command." Finally, echoing Mixson, Power declared, "In the event of need, SAC can be expected to contribute its share to this effort by putting into space strategic weapon systems . . . [and] manned spacecraft which would orbit the earth in a continuous space alert." However, Power did not overpromise. "The day when such weapons become a reality may still be far in the future," he said, "but regardless of the dramatic challenges that lie ahead, it is safe to predict that the American people can always count on SAC and its men to do their part—on the ground, in the air, and in space."[25]

There is some evidence that Power took organizational action to ensure SAC would be effective in those three domains. A little-known and unappreciated organizational innovation occurring at SAC at this time was the concept of strategic wings. When missiles first started to enter SAC in 1957, the strategic wing was developed that merged a strategic bomber squadron and one or more missile squadrons assigned to the same air base. Later, strategic wings could be a combination of bomber, tanker, or missile squadrons (for instance, the 92nd Bombardment Wing became the 92nd Strategic Wing when Atlas E missiles were added to the wing's B-52D bombers). By the end of 1958 there were fourteen strategic wings in SAC. In 1962 Power redesignated the strategic wings as strategic aerospace wings, to support General White's aerospace construct. Most SAC historians consider the strategic aerospace wing to merely be a method to reduce the number of wing headquarters that would have been necessary to maintain the traditional air wing construct.[26] However, given Power's emphasis on SAC personnel to adapt to any weapons system no matter how revolutionary in nature (such as in his 1957 memorandum to the alert force), his dedication to building a combined bomber/missile/aerospace team in the 1958 SAC space plan, and his plan to integrate truly revolutionary manned spacecraft into SAC in only a decade's time, the strategic aerospace wings may also be seen as an organizational experiment by Power to explore how a hybrid wing of dissimilar strategic weapons could be managed. One can easily imagine the first SAC Orion spacecraft attached to a strategic aerospace wing with its crew drawn from the wing's mix of pilots (as spacecraft commanders), missileers (as weapons officers), and aircrew (to serve other duties) to form the first combat crews for the strategic space forces.

Power's support for Orion coincided with one of the Air Force's most enthusiastic attempts to express its vision for the national space program and the Air Force's role in it. In reaction to many Soviet firsts in space, especially Yuri Gagarin's space flight on 12 April 1961, the Air Force believed that perceived weakness in the U.S. national space program would make a more aggressive military space plan widely popular with the American people. The Air Force began by updating its space plan of 1961. It stated that the Air Force's two primary space missions were "to enhance the general military posture of the United States through [the] military use of space" and "to provide a military patrol capability within the space region." Ultimately, the Air Force would develop the capabilities that could deny to any hostile power "the uninhibited military exploitation of space, and to provide a system of protection for U.S. scientific activities in space."[27] The details and funding requirements of how the space plan would accomplish that mission were to be developed in the five-year 1962 Air Force space program for fiscal years 1963–67. The 1962 Air Force space program would be the high-water mark for Project Orion.

The debate over the 1962 Air Force space program lasted from April to November 1962 as Air Force Systems Command officers and Power allies pressed for operational space requirements against civilian scientists on the Air Force's Scientific Advisory Board who favored funding modest technological advancements in space. Orion bounced back and forth from being lavishly funded to zeroed out over seven iterations of the plan. Finally, on 1 November 1962 LeMay—now Air Force chief of staff and an Orion believer—decided in favor of operational requirements, sending a proposal to Secretary Zuckert asking for a $7.9 billion Air Force space program, with Orion alone funded at $1.4 billion, or 18 percent of the budget.

However, the civilians were not defeated. Launor Carter, a member of the scientific advisory board, believed "it was their unanimous opinion that the program was much too ambitious, was in many ways technically unfeasible, and could not be sold to DDR&E [director of defense research and engineering]."[28] Carter further claimed the programs the Air Force wanted "were not with the state-of-the-art and that, at best, exploratory development was all that could be justified" and that the operational commands (meaning SAC) were pressing unrealistic requirements "that put great pressure on AFSC to come forward with proposals which were either unsound or not fundable."[29]

Zuckert decided not to present the 1962 Air Force space program to McNamara, preferring to send a much smaller funding request for only the most modest of Air Force space projects. Orion was completely removed.[30] Zuckert was undoubtedly influenced by McNamara's and DOD's general mistrust of the Air Force's space ambitions. McNamara did not believe that space operations could provide the revolutionary military advantages that the Air Force thought possible, saying the "prospect that remarkable new weapons can provide a sudden change in the margin of superiority is not, in my judgment, likely."[31] "Unfortunately, the five-year program—which served the useful function of crystallizing Air Force thinking on its space goals—made no great impact upon the OSD," historian Gerald Cantwell remarked; "McNamara for all practical purposes ignored the document."[32] Of interest, of the sixteen original programs and the six that the Air Force ultimately requested funding for, only one—Midas, the precursor to the Defense Support Program missile warning satellite—was ever fielded. The Air Force did not pursue space power as Mixson, Gorschboth, and Power envisioned.[33]

Power, however, was not going to accept the loss of Orion lying down. He was astute enough to know Zuckert was not the real obstacle.

The DDR&E, Dr. Harold Brown, was the face of the McNamara DOD research and development effort, and he held the real power to get Orion funded. Only two days after Zuckert's decision, Power wrote to Brown, "The capability to launch and maneuver truly large payloads [in space] could provide the operational flexibility which has always been the key to effective military posture. Unilateral ORION capability gained by either ourselves or the Soviets could be a decisive factor in achieving scientific and commercial, as well as military supremacy. . . . I understand you have recommended disapproval. I believe these [ORION] experiments should proceed without delay."[34] A few days later, Brown explained his disapproval of Orion: "This development program would be a very high risk one. . . . If we accept the possibility that military operations will require large maneuverable payloads in space, it is still far from clear that substantial investment in ORION is warranted *now*. . . . Very large chemical boosters are under development. . . . They could launch other large military payloads, if required."[35]

Brown's letter reveals a significantly different attitude from Power's. Instead of seeking capability, as Power did, Brown instead focused on risk. Brown, and the rest of McNamara's DOD, saw Orion and other ambitious programs as high-risk, high-cost gambles. Interestingly, Brown mentioned large chemical boosters as potential substitutes for Orion, which he must have known were vastly inferior to nuclear pulse propulsion, and an argument that Maj. Gen. Hewitt Wheless anticipated and rejected months earlier. Wheless, SAC's chief of plans, wrote in March to the air staff, "Nuclear pulse propulsion (ORION) is not an alternative approach to large boosters. ORION is a complementary propulsion vehicle which offers the capability to orbit massive payloads with the high thrust/weight ratios and large velocity reserves for maneuver. These mission capabilities far exceed those which will be available from the best practical chemical systems. . . . The 'payoff potential' of this concept is vastly superior to anything else presently contemplated."[36] Power thought the sheer capability Orion offered in space was worth the risk. Brown did not see that an Orion-type space capability was worth purchasing, even if it were possible.

The civilian decision to reject Orion seems to have been based on the assumption that the capability Orion represented was unnecessary even if it worked. Therefore, two different potential flaws can be identified: Power may have overemphasized capability and downplayed risk, and Brown may have overemphasized risk and downplayed military capability. In any case, the most ambitious attempt by the Air Force to realize Thomas Power's space vision was blocked by Harold Brown and Robert McNamara's defense department. However, Power would not stop fighting, nor would he soon forget what he saw as civilian betrayal of the Air Force's destiny in space.

Orion may not have been made a flagship program, but the program nonetheless continued. Shortly after the loss, Power wrote to LeMay and Schriever on 20 February 1963 to outline his reasons for continuing to support Orion: "Space is now just opening up an entirely new arena where nations will eventually develop new weapons as they have done for the land, sea, and air. We must plan today for the Space Power of tomorrow. Unfortunately, there is not today any single space program designed to provide this nation with the foundation of a predominant military space superiority."[37]

Power stressed that predicting "precise combat operations, tactics, and weaponry is, of course, impossible in detail," but, he maintained, "military preparedness for the future must be not based on the capabilities and limitation of today's conceptual weapons systems. It is clear that a new dimension of warfare is open for those bold enough to accept the challenge. . . . The Orion propulsion technique offers the 'Best Bet' to approach the nearly unlimited propulsive power we must have if we even hope to do the things we know the USAF must do in order to discharge its responsibilities in the post 1970 time period." Only Orion could provide a level of freedom of action in space that the Air Force currently enjoyed in the air.[38]

Additionally, Power made a new argument. If a complacent United States ignored the technology behind Orion, a confident Soviet Union might not. Power claimed that "during the post 1970 time period it may be necessary for the United States to fight its way into space against a previously deployed enemy to prevent space being permanently denied to us. Under these conditions it would be imperative to enter space with a vehicle immediately capable of conducting offensive/defensive operations in a sustained conflict. The Orion project offers such a capability."[39] For all these reasons, Power maintained, "I view the Orion Program as essential to the future welfare of the nation and urge that it be pursued with the utmost vigor consistent with the technical state-of-the-art. Such a breakthrough in the art of propulsion will produce revolutionary improvements in the science of warfare."[40]

Power mentioned Project Orion in a speech to the Union League of New York on 10 April 1962 and explained why such a capability was essential for SAC. Power declared that to adjust to new strategic realities, SAC might need to evolve from a strategic bomber command into a "Strategic Aerospace Command."[41] He then told the audience, "There is as yet no manned space system under development that would meet SAC's future needs to . . . achieve and maintain 'mastery in space.'" To achieve true space mastery, Power explained, "will require intensive and coordinated efforts in many areas, including the development of radically new power plants—possibly of the nuclear pulse type—and perhaps of revolutionary new weapons."[42] Then Power assured the audience, "Given the tools, SAC stands ready to accomplish its strategic aerospace mission as effectively as it has accomplished its strategic air mission."[43]

Unfortunately, Power's enthusiastic support may have inadvertently hurt Orion as he struggled to keep it alive after the 1962 Air Force space program effort. Ted Taylor believed that "those big briefings by SAC with a hundred slides of variations, themes, and more variations on the theme 'whoever develops Orion will rule the world' had a very negative effect on a lot of people, and I think that had a lot to do with it being easy to kill."[44] Fred Gorschboth, who wrote an entire book developing the Orion concept as a military vehicle, believed that scientist Freeman Dyson turned against Orion immediately after the team approached SAC.[45] There is some evidence to think Dyson might have been against SAC involvement. Dyson had served in the Royal Air Force Bomber Command during World War II and reportedly did not like the organization or its leader, Arthur Harris.[46] It seems entirely possible that Dyson saw much of "Butcher" Harris in Thomas Power, and that might have dampened Dyson's enthusiasm for the project. Even Mixson came to regret the implications of taking Orion to SAC. After Dyson's book *Disturbing the Universe* brought Mixson's paper to light in 1979, Mixson responded to Dyson, "[*Military Implications*] was written not to make Orion a military machine, but to con a military machine into yet another installment of funds to keep your big beautiful dream alive."[47] Whether these are after-the-fact laments or a true sentiment, Orion did run into some setbacks for what appears to be Power's overly aggressive selling of the idea.

One semilegendary event in the history of Project Orion was a meeting at Vandenberg Air Force Base on 23 March 1962 when Power presented a large model of an Orion vessel to President Kennedy and his entourage, including Harold Brown. This model was "Corvette sized" and cost $75,000 to produce.[48] Some Orion veterans remembered the model as "bristling with bombs," while others recalled that it was equipped with five-inch guns.[49] Kennedy was bewildered by the scope of Orion and the model but apparently was impressed with the dozens of landing craft that were attached to the ship as if Orion was a gigantic space carrier: "They'd hold about as many people as I'd ever put on a PT boat."[50]

By most accounts the sheer scale of Orion appeared to leave Kennedy questioning the sanity of the project, and it certainly did not win his support as Power had hoped. According to Taylor, "Not everybody greeted the project with enthusiasm. They did when it was presented as a way of exploring space and mostly were very disapproving when it was presented as a space battleship or anything like that."[51]

Harold Brown recalled the event, saying, "The model of the Orion thing had about 50 Dyna-Soars in it, and I was appalled, and President Kennedy was obviously appalled, and amused, too, and he asked me what the devil the Dyna-Soar was for." Brown explained that the Dyna-Soar was a "better way of getting down" from space.[52] Kennedy then mentioned he wanted to know what Orion was for, "but we didn't have any time to discuss it afterwards."[53]

The model disappeared shortly thereafter. Aerospace historian Scott Lowther quipped of this briefing that "the display model in fact turned out to be a really bad idea. . . . rather than helping to sell the concept, it apparently helped kill it. When the President of the United States thinks what you are working on is an evil monstrosity, your chance of further funding may tend to decrease."[54]

Power never let Orion stray far from his attention. He alluded to Orion frequently in a speech to the Second Manned Spaceflight Meeting in Dallas, Texas, on 24 April 1963, though he never mentioned it directly.[55] Power's speech was quite visionary. However, it was only a fraction of the speech he wanted to give. On 16 April 1963 Charles W. Hinkle, director of security review in the office of the assistant secretary of defense, informed Power that his proposed speech was "reviewed at the highest level" and Hinkle's office "concluded that it is impractical to make amendments."[56] Power's original speech included the statement, "I believe that an adequate space capability will require a vehicle that is equipped with a nuclear or nuclear-pulse powerplant to afford wide maneuverability over extended periods of time . . . and I am convinced that such a vehicle will have to be manned for the same reasons which make the manned bomber such a potent and flexible strategic weapon."[57] Power had not given up on Orion, and he intended to take his case to the public time and again after the loss to Harold Brown and OSD over the 1962 Air Force space program. However, OSD had finally muzzled Power from bringing his case to the American people.

For his part, Power was often a thorn in the DOD intellectuals' sides. He was unique among all serving senior officers in that he openly opposed the ratification of the 1963 Limited Test Ban Treaty (LTBT) and was the only uniformed officer to voice his opposition on public record. Not even LeMay voiced opposition to the treaty, though his support was at best lukewarm, and his support likely due to political pressure rather than honest military belief. Power, however, appeared before the preparedness investigation subcommittee of the Senate armed services committee to discuss the LTBT on 19 August 1963.

Power was apparently called to the Senate on very short notice, as he had no prepared statement to give. Senator John C. Stennis quickly began by asking, "Are you in favor of the Senate ratifying and committing the Nation to this treaty or not?" Power replied directly, "I am not in favor of the test ban treaty." When Stennis asked for Power's rationale, Power continued, "I don't think it's in the best interests on the United States. That is the basic reason . . . I feel we have military superiority now, and I feel very strongly that this has resulted in a world that has been free from nuclear warfare. I have a low confidence factor that we can and will maintain that military superiority under the test ban treaty than I have under a condition in which we do not have a test ban treaty."[58]

Power went through a number of objections to the treaty, some concerning perceived Soviet superiority in antiballistic missile technology, "clean" and small nuclear explosives, atmospheric testing, high-yield (fifty to one hundred megaton) nuclear weapons, and "weapons effects," or the study of nuclear explosions beyond their destructive capability.[59] Power also argued that, in the field of strategic nuclear warfare, no weapons that SAC fielded had been operationally tested, and "hardened" silo capsules had never been tested against a nuclear weapon strike. Power explained, "I have some [deleted] different types of nuclear weapons in the Strategic Air Command arsenal. None of them have been tested operationally from stockpile to detonation. I think it is a mistake. They should be tested."[60] The fact that the nation relied on a system never operationally proven disturbed him greatly.

Power concluded his philosophy with the reason why operational testing, which was distasteful to many and would be illegal under the proposed treaty, was necessary: "We could not be in the position of talking with confidence that we could prevent a thermonuclear war unless we were strong. . . . I just feel that the surest way to prevent war—and that is my goal, and I feel very strongly about it—is to have overwhelming strength so that it is ridiculous for anybody to even think of attacking the United States."[61]

Power then voiced his acknowledgment of public distaste and his concern for the American people. "It has unpleasant features, yes," he conceded, "but the surest way in my opinion of preventing a thermo-nuclear war is to have an overwhelming strength, and I think this is one area in which we can beat anyone. I think our science, our economy, and everything else can help us win this race. We have won it in the past, and I think we can continue to win it. But it takes the will to do it!"[62]

The discussion eventually turned to disarmament, and Power gave another stark opinion: "I have studied [previous disarmament measures], and in my opinion disarmament is a proven concept to get you into a war. ... And the surest way to cause a war, nuclear war or any war, is to disarm. That is my own personal opinion. There are people that disagree with that, and they are entitled to their opinion. You asked me for my opinion, and I have given it to you."[63]

Near the conclusion of his testimony, Power offered his final thoughts on the contest between the Soviet Union and the United States. "This is an arms race. You have had it since history started and you will have it forever, in my opinion. Now if you are in a race, win it," Power implored. "Granted it costs money, but it costs more than money. Money is not what makes the Strategic Air Command. It is the realiza-tion of the importance of the mission. It is the desire to maintain this superiority." Finally, Power issued a dire warning: "Now this is a very fragile thing. This can be destroyed very easily, but not by the Soviet Union. The Strategic Air Command cannot be destroyed by the Soviet Union but it can be destroyed by the American people if they desire it, and very quickly."[64]

Power received a great deal of mail in support of his testimony, from Air Force officers to workers to housewives to congressmen. Official Washington was not as supportive. Harold Brown dismissed Power's tes-timony: "He was not [inhibited]. I think he was not very well informed, either, but he was not inhibited."[65]

Power did not mention Orion or hint at anything similar in his testi-mony to the Senate regarding the Limited Test Ban Treaty, but he surely knew that the treaty would make developing, testing, and operating an Orion flight system impossible. After his testimony, he took measures to retain the Air Force's commitment to the technology. In a 14 October

1963 letter to Headquarters, USAF, Power argued, "The Strategic Air Command's requirement for the space vehicle performance represented by the ORION concept remains valid regardless of the treaty banning nuclear explosions in the atmosphere or space. The treaty, far from removing nuclear pulse propulsion from serious consideration, serves only to increase the urgency of the proposed underground test program and allied non-nuclear research and mechanical test programs."[66]

Power stressed the importance of nonnuclear testing, which would be unaffected by the treaty: "Logical progression of an ORION research program will not be impeded by the test treaty until possibly 1966. Nor does the treaty affect in any way the requirement to design, develop, and mechanically test by high explosives a research vehicle capable of high altitude flight. If the national policy of preparation to test on short notice is applied to ORION, these three years of preparation are vital."[67]

Power next argued that the reason he was so insistent on continuing Orion was that the Soviet Union might gain the capability first. Power claimed, "The ease with which the USSR could conduct clandestine testing leading to the development of a full-scale ORION prototype places further urgency upon the conduct of our own program. The practicality of the concept is susceptible to demonstration with a flight research vehicle of between 20 and 200 tons gross mass. Multiple shot dynamic free flight engineering tests could be conducted within the lower atmosphere with nuclear yields ranging from one to ten *tons*. Such low yields would not be detectable beyond the boundaries of a remote test site, let alone the borders of the USSR." Exhibiting a firm grasp of the technical issues associated with Orion, Power explained how the Russians could overcome many barriers to the system without being detected by U.S. forces. From his analysis, Power offered, "Thus, if the treaty were to be abrogated for any reason, the Russians could be in a position to conduct a full-scale prototype orbital test as the first order to business. This could give them a technological lead of as much as six or eight years and guarantee them military dominance in space."[68]

Power concluded, "In view of the consequences of a clear Russian lead in ORION propulsion technology, as applied to manned military systems, your continued support for an adequate ORION program is urgently necessary."[69] Power then demanded a robust theoretical, non-nuclear, and underground nuclear test effort focused on overcoming Orion's technological hurdles to ensure the United States could field an Orion spacecraft when the Russians broke the treaty, which Power was sure they would do.

Even though Power stood alone as the single military leader to oppose ratification of the LTBT, he was far from the only senior officer to think poorly of the OSD Whiz Kids. On 4 May 1963 Gen. Thomas White, then retired from the position of Air Force chief of staff, wrote a scathing article in the *Saturday Evening Post* entitled "Strategy and the Defense Intellectuals," in which he wrote: "I am profoundly apprehensive of the pipe-smoking, tree-full-of-owls type of so-called 'defense intellectuals' who have been brought into this nation's capital. I don't believe that a lot of these overconfident, sometimes arrogant young professors, mathematicians and other theorists have sufficient worldliness or motivation to stand up to the kind of enemy we face."[70] Power was not the only senior military officer to congratulate White on his article, but he did it in writing, on letterhead that read "Headquarters Strategic Air Command, Office of the Commander in Chief."[71]

The animosity between Power and his civilian superiors was definitely requited, even to the highest level. Harold Brown recalled one 1962 meeting in which a proposed U.S. one-hundred-megaton bomb was being discussed. Kennedy quipped, "I know someone who I know would be willing to test one, and I even know where he would be willing to test it."[72] It was clear to Brown that Kennedy "was talking about General Power and he was talking about Moscow." However, Brown was quick to point out in his interview that Kennedy did not seem overly concerned about Power, and that Kennedy appreciated Power's opinion. "[Kennedy] never seemed to me to have any doubt about his ability to handle or to assert civilian authority over the military," Brown recalled. "I think he made it clear that he wanted his military people to be aggressive in the sense of being willing to do what was necessary if it were necessary, but that he had no doubt of his ability to control them."[73]

In his daily activities, Power attempted to keep SAC's morale high and his men in public view. On 4 March 1962 Power spoke at the Screen Producer's Guild milestone dinner in Los Angeles honoring entertainer Bob Hope, who had toured Thule Air Base in Greenland a few months earlier. Power said that "we are fortunate indeed that we [at SAC] can rely on the patriotism and selfless dedication" of comedians like Bob Hope. Humor, Power said, "is the best tonic for those who must man the distant and lone outposts of our defense line."[74] Hope, who had thanked Power for his kind words, added, "I hope you're keeping your golf game in good shape."[75]

Power wanted to present SAC to the public as a disciplined, professional force, and it took showmanship from the men and the commander. He gained a national audience for the command in a special report on ABC, "SAC: The Big Stick," which aired on 8 May 1962. It received very good reviews, and Power was lauded by the national news specifically. The *New York Herald Tribune* noted Power's "dry humor" when explaining the new SAC airborne command post aircraft, recounting Power's statement that "If the general officer [on the aircraft] should look down and see a large hole in the ground where SAC headquarters used to be, he would naturally become suspicious."[76] Power also received a great deal of mail due to the show. An "average American mother" wrote Power, "I want to thank you, sir, and your men of the Strategic Air Command for allaying my fears. I truly did sleep in peace for the first time in a long time last night" after watching the program.[77] Thomas McKnew, vice chairman of the board of the National Geographic Society, thought "it was a splendid program and one that every American should have seen."[78]

On 6 June 1962 the *Saturday Evening Post* asked Power to contribute his favorite quote to the magazine for use in a new feature. Instead of invoking an airpower quote, Power chose the words of British explorer Sir Richard Francis Burton: "Do what thy manhood bids thee to do, from none but self expect applause; He noblest lives and noblest dies who makes and keeps his self-made laws."[79]

Unfortunately, Power bristled under laws he did not make. McNamara consistently refused to give SAC control and operation of the deterrent for the "emergency capability" that Zuckert and Power desired. On 29 January 1963, shortly after the Cuban Missile Crisis, McNamara insisted the nuclear deterrent would always be under the basis of policy decisions at the highest level of government and that under no circumstances "should SAC have the unilateral decision as to whether an operation should be conducted or not."[80]

However, McNamara was not opposed to Power leading SAC. In April 1963 McNamara approved an extension to Power's tenure as CINCSAC until Power's retirement on 30 November 1964.[81] In July McNamara thanked "Tommy" for his work in preparing a summary SIOP reference book: "I was impressed by the useful form in which significant aspects of the SIOP are treated and also by the fact that you plan to keep the tables current through monthly revisions," and he called the summary a "job well done."[82]

In June 1963 the University of Akron conferred upon Power an honorary doctor of laws degree. Power received the honor as the commencement speaker in addition to presenting the graduating Reserve Officers' Training Corps cadets their commissions.[83] When preparing his speech, Power detailed the moments in his career of which he was most proud: planning and executing the 9 March 1945 Tokyo raid, commanding ARDC and producing the Atlas missile, and creating the Joint Strategic Target Planning Staff.[84]

On 4 June 1963 Power was made aware that 1st Lt. Roger Edwards of the 578th Strategic Missile Squadron decided his Catholic beliefs prevented him from performing nuclear duties. In contravention of his popular reputation, Power did not reprimand or censure the lieutenant. Noting Edwards' strong religious convictions, Power recommended an honorable discharge.[85] Norman Cousins, the editor of the *Saturday Review* and a staunch advocate of nuclear disarmament, liberal causes, and "world peace," wrote to Power thanking him for his "equitable, humane solution of what might have easily been a situation diminishing and hurtful to all concerned."[86]

During an inspection conducted from 28 April to 3 May 1963, Air Force inspector general Maj. Gen. S. W. Wells found that the 548th

Strategic Missile Squadron's technical order familiarization program directed by SAC on 6 March 1963 "had not been implemented. Under LeMay, an inspection failure was a swift and devastating blow to a career—a blow often delivered by Power himself. The squadron's commander viciously protested to Power. Power wrote back confirming Wells' findings but also offered, 'I have been advised that positive action has been taken to correct these deficiencies, and I am confident that, as a result, subsequent inspections will find all requirements being met satisfactorily.'"[87] The squadron commander retired in 1972 as a brigadier general commanding the Civil Air Patrol.

Power was not willing to save every career. In late 1963 a SAC missileer was charged with an incestuous relationship with his daughter. However, the daughter recanted her statement, eliminating any proof of crime. Power then personally sought to discharge the officer through "administrative elimination proceedings." Due to political debate over the legal authority of senior officers, Zuckert overturned Power's decision, and the officer was medically retired.[88] Power could be a hammer, but often for much better reasons than his detractors credit him.

On 17 February 1964 Elizabeth Cowles of the Vital Issues Group of New York wrote to Power asking his opinion of the recently released movie *Dr. Strangelove*. Cowles called the movie a "slashing broadside thinly disguised as good-natured lampooning . . . so vicious as to give pause even to the leftist reviewers." She asked how the government could allow *Dr. Strangelove* to be shown.[89] Power quickly replied, "I can assure you that neither the Strategic Air Command nor the Department of Defense has assisted in the production of this picture in any way," but reminded Cowles that "the Government is in no position to prevent the production and distribution of any literary or pictorial venture of this type. We can only hope that the great majority of the American people will retain their faith and confidence in their Armed Forces despite *Dr. Strangelove* and similar films and books."[90]

Power, consistent with his belief that communication was the best policy, took time to respond to a questionnaire sent by a citizen in February 1964. Circling his answers to the questions on a postcard,

Power revealed to the interested taxpayer that he thought the chances of an "accidental war" were "too remote to worry about." Power was also in favor of the public building fallout shelters, and did not find such shelters "provocative." Lastly, Power responded that the recent test ban treaty was "very risky" and in response to the question, "Are we winning the Cold War?" Power simply circled "No."[91]

On 10 April 1964 Creighton University notified Power that they would confer upon him an honorary doctor of laws degree by unanimous vote. University president H. W. Linn wrote, "In our opinion, no military leader in this country has fulfilled his highly responsible role over a long period of years more competently than you."[92]

On 7–8 April 1964 Power hosted a number of retired Air Force officers at Offutt Air Force Base, including Lt. Gen. Harold L. George, who led the air war planning effort prior to World War II and was the lead writer of Air War Plans Division-1, the plan that, among other results, committed the United States to a strategy of strategic bombing. George wrote to Power that his presentation "will be remembered by me as one of the outstanding summations of this nation's security and survival problems that I have ever heard discussed so fluently and intelligently by a senior officer of our military forces."[93]

General Power had served more than thirty-five years in uniform and was notified that he would be retired from service on 30 November 1964 because he had reached the maximum service age. Not everyone was happy with Power's impending retirement. Aviation public relations expert Harry Bruno wrote, "I just saw the [Associated Press] story about your planned retirement. My personal feeling is that this country can ill afford to lose your services at this time."[94] SMSgt. Henry Lacour relayed, "I hate to see the day come when you and General LeMay leave our Air Force."[95] Maj. Gen. C. F. Necrason wrote, "Your name will be spoken in military circles for a long time to come."[96] Lawrence Spivak, the host of Meet The Press who had been trying to get Power on the program for years, again wrote "to renew my invitation in the hope that [Power] can appear immediately upon retirement before you do any other national interview programs."[97] This time, Power responded, "It would be a pleasure indeed to appear on your program at that time" and referred Spivak to Carl Brandt, Power's new literary agent.[98] Power also attempted to shift some assets to prepare for his retirement, transferring $75,000 (about $575,000 in 2018 dollars) in stocks for California tax-free bonds, indicating that the Power family was well prepared for retirement but not necessarily wealthy.[99]

By 5 May 1964 DOD agreed to release a copy of *Design for Survival* to Power to prepare for its publication upon his retirement. Carl Brandt read the copy and wrote to Power that "I now can understand, at least in part, why you have been entrusted with the responsibilities that you have had over the years. This is an important book, and a book with a point of view which will provoke great discussion in that it is a serious and responsible challenge to so many people who are now supporting a 'liberal' approach to our national security." Brandt suggested that Power and Arnhym consider simultaneous publication in book form as well as magazine publication in early 1965.[100] On 18 May 1964 Brandt recommended Random House be offered the manuscript first because of its earlier contract that DOD had invalidated, but that they should contract with Random House only if "their enthusiasm is reflected properly in a contract." Doubleday was Brandt's second choice, but he also warned against dealing with Coward-McCann, who "has had some real recent success" but was not "set up to do the kind of publishing job which this book deserves."[101]

Just two days later, Brandt received Random House's reply. Editor Robert Lewis "was somewhat disappointed" in the book. The six-year-old manuscript had not aged well. Power's book read "as if the B-70 were going to join SAC almost any day" instead of it nearing cancellation, and the book had many outdated statistics. The manuscript may have been most damaged, however, by the fact that "the tremendous influence of our strategic forces on world events has been greatly diminished" and that defense analysts in 1964 were concerned about being "somewhat slow in creating a special kind of force to meet situations such as we now have in Vietnam."[102] SAC was rapidly disappearing from the public's imagination, and limited war was now the nation's focus. Brandt notified Power that there would need to be significant additional revisions to the book before Random House would reconsider. Doubleday was more final in its assessment of *Design for Survival*, concluding, "General Power's position is too well known for us to envisage much success for this book."[103]

General and Mrs. Power always held a deep devotion to Strategic Air Command personnel. The Powers were devout Catholics and did not hide their Christian faith, and on 14 July 1964 they were honored with the highest awards the Catholic church can bestow on laymen for their efforts in assisting Catholic SAC families. Their efforts had been more than five years in the making. In 1959 a young Air Force Catholic chaplain, Capt. John J. Ruef, arrived at Offutt Air Force Base. As SAC grew, so did Offutt. Between the late 1950s and early 1960s, more than 13,000 homes were built for personnel over all SAC bases, and Offutt had grown more than most. In 1962 Offutt had 450 Catholic families on base, and Father Ruef was already overwhelmed by the number of students in his catechism class. By 1964 Father Ruef had 750 families to support. He decided that a Catholic parochial school was needed at Offutt. The school had to be privately financed but operated by the Catholic military parish to serve a specific military base, something that had never before been attempted.[104]

Father Rueff approached SAC headquarters with his scheme. Maj. Gen. James B. Knapp, SAC's chief of civil engineering and a Catholic layman, agreed to help. Mrs. Mae Power, a devout Catholic who dedicated a great deal of time to Offutt family services and the officers' wives club, also joined the project. Together, Major General Knapp and Mrs. Power began the Catholic Education Association (CEA) of Offutt, as president and vice president, respectively.

The CEA immediately began soliciting donations. The association estimated that they would need $130,000 to build and run the school. Father Rueff, General Knapp, and Mrs. Power engaged the local community. Omaha archbishop Gerald T. Bergen and military vicar Francis Cardinal Spellman provided support from the larger Catholic community. Power personally approached many of his national-level contacts to help fund the school. After months of seeking donations, Catholics from all the bases of the 16th Air Force raised $4,000, the local Omaha community raised $63,000, and local architect Leo Daly waived his usual $15,000 fee to design the unique pod-like structure of the building. National contributors included Brig. Gen. James "Jimmy" Stewart—movie star, SAC reservist, and personal friend of Tommy Power—and Conrad Hilton of the Hilton hotel chain. But it was SAC personnel who donated the most to the school: $67,000. [105]

Once they had the money, the CEA decided to name the school after Francis Spellman. He was nearing his twenty-fifth anniversary as military vicar, and having the school named for him was considered "an appropriate physical demonstration of progress that Spellman has made in providing better facilities for military Catholics [going] from tents to permanent chapels, and now schools."[106] Spellman himself dedicated the school on 18 August 1963 in a ceremony with the Powers, SAC senior officers, local dignitaries, and the Catholic families of Offutt Air Force Base in attendance. The school still exists.

Almost a year later, on 14 July 1964, Omaha archbishop Gerald T. Bergan presented papal honors to both the Powers for their efforts on behalf of the Catholic community. For their distinctive service to the Church, Gen. Thomas Power was invested as a knight commander with the Grand Cross of the Order of St. Sylvester, and Mrs. Mae Power was presented a *Pro Ecclesia et Pontifice* ("for Church and Pope") medal.

"It is a distinct honor, and one of the most joyous events of my entire episcopacy to render this public ecclesiastical recognition to you," Archbishop Bergan said as he conferred the honors in a noon ceremony at his personal residence. "This ceremony is the climax of the activities of those laboring as peacemakers in a troubled world: the Holy Father, the representative of the Prince of Peace at the Vatican; and you, General Power, who so capably command the military force which preserves the world from its own destruction."[107] Bergen added that SAC's motto "Peace is Our Profession" might as well be considered the pope's motto, since he also worked untiringly for peace among all nations.[108]

Power's citation accompanying the award was forwarded by Amleto Cardinal Cicognani, the papal secretary of state. The SAC commander was lauded for "outstanding consideration manifested to the Church" and for having "generously seen to the erection of a parochial school for Catholic children of members of the United States Air Force." Mrs. Power's medal, a gold cross decorated with comets and lilies on a red, white, and yellow ribbon, was awarded for her "outstanding service to the Church and to the Pope." Power wrote to Spellman, "Mrs. Power and I are greatly honored by these distinguished awards and are deeply grateful to you for the renewed expression of your personal and active interest in the educational project at Offutt Air Force Base for whose pursuit we have been so richly rewarded. The honors we received will serve as a lasting incentive to always prove worthy of the high ideals which these awards represent."[109]

On 10 November 1964 Omaha television station KETV aired a special production highlighting Power's long and storied military career. In it, many notable figures such as Senator Barry Goldwater, Gen. Carl Spaatz, and Brig. Gen. Jimmy Stewart were interviewed regarding what Power had done for the Strategic Air Command, the Air Force, and the nation.[110] A congressman called Power one "of the half-dozen most outstanding men in the world."[111] Power was in the national spotlight again, but *Design for Survival* was not doing as well. Power's literary agent Carl Brandt informed him on 18 November that many magazines, including the *Saturday Evening Post*, *Life*, and *Look*, had turned the book down. Brandt held hope that *Reader's Digest* would accept it for serial publication.[112]

Between operationally standing off against the Soviet Union during the height of the Cold War and warring against Washington bureaucrats for SAC's future, Power's herculean responsibilities began to wear him down, and he was showing his age. Power had been on a flying waiver since 1959 for substandard hearing (hearing loss is common among fliers), substandard near vision, and hypertensive vascular disease.[113] The hypertension was most serious. Both his mother and father had suffered from heart disease. His mother died of liver cancer at sixty-seven, and his father died of a heart attack at seventy-four. Power was advised to limit his exposure to stress as much as possible, but doctors agreed his hypertension was not advanced enough for treatment. In a 1962 memo, Power's doctor, Brig. Gen. Alonzo Towner, had written to Air Force surgeon general Oliver Niess that Power was "a little sensitive about any physical defect that would imply weakness. This is understandable for a man of his strength and position. I only hope to be in as good health as he is when I pass the 56-year mark."[114]

Power had advocated for SAC's role in space as much as he could, but his retirement in 1964 brought large-scale support to Project Orion in the Air Force to a close. Dyna-Soar and Orion both had prominent sections in official SAC annual histories between 1961 and 1964, but their coverage ended in 1965, shortly after the end of Power's tenure. Neither program would fly. Dyna-Soar would be remembered, but Orion was promptly forgotten. Gerald Cantrell wrote the official history of the 1962 Air Force space program and did not make any mention of Project Orion. It appears that even the Air Force attempted to bury or ignore Project Orion in the official histories. For all intents and purposes, Orion in the highest levels of Air Force and DOD discussion ended in November 1962. Orion had reached its high-water mark and slowly subsided until the project entirely disappeared from the Air Force's collective memory.

Power's greatest contribution to Air Force space power was to communicate clearly an operational definition of what superior space power looked like—it was a weapon that could propel thousands of tons into orbit in a single launch, maneuver in space as easily as an airplane in the air, carry out any payload and mission asked of it, and send a payload anywhere in the solar system. Power did not need the weapon to have a nuclear pulse propulsion system like Orion, but he did want the performance that only an Orion system provided. It was a desire the post-Power Air Force did not share.

General Power retired from the Air Force on 30 November 1964, after thirty-six years of service. On his last day on active duty, chief of staff General LeMay wrote to Power, "In leaving, you may look back with justifiable pride upon your myriad achievements, confident that your example will inspire us to the great task of building adequate aerospace power for national security."[115] His more than seven-year tenure as SAC commander was exceeded only by that of General LeMay. During his time, Power "polished the command" that LeMay had built.[116] Power had perfected the alert force, deployed the airborne command post, enhanced SAC's reconnaissance capabilities, and managed SAC's transition from a bomber force to a mixed aerospace force of bombers and missiles. He fielded three new bombers, three new ICBMs, and a whole new command and control system. He created and matured the Joint Strategic Targeting and Planning Staff.[117] He oversaw SAC during the Cuban Missile Crisis, arguably the command's finest hour second only to the end of the Cold War. One author credits him with "hon[ing] SAC into a multi-faceted combat organization capable of going to war at a moment's notice."[118] Fortunately, SAC never had to fight using nuclear weapons. However, Power's vision of SAC as a true aerospace force capable of defending the free world while also conquering space remained unfulfilled. Furthermore, the same men who had thwarted his plans were still in Washington.

Power did not stop defending the country simply because he had hung up his uniform. The defense establishment could no longer muzzle him, a private citizen, the way they had when he was SAC commander. He could take his message directly to the American people. As Thomas Power mustered for battle (as well as playing a bit more golf in Mae's and his new home in Palm Springs), the wheels of the DOD and the Air Force machines kept on going with a momentum that might not be easily stopped. The Cold War was not yet over, so the coldest warrior sallied forth in his new position as civilian.

CHAPTER 8

The War of Remembrance

Civilian Life, 1965–70

On 1 December 1964 Thomas Power woke up as a civilian for the first time in thirty-six years. But his war was not over. The Soviet threat still existed, and Power knew where and how he would continue the fight.

First, however, Power established his civilian life. Originally intending to retire to the Gulf coast of Florida, Thomas and Mae instead chose to build a home in the Thunderbird Country Club of Palm Springs, California. Five years earlier, Power had visited the high desert en route to La Jolla, California. "I liked it the minute I saw it," he recalled of Palm Springs. "I've been all over the world, and there's just no place like this."[1] He and Mae began visiting Palm Springs in their precious free time and ultimately decided to buy. Their home was a cozy, modest "off-white house of simple lines and a charcoal roof, with a swimming pool and a magnificent view."[2]

The Powers' modest retirement lifestyle, and Power's disciplined investing during his time in service, allowed him abundant free time to hunt, play golf, write, and speak. Power's life-long investment adviser was Harry W. Besse, his intelligence officer at the 314th Bomb Wing who flew with Power to sketch the results of the first incendiary raid against Tokyo in 1945. Colonel Besse became a successful investment banker and president of the Boston stock exchange after the war, and he always helped Thomas and Mae with investment decisions.[3]

Unlike so many famous and important generals, Power did not write his memoirs, but instead devoted his writing to convincing America to remain vigilant in defending against communist aggression. As a civilian,

Power was finally able to release *Design for Survival*. Power and coauthor Albert Arnhym heavily revised their original 1959 draft in Power's final months in uniform, but Power waited until retirement to conclude a contract with a publisher. Even though McNamara was in far more disagreement with Power than McElroy had been, Washington made no attempt to resist the book's publication.

Design for Survival was Power's largest project, and he began working with Coward-McCann to publish it. Ira Eaker promised to purchase one hundred copies to distribute to senior leaders.[4] Oil wildcatter millionaire William "Monty" Moncrief bought five hundred copies to send directly to the editors of small-town rural newspapers in order to "spread the message of the book" among "grass-roots" citizens.[5] Coward-McCann sent advance copies of the book to Walter Cronkite, former Air Force secretary Stuart Symington, broadcaster Arthur Godfrey, Senator John Stennis, defense correspondent Hanson Baldwin, actor Desi Arnaz, and others.[6] To publicize the books, and to bury any remaining hatchets, Power even had dinner with former President Eisenhower, even though the Eisenhower administration had banned the "parochial" general's book to begin with. Arnhym confidently told Power that Eisenhower "will be among your staunchest supporters" from that point forward.[7] Both *Cosmopolitan* and *Reader's Digest* ran articles on SAC and Power, and *U.S. News and World Report* printed an extensive interview with Power to close out 1964.

Many peers lauded Power in retirement. Gen. John D. Ryan, the new CINCSAC, told Power on 23 December 1964 that Robert McNamara told Ryan, "If the rest of the Department of Defense ran as efficiently as Strategic Air Command, half my troubles would disappear." Ryan "thought it a mighty fine compliment to [Power's] leadership."[8] Longtime friend and retired Lt. Gen. D. M. Schlatter wrote, "I just can't imagine our Air Force without you on the active list."[9] Gen. J. P. McConnell, recently elevated to Air Force chief of staff, told Power, "I need and want any advice or suggestions you may have from time to time."[10] Hewitt Wheless wrote Power thanking him for Power's help in being promoted to lieutenant general.[11] Wheless retired as assistant vice chief of staff a few years later.

Civilian think tanks eagerly sought out Power's advice. On 2 December 1964 Hudson Institute president Don G. Brennan approached Power to work on a study about nuclear communication. Brennan had asked Power in September 1963 to share his thoughts on the possible role of Soviet observers at SAC headquarters. At that time, Herman Kahn and others wanted to consider the problem of "intrawar deterrence and war termination." After a major nuclear exchange, the United States could have many missiles and bombers that had not been launched. How, then, would the United States be able to provide "convincing information about retained capabilities" to the Soviets in such an event? The Hudson Institute believed that Soviet observers could be a better solution than the standard U.S.-Soviet "hotline," which would provide verbal assurance that might not be sufficiently believable to deter the Soviet Union from continuing the war.

As CINCSAC, Power was interested, but he wanted the study authors to go a little deeper. Power asked them to consider "more general methods of information transfer and displays than the mere emplacement of hostile observers." Instead, they should "ask more generally just what information we wish [the Soviets] to have, with what kind of reliability and credibility, and what the costs and gains of various possible ways of providing this information seemed to be."[12] Power's interest in the study is unsurprising, because communicating was key to his concept of deterrence. What better way to make sure your adversary knows your strength than to invite him into your organization? Unfortunately, SAC could not sponsor any outside studies, and Power recommended Brennan approach DOD and, upon approval, SAC would support the study as much as possible.[13]

The Hudson study did not come up again until Power was retired. On 2 December 1964 Brennan sent Power a study proposal to DOD that contained an unidentified quotation from Power's earlier letter to Brennan about the study. Power again expressed interest but required remuneration since he was now retired. Brennan readily agreed.[14] Brennan doubted "there is anyone else who has thought about the roles and uses of the strategic forces and who also knows as much about the operating practices and details that we should have to be concerned with" and hoped Power could become a principal researcher. However, Brennan was happy to accept any time Power could devote to the study.[15]

Brennan attempted to sell the study idea to Harold Brown and enlisted his many contacts to help. Famous nuclear theorist Thomas Schelling on 27 January 1965 said he was eager to work on the project and urged Brown to approve the proposal. Schelling added, "I do not often write unsolicited recommendations of this sort."[16] But, perhaps still sore over previous battles with Power, Brown declined to fund the Hudson Institute study. Brennan kept searching for funds, but Power had to withdraw his commitment to the project on 13 March to focus on other projects.[17]

Power's other effort was his public speaking tour, with engagements starting at an average honorarium of $500. Arnhym worked diligently to take Power's many quotations and statements and turn them into public speeches.[18] An audience member at Power's speech to the Midwest Gas Association in Minneapolis wrote, "I've been to a lot of conventions, a lot of meetings, but I've never before witnessed such an example as yours of holding an audience in the palm of one's hand."[19] Power's speaking tour kept him very busy, especially after *Design for Survival* hit the shelves shortly after he retired.

Power also explored board membership positions in various companies. General Dynamics president Roger Lewis promised Power, "I will most definitely explore the directorships idea. The right ones would be mutually beneficial but they must be selected with some care," adding, "Tommy, the country owes you a great deal for your long and dedicated service. . . . You may not get the public recognition you deserve but it lies in the hearts of your friends and you must know in your own mind that this is so."[20] Meanwhile, Power had been approached to become of director of Houston Fearless, a photographic film company and contractor with the Central Intelligence Agency, but ultimately did not take the role after his inquiries about the company left him unsettled.[21] Friends put in good words for Power at Sears, Illinois Central Railroad, and Goldman Sachs, none of which panned out.[22] In April 1965 George Todt, a friend and public relations consultant, noted he met Patrick Frawly Jr. of Schick Safety Razor Company and "put the idea we discussed in his mind."[23] Power became vice chairman of the board of Eversharp, Inc., a Schick subsidiary, in 1966.[24] In addition, that April, Power was honored with the Arnold Air Society's H. H. Arnold Award, and *Air Force Magazine and Space Digest* published selections from *Design for Survival*.[25]

However, there were indications that the tide was shifting in the Air Force away from Power's view of strategic deterrence. Colonel Arnhym left SAC to work for chief of staff General McConnell in March 1965, but Arnhym was weary. "I hated to leave SAC and Offutt, but although everyone from General Ryan down was very nice to me, I was a 'hold-over from the old regime,'" he wrote Power. "As you may have noticed during your visit to SAC last week, there have been some basic changes in overall philosophy and mode of operations."[26] The change in overall philosophy, most notably sending SAC bomber crews to Vietnam, held grave consequences for SAC. Once at the Pentagon, Arnhym wrote Power, "Curiously enough, very little is being said about the book in the Pentagon, although it has been doing well in the Brentano book store in the Concourse. Perhaps the people here may agree with what you said but, for obvious reasons, hesitate to side with you openly."[27]

Power remained committed to efforts to tell the SAC story. He finally appeared on *Meet the Press* on 21 March 1965, the eve of *Design for Survival*'s publication. Moderator Lawrence Spivak was joined by panelist journalists Floyd Kalber, Hanson Baldwin, Charles Corddry, and Warren Rogers. Power described his book as an urgent report to the American people about keeping the peace through overwhelming military superiority instead of general and total disarmament, warning readers, "You cannot go down both roads at the same time."[28] The discussion, however, quickly turned to Vietnam. When asked if he thought SAC bombers should be deployed to Southeast Asia, Power responded that it "would be catastrophic" to pull out of South Vietnam and that he would like to see the bombers used (backing down from his initial refusal to send SAC bombers as CINCSAC) but not "to the point where it would interfere with their primary mission of deterring nuclear aggression."[29]

After discussing Vietnam, Power described his "mixed force" missile and bomber deterrence concept as important because of the risk of an all-missile force to an anti-ICBM system. "Let's assume that an aggressor, the Soviet Union, develops an effective anti-ICBM, or let's assume that they think they have an effective anti-ICBM. You could lose your deterrent." When Corddry challenged him, saying that the Air Force position was that an effective anti-ICBM was "out of the question," Power replied, "Well, I think an effective defense against any kind of an effective offensive system is not out of the question."[30]

Corddry then challenged Power with a quote from McNamara, saying that even after being hit by a first strike, the U.S. missile force in 1970 would be able to destroy 80 percent of Russian industry and kill one hundred million Russians. If missiles could do that after taking a first strike, "What do you need a bomber for?" Power responded, "Well, [McNamara's] is a very authoritative statement. . . . I don't know how anybody can be that sure with a number of variables there are. . . . I don't see how anybody can speak authoritatively about the future."[31]

Power was asked about the space program and the military's role in it. Power worried that the United States was not pursuing an aggressive military space program and argued, "Of course this won't affect you tomorrow, but we still have to live in this world ten or fifteen years from now, and if you believe in my philosophy of deterrence through the maintenance of a posture of overwhelming military superiority, then I feel you must exploit space for military purposes." When asked about his thoughts on the moon program, Power responded with a refrain similar to his thoughts on limited war: "I have no objection to exploring the moon, as long as it doesn't interfere with . . . our maintenance of a solid military position in order to deter."[32]

Rogers asked Power what he thought of the charge that DOD was silencing dissenting opinions in the military and creating a generation of "yes-men." Power hedged: "No, I don't think so. It's a very difficult problem that they're faced with. . . . I do feel that the public is entitled to know what some of our top military men are thinking," but restraint was also necessary because military leadership publicly disagreeing with the president "wouldn't be good for the country."[33]

As the program went on, the men discussed how strategic bombing could be used in Vietnam. Power said if SAC had been used in Vietnam like the Strategic Air Force was used against Japan in 1945, "within a few days, and with minimum force, the conflict in South Vietnam would have been ended in our favor." He also supported dropping leaflets on Vietnamese cities slated for attack in order to warn civilians to leave, just as his B-29 crews had done in Japan twenty years earlier, because "psychologically this has a tremendous impact, when you tell somebody you're going to do something and then you do it. We're not interested in killing civilians."[34] Power even warned that ending Vietnam might require nuclear weapons, even if it meant antagonizing China. "There's no easy way to win a war, there's no cut-rate prices," Power warned.[35]

And if China developed nuclear weapons, Rogers asked? "Well," Power responded, "you've got a real situation on your hand [sic]. Now people worry about China coming in today. I say if China should decide to get into this action, if it escalates, we are in a better position to handle China today than we will ever be again. When they get nuclear weapons and the capability to deliver them this equation is going to change, and change radically."[36]

Finally, Baldwin, a 1924 graduate of the United States Naval Academy, asked, "How do you define a military victory in a nuclear war?" Power replied, "Very simply . . . You have sufficient strength to stop that military action, destroy him militarily and still retain a superior military posture. That's what I mean by a victory. In a true sense there wouldn't be any winner, it would be a hollow victory. But you can stop the military action and retain control. That's what I mean by a victory."[37]

Public reaction to the interview was mixed. A viewer from Power's hometown, Great Neck, New York, wrote to Power that he had "seldom been so shaken. . . . I can only offer you my profoundest pity that you are so utterly unaware of the evil demon that lurks within you."[38] A housewife and grandmother from Reno, Nevada, wrote, "I love you!"[39] Another woman wrote, "What a MAN!"[40] Another viewer advised Power to run for president.[41] Ira Eaker was impressed with Power's performance: "I thought you fielded the hard ones better than Joe DiMaggio ever did."[42] A former SAC B-36 pilot claimed, "Although you were outnumbered I was happy to observe that you had them badly outgunned."[43]

In a publicity event for *Design for Survival* on 22 March 1965, Power told a news conference in New York that SAC would not be deterred by poor weather and should be used to immediately destroy targets the communist government valued in North Vietnam. To limit civilian casualties, Power argued Vietnamese civilians should be warned ahead of time by leaflet to flee targeted areas. Further, Power urged the continuance of atmospheric nuclear tests, claiming opponents were warning "the health angle . . . to a point of hysteria" and that "this little bit of radiation . . . is certainly very minor in comparison" to the "hazard of being blown to bits by a Soviet missile."[44]

Two protesters had intended to disrupt the press conference, but Alice Widener, a conservative syndicated columnist, had spotted them in the crowd before the event. She passed a note to Power warning him just as he began to speak. No news story appears to have reported exactly what happened, but Widener congratulated Power on his reaction, saying, "You really put those two little subversive squirts in their place." Widener also complimented Power, "You did just grand at the press conference and it was so good to see you looking so fit and ready to GO!"[45]

Reviewer James D. Atkinson said in *Military Affairs* that with *Design for Survival*, Power "has written one of the most significant books in the field of national security affairs of this decade. Writing with all the authority of his distinguished career . . . [he] discusses in concise and cogent fashion the principle problems relating to our defense posture. . . . His book is *not* a war-inciting book; quite the contrary, it is a lucid and penetrating contribution to an understanding of how the United States can best act to create the conditions leading to a viable peace."[46]

Alternatively, Ronald Steel in the *New York Review of Books* called the book "part Air Force brochure, part lecture on why you can never trust a Communist, part critique of current defense policy—[Power] gives us carping laymen just a hint of what Secretary McNamara and his civilian helpers must be up against. . . . [Power] has chosen to treat us to his quaint views on foreign policy and explain how SAC can do everything—except wrong. In so doing he has convinced us of his patriotism and sincerity, but also made us once again agree with Clemenceau that war is, after all, too serious a matter to be left to generals."[47] Hanson Baldwin warned that "those who seek the sensational here will not find it in these pages; *Design for Survival* is the pragmatic philosophy of the realist."[48]

Design for Survival's impact was not limited to public debate in the United States. On 17 May 1965 Power received a handwritten letter from British field marshal Bernard Montgomery of World War II fame. Montgomery thanked Power for a copy of his book and asked Power if he could quote some material from *Design for Survival*—which was "quite first class"—for use in a book Montgomery was writing on "the study of the science of war and my practical experience of the art in battle."[49] Power readily agreed. In his 1967 book *A History of Warfare*, Montgomery wrote Power "is a friend of mine [and] a very great airman." In classic British understatement, Montgomery added, "I found his book helpful" and among the two most instructive of the books sent to him from various authors.[50]

Regardless of the polarity of its reviews, *Design for Survival* became a national bestseller. It debuted on the *New York Times* nonfiction bestseller list on 18 April 1965 at number ten. For five weeks it was in the top ten, reaching its highest point at number six the week of 9 May.[51]

President Lyndon Johnson, who had sometimes accompanied Power on hunting trips in Texas, ordered air strikes in Vietnam beginning in March 1965 under the codename Operation Rolling Thunder. On 7 May Power wrote to Johnson: "Your recent decisions to use air power effectively in Vietnam . . . were like a breath of fresh air. . . . Keep strong—do not let the bleeding hearts, the incredibly naïve or the fellow travelers or your critics overly concern you." Power ended by pleading, "Keep our nuclear strategic forces overwhelmingly strong and our limited war forces adequate."[52] Johnson thanked Power warmly for his support.[53] Power was a Republican but believed Johnson would do what needed to be done to keep America strong. However, just as time would indicate that Rolling Thunder was not an effective use of airpower, Power eventually became disillusioned with Johnson's leadership as well.

A significant "what might have been" is hinted at in a 7 May letter from Coward-McCann offering Power a $7,500 advance (almost $60,000 in 2018 dollars) to write a book on space that Power had pitched to them earlier. Three weeks later, Power wrote that he was "planning to start, very shortly, on a second book—a sequel to Design for Survival."[54] Unfortunately, Power apparently dropped the project. No manuscripts, outlines, or other mentions of this project appear to exist. Power might have decided to abandon the project when he heard about his friends Phyllis Schlafly's and Rear Adm. Chester Ward's book Strike from Space that was being published in November, which covered most of Power's beliefs about space.

Strike from Space might even be considered Power's abandoned space treatise. It lays out Power's aerospace power plan for strategic superiority that he advocated at SAC, offering a mix of B-70 bombers and Polaris ICBMs to be augmented by a "second generation" force of Orion spacecraft, embodying "the most advanced space nuclear propulsion system ever devised, with great military as well as scientific potential." These systems, Schlafly and Ward claimed, "will keep America safe from the terror of a strike from space."[55]

Power certainly had a large hand in the project. He penned an extended blurb for the book, praising Strike from Space's "very important message . . . that the road to world peace does not lie in the direction of disarmament, but rather in the posture of overwhelming strategic nuclear superiority."[56] Power even wrote a letter for Schlafly to enclose with her book to send to prominent businessmen around the United States.[57]

Perhaps due to his heavy workload, Power in mid-May 1965 suffered from a vitreous hemorrhage, a leaking of blood into the clear gel space between the lens and retina, in his left eye. He remained hospitalized for a week at March Air Force Base, near his home in Palm Springs. By 7 June his eye had cleared up, and he recovered most of his vision. Over the next few weeks he recovered fully, but his doctor warned Power to avoid any "unusual exertion" for ninety days.[58]

In early 1966 Robert McNamara began to accelerate the phase-out of many of SAC's B-52 and B-58 bombers and replace them with the new FB-111. Congressman F. Edward Hebert, of the House Armed Services Committee and chair of subcommittee number two, asked Power to provide testimony to the subcommittee, adding, "General, we need you badly!"[59] Because of his speaking tour, Power had to decline. George Todt quipped to Power, "In the name of adequate national security, I think we should phase out McNamara instead of the bombers!"[60]

Rolling Thunder quickly disappointed Power; the graduated response of the Johnson air plan was very different than what he had recommended on *Meet the Press* a year earlier. In January 1966 Power recommended that if the Viet Cong or North Vietnamese broke or otherwise balked at the proposed peace talks Johnson was currently engaged in, the United States should destroy the physical plant of North Vietnam, presaging the later aerial campaigns Linebacker I and II.[61]

Power also kept up with judo as best he could. In February he became the honorary chairman of the United States Olympic judo financing committee at the request of Philip Porter, who had worked with Power in promoting judo in the Air Force years earlier.[62]

Power became active in Republican politics after becoming disillusioned with Johnson's leadership in Vietnam. Power introduced California gubernatorial candidate Ronald Reagan at the Republican Women's Club of Indio on 19 May 1966.[63] Power presented Reagan with a copy of *Design for Survival*.[64] Power also began briefing Richard Nixon on defense issues, as he had enjoyed Power's *Design for Survival* as well.[65] Power began an extensive correspondence with Washington, D.C., lawyer Robert Ellsworth and former assistant secretary of defense Franklin B. Lincoln Jr., Nixon confidants who often passed Power's thoughts on defense to Nixon.[66] On 21 July 1967 Power joined an unofficial group to advise Nixon on defense matters.[67] Regarding escalation in Vietnam in October, Power wrote to the group that you "don't prevent [a nuclear war] by wishful thinking. The easiest thing in the world is to get into a war, a nuclear war, particularly a fat, soft, rich nation. It takes a lot of courage, a lot of hard work, a lot of brains and fortitude to stay out of one on honorable terms."[68]

In January 1967 Power was elected as chairman of both Eversharp Corporation and Schick. He was also a director of the Bucyrus-Eire Company, an underground mining equipment company.[69] Power convinced Schick to sponsor a $100,000 essay competition on how business could fight communism.[70] Power's speeches as chairman of Schick often drummed up a great deal of business, improving the company's bottom line.[71] Phyllis Schlafly's husband Fred also congratulated Power for his skills as chairman in shutting down Lewis Gilbert at a Schick stockholder meeting. Gilbert was notorious for buying a single share of a company and then "standing up for the small shareholder" by grandstanding at stockholders' meetings. Schlafly believed Power "handled the aggressive Mr. Gilbert more skillfully than any other chairman he has faced including his celebrated exchange with General [Douglas] MacArthur when the latter was board chairman of Remington Rand."[72]

Power also joined the American Security Council, a nonprofit corporation dedicated to "peace through strength," as part of their national strategy committee, later as an interviewee for their radio show *Washington Report* and eventually writing and performing in a new show called *Washington Report of the Air* starting on 15 July 1967. In the ten-minute weekly radio broadcast, Power often commented on familiar subjects such as Vietnam, nuclear superiority, space weaponization, and his time in the Air Force. In his first show, Power defended the need for a new heavy bomber, recalling his almost four decades of experience. "The B-29 raids against Japan caused their surrender and [are] credited with saving hundreds of thousands of American lives that would have been lost in a costly invasion," Power argued. "I never thought that after all this we [would] ever have to defend the requirements for a heavy bomber."[73] Power was not above sarcasm in his speaking. He opened one report with the comment, "Everyone today understands the horror of a nuclear war. Our pacifists, one-worlders, and communists have seen to that!"[74] After only a few weeks, *Washington Report of the Air* was renewed for another year, with Power as American Security Council's military affairs editor, and was broadcast on more than five hundred radio stations nationwide.[75]

Power became much more active with Nixon in October 1967, shortly after Nixon decided to run for president. On 4 October, Power sent Nixon a series of defense questions, as well as a recent speech, to prepare for debates.[76] Nixon wrote Power that "it is not parity but American superiority which has kept the peace for two decades, and it is essential that we maintain it."[77] On 22 November Nixon sent a letter to his unofficial defense think tank about the balance of power between the United States and the Soviet Union, defense manpower, Vietnam, and guerrilla warfare. Nixon sent Power's questions to many retired senior officers including Arleigh Burke, Victor Krulak, Matthew Ridgway, Bernard Schriever, Nathan Twining, and others.[78] Power kept an avid correspondence with Frank Lincoln through February, especially concerning Vietnam.[79] Power advised closing off the port of Haiphong immediately and removing any restrictions on targets in North Vietnam.[80] On 12 February 1968 Power advocated the mining and closing of Haiphong and attacking Hanoi directly with SAC B-52s, a plan very close to Nixon's original conception of Linebacker I in May 1972, before Henry Kissinger convinced Nixon to remove the B-52s due to political concerns over the Strategic Arms Limitation Treaty. Linebacker II in December 1972 centered on the use of SAC B-52s. Power's advice may have been the genesis of Nixon's Linebacker campaigns.

On 22 March 1968 Power sent a letter with some recommendations to Nixon regarding campaigning. Power advised Nixon not to explain how he would end the Vietnam War and recommended Ronald Reagan as his running mate. Power thought Nixon should switch the military to an all-volunteer force by eliminating the draft and raising military pay. Then, Power advised taking "a crack" at "[Charles] DeGaulle, Sweden, the nihilists in our colleges, the Negro black power communists, and the black power gangsters who want riots, destruction, and anarchy." Power concluded, "It seems to me that we, as a people, have to decide—do we want a nation that improves things peacefully and legally or do we want a nation where the violent minorities through terror and destruction force their will on the majority? . . . Vote for Nixon and law and order."[81] Although they shared some correspondence, Power never mentioned Curtis LeMay's decision to run as George Wallace's vice presidential candidate during the 1968 election. Power remained a Nixon supporter, but he did support his old boss in a *National Review* book review of LeMay's book *America Is in Danger*, calling it "a damning exposé of Secretary McNamara's obsession with cost effectiveness as a substitute for sound military doctrine."[82]

In late March 1968 President Johnson canceled the Rolling Thunder campaign and announced that he would seek peace talks with North Vietnam. Just before Johnson's announcement, NBC News taped an extensive interview with Power on airpower in Vietnam. On 5 April NBC notified Power that they would not air Power's interview, with correspondent Roy Neal writing to Power, "I'm truly sorry. . . . Everything about it was good except for the timing of international affairs!"[83] Power, along with a number of other retired Air Force generals, kept assisting Nixon. Nathan Twining and Pete Quesada informed Power that they thought they might have finally convinced President Eisenhower to endorse Nixon in the primaries, which Eisenhower did in mid-July.[84]

On 30 July 1968 Frank Lincoln asked Power to list the various items Nixon's "military advisory committee" should explore in devising Nixon's strategy for the military posture of the United States.[85] Power generated a series of questions and responses in conjunction with the current vice commander of SAC, Lt. Gen. Keith Compton (Power's SAC chief of staff who had also served with Power in the 15th and 2nd Air Forces in World War II), for submission to Nixon on 20 September 1968. The extended memorandum commented on twenty-one issues, including Vietnam, Russia, China, the "blunders" of the Johnson-Humphrey-McNamara team, and other standard political issues such as the budget. On Vietnam, the memorandum recommended the United States present an ultimatum to North Vietnam to de-escalate the conflict and, if they did not within thirty days, to resume immediately unrestricted bombing of North Vietnamese military targets "regardless of location." Additionally, the United States should blockade or mine the port of Haiphong and any other North Vietnamese waterways in order to "achieve a military victory in the shortest possible time."[86]

Regarding McNamara and the Whiz Kids, Power held nothing back: "Blunders of the team actually began with the assumption of office of President Kennedy and the influx into his administration of members of the intellectual and academic communities who had long abhorred the philosophy of overwhelming nuclear superiority vis-à-vis the USSR." Power continued that the "group maintained that such a national posture, while it had succeeded in past confrontations involving 'brinkmanship,' was in fact provocative in nature, would lead to a nuclear arms race, and would ultimately bring on the destruction of the entire civilized world. They, therefore, began a series of moves which, if continued indefinitely, would result in the unilateral disarmament of the free world, in particular, the U.S." Finally, Power charged that "our one-sided reduction of strategic nuclear offensive arms was actually interpreted by the Soviets as a sign of weakness, and a lessening of our national resolve has been amply demonstrated by events of the past few years."[87]

The memorandum offered further specific charges, including that McNamara's concept of assured destruction was dangerously speculative in nature, that its emphasis on a minimum deterrent might not "provide military forces for terminating [a nuclear] war short of all out exchange," and that threatening an all-out exchange was not credible for deterring low-intensity conflict. Next, McNamara's gradual escalation strategy in Vietnam "would be alright if applied promptly and with sufficient force to be significant—and before the enemy has time to prepare defenses or countermeasures," but McNamara's insistence on running the operation "piecemeal fashion" based on a false interpretation of "civilian control of the military" had invalidated its effectiveness. McNamara was also accused of ignoring the opportunities presented by the Bay of Pigs incident and the Cuban Missile Crisis to remove the communist foothold in Cuba, giving up the Jupiter missiles in Turkey, signing the Limited Test Ban Treaty "after a similar agreement had previously been abrogated by the USSR," and canceling the Skybolt nuclear standoff missile, thus killing "the one program that would have kept the [United Kingdom] in a viable strategic nuclear offensive role and, very likely, caused the conservative government to lose a general election which followed."[88] Further, McNamara's insistence that the F-111 be "all service" had created an aircraft that was unsuitable for any envisioned role, and his cancellation of the Dyna-Soar program, which "represented this nation's only effort for utilization of space by manned systems for other than strictly peaceful purposes," had made the United States dramatically weaker.[89] The memorandum stressed that Nixon should repudiate assured destruction in favor of developing a clear strategic superiority in terms of both quality and quantity that would assure the United States a war-winning strategic nuclear capability.[90]

The memorandum was quintessential Power, but it was also a statement from General Compton, vice commander of SAC. It may be significant that CINCSAC Gen. John Ryan was not involved in the document and could indicate that while Ryan—who had, unlike Power, authorized SAC bombers deployed to Vietnam—was interested in developing a new approach to SAC more in line with the McNamara defense department, there was still a significant "Old Guard" contingent in the service pushing for the Power vision.

Shortly after Nixon's victory in the election, Frank Lincoln wrote to Power thanking him for his dedication during the campaign and especially for his service on the military advisory committee, writing that "we more than welcome your continued advice and counsel over the next few months." Lincoln also complimented Power on a recent speech he gave supporting Nixon in the closing days of the campaign.[91]

Power's efforts on behalf of president-elect Nixon seemingly paid off, as suggested in a letter dated 2 December 1968 from C. Calvert Knudsen, a member of Nixon's transition team: "Your name has been suggested to the incoming Administration for appointment to high Federal office. . . . If you might under any circumstances be available to accept such an appointment and serve in the new Administration, either now or in the future, we would greatly appreciate your prompt completion and return of the enclosed form to this office." Given Power's leadership on the military advisory committee, it seems reasonable to assume that he might have been considered for secretary of defense or another defense position. On 11 December as a handwritten note on the letter records, Power responded, "No."[92] Power seems to have left no reason for refusing this offer.

In 1968 the American Security Council released *Design for Survival* in comic book form, an early example of a graphic novel, though Power described it as an "informational pamphlet" like those popular with GI education in World War II.[93] Power collaborated with cartoonist Emil "Zeke" Zekley of the newspaper strip *Bringing Up Father* to shrink Power's 255-page tome into a 38-page illustrated booklet, and secured a $32,000 advance from Eversharp to cover the production and distribution expenses.[94] All other proceeds from booklet sales were to cover shipping expenses and to send free copies of the book for wide distribution. Power received no money for the project and simply wanted the illustrated *Design for Survival* to reach as many people as possible. Power explained the purpose of the illustrated booklet was "to broaden public understanding of this vital subject" of deterrence. "Unfortunately," he continued, "not many people read books, but it is hoped that an easy-to-read pictorial format could reach a vast mass audience."[95] Power did not limit his distribution to the nonreading public. He also sent copies to William F. Buckley, Richard Nixon, Ronald Reagan (who, by 1 August 1968, Power called "Ronnie" in correspondence), and many others.[96] Phyllis Schlafly, Barry Goldwater, and Lt. Gen. Dale O. Smith (who ghost-wrote *America Is in Danger* with Curtis LeMay) all thought the booklet very useful and sent copies to as many people as they could. Governor Reagan thanked Power for the booklet, finding it "very readable and very informative. . . . You and I are certainly in agreement about the situation."[97] Even Power's one-time nemesis Arleigh Burke admitted, "I read General Power's illustrated pamphlet with great interest. . . . I would imagine it will have considerable influence."[98]

Power's significance in military debate had slowly waned in the years after his retirement, but he still carried enough weight in 1970 to write an editorial for the *New York Times* on 23 May 1970 titled "In Defense of the Pentagon." Power posed two questions, one familiar and one perhaps less so, to the American people: "First, do you think both the Soviet Union and Communist China have abandoned their stated goal of world domination and destruction of the capitalist system? Second, can you guarantee that they or some other 'ism' will not sometime in the future resume such a goal?" After asking these questions, Power then stressed that the primary mission of the U.S. military was "the prevention of war" through nuclear deterrence. He implored America to keep focused on what was important: "We must keep all potential aggressors convinced that if they resort to the use of nuclear weapons they will be defeated."[99] Only by keeping America strong could the nation defend the free world, whatever adversary may come.

All indications were that he would keep leading the charge, but Thomas Power's crusade came to an abrupt and tragic end when on 6 December 1970 he suffered a fatal heart attack while playing golf near his home. Even though he had a family history of heart trouble and his own heart had some issues, Power's end was sudden and unexpected. Mae Power buried her husband at Arlington National Cemetery with full military honors a few days later.

Air Force Magazine's obituary stated that Power was "known as a spit-and-polish commander in the traditional ramrod straight manner" and noted his roles in World War II, the development of missiles, and his efforts to strengthen SAC: "Before retirement in 1964, he was to see SAC become the most powerful military force in history."[100] And that was it. Gen. Thomas Power, who had risen from high school dropout to four-star general, who had served in many of the most iconic missions of U.S. airpower, who had flown everything from the earliest biplanes to the fastest supersonic bombers, and who ended his career as commander in chief of one of the most powerful military forces in human history, was gone.

Who was Thomas Sarsfield Power? He was cruel and sadistic to some, and an inspiration to others. He was the last non–college graduate general officer in the U.S. military, but his high-technology vision suggested a keen military mind. It would be easy to say he was a man of contradictions, but this is not the case. It is more accurate to say that Power was a man easy to caricature. As both the last true "bomber baron" CINCSAC and the most outspoken and well-spoken proponent of "keeping America strong" through overwhelming nuclear superiority, he was an incredibly valuable and vulnerable target of those who were uncomfortable with SAC's strength, who wanted to discredit "air-atomic age" strategic thinking, and who sought nuclear or general disarmament. Discredit Power, they reasoned, and you discredit SAC itself.

Power's most egregious vulnerability, especially to the emerging elite in the 1960s that championed academic credentialism over experience, is that he was the last U.S. general officer without a college degree. Stephen Budianski used this fact to claim that "there was certainly more than a little brash, I-don't-give-a-damn anti-intellectualism in the attitude of SAC commanders."[101] Fred Kaplan went further in *Wizards of Armageddon*, in which he described Power as "a brutal, easily angered man who struck Air Staff officers outside SAC as dim-witted and insensitive to the dilemmas that the bomb raised."[102] By using Power's lack of formal education to accuse him of being anti-intellectual and dim-witted, his detractors may ironically have given Power too much credit. There is little evidence that Power even graduated high school. However, this shortcoming was a consequence of his parent's divorce, not of his lack of aptitude or intelligence. Aside from his lack of credentials, Power emerged as a highly disciplined, bright, and forward-thinking officer. Power did have some college experience through the Cooper Union night school. Moreover, he passed the very difficult flying cadet entrance exam—meant to weed out anyone but college students—through only a scant few months of self-study at the New York Public Library. He graduated from the best aeronautical mechanics course in the United States, developed ideas for advanced weapons in air warfare, showed himself to be an innovative commander in World War II and an able administrator and senior air commander during the Cold War, and penned some of the most advanced military space thinking ever exhibited by an Air Force officer. These facts are virtually unknown.

The little that is known about Power is from books with an anti-SAC slant, all published by mainstream presses with large audiences.

By contrast, pro-SAC publications have been limited to publication by smaller, independent presses. Carroll Zimmerman, a civilian SAC operations analyst under both LeMay and Power, in his book *Insider at SAC*, remembered Power "always looked to the future, while making certain that present-day operations were under control—whether it was by listening to Dr. Percy Carr [Iowa State University Operations Analysis Standby Unit] explaining Einstein's Theory of Relativity and related space topics, or directing me to contact the top nuclear physics experts in the country in order to collect their thoughts and opinions related to new developments possible in nuclear weapons and devices." His detractors ignore these aspects of Power's career.

As a speaker, Zimmerman claimed that "not only was General Power a dynamic leader of military men and women, he was an articulate advocate of strong strategic forces. He could persuade audiences that his viewpoint was rational and correct—a real spellbinder."[103] Even such detractors as Lt. Gen. Lloyd "Dick" Leavitt learned from Power. He wrote that listening to Power's "inspirational talk heightened my interest in the writings of Herman Kahn, Albert Wohlstetter, and others. By 1961 I understood the political and military consequences of nuclear deterrence and believed that a well-equipped, highly trained SAC was the best hope for peace."[104] Accusations that Power was uneducated or dim-witted simply do not hold up to scrutiny.

The next avenue of attack against Power centers on supposed sadism. Here again is much to caricature. Kaplan leads the pack in *Wizards of Armageddon* by recounting some anecdotes about Power from the perspective of the civilian Whiz Kids of whom he was writing. Describing one meeting, Kaplan wrote, "Once, when Herman Kahn was briefing Power on the long-term genetic effects of nuclear weapons, Power suddenly chuckled, leaned forward in his chair and said, 'You know, it's not yet been proved to me that two heads aren't better than one.' Even Kahn [who was a model for Dr. Strangelove] was outraged, and sternly lectured Power that he should not discuss human life so cavalierly."[105] Power was known for having a very dry sense of humor about nuclear warfare, which he felt necessary to maintain morale in the tough nuclear business.

Kaplan had a slightly differently take on John Rubel's recollection of another Power comment. He recounts Power approaching McNamara after a meeting on 3 February 1961 and saying, in a clearly sarcastic deadpan, "Well, Mr. Secretary, I hope you don't have any friends or relations in Albania, because we're just going to have to wipe it out." Kaplan says McNamara "stopped in his tracks for a moment and glared at Power with all the contempt he could muster."[106] Kaplan believed it "appalling" that SIOP-62 targeted Albania because "it had dramatically dissociated itself from the policies of the USSR" even though the Soviets still operated the radar in question, showcasing Kaplan's moral grandstanding and military ignorance in equal measure.

Perhaps the most well-known example of Power's so-called evil was his reaction to a counterforce briefing he received from a RAND civilian in 1960. Counterforce was a strategy intended to remove Soviet cities from deliberate targeting, hopefully prompting the Soviets to refrain from targeting U.S. cities in like fashion. With luck, the civilian offered, such a counterforce war would only cause "a few million casualties on both sides, versus hundreds of millions dead if SAC executed its preferred 'maximum effort' attack plan." At this, Power burst into a rage. "Why do we want to restrain ourselves?" Power shouted back. "Restraint! Why are you so concerned with saving *their* lives? The whole *idea* is to kill the bastards! Look, at the end of the war, if there are two Americans and one Russian, we win!"[107]

It is easy to take these anecdotes at face value, and historian Richard Rhodes does exactly that. Rhodes describes Power as "at least as eager as LeMay to 'get World War III started.'" Rhodes quotes from an interview of a SAC officer who said Power was "a hard, cruel individual. . . . I used to worry that General Power was not stable. I used to worry about the fact that he had control of so many weapons and weapon systems and could, under certain conditions, launch the force. Back in the days before we had real positive control, SAC had the power to do a lot of things, and it was in his hands, and he knew it."[108]

The officer was Gen. Horace M. Wade, deputy commander of the Eighth Air Force under Power, whose opinions on Power must surely be respected. But Rhodes leaves out much of General Wade's thoughts on Power. When asked why Wade thought Power was hard and cruel, Wade replied, "I think he thought this was the way to make good leaders, was to make it tough for those people who are growing up and then they would be tough when they got in command positions."[109] When asked if he got along with Power, Wade said:

> I got along fine with him. . . . I have to attribute my success with Power to the fact that I never took an audience in with me when I got ready to brief him on something or tell him about something. I went by myself. I went by myself so he didn't have an audience to perform in front of. . . . We always found that if he had a room full of people he liked to perform. If you were just one on one, well, then he didn't try to work you over because nobody was there to witness what he was doing to you so he didn't receive the gratification of having performed in front of people.[110]

Power may have had a lot of bark, and he did indeed toy with briefers, but there is significantly less evidence that his "playing to an audience" carried much bite. Carroll Zimmerman was on the receiving end of Power's cruelty after Power had tried to talk him out of following LeMay to Washington, D.C., when he became Air Force chief of staff. Zimmerman politely informed Power that he would go with LeMay. "So when I went to General Power to tell him I had decided to go to Washington," Zimmerman recalled, "he royally lit into me. He racked me up one side and down the other. Remember, he was an expert. He always thought I had more sense than to go to Washington." The next day Zimmerman learned that immediately after their uncomfortable meeting, Power had Zimmerman written up for the "highest award the Air Force can give to a civilian" and awarded it to him personally before Zimmerman left Omaha.[111]

There is no doubt that Power had a tendency toward theatrics during briefings. If he liked to perform in front of an audience out of vanity, he performed as a cruel taskmaster to toughen up his men. Combine Power's self-perceived role as a hard and unyielding commander with his deeply held disgust with civilian intellectuals such as McNamara's Whiz Kids, who kept him from achieving his vision of an invulnerable space-borne SAC defending America, and there is a powerful explanation for Power's outrageous statements made to defense intellectuals. Instead of being an unstable and vicious individual wanting to start World War III, Power instead needled Herman Kahn and Robert McNamara with his dry and sarcastic wit because he wanted them to know he found them as contemptuous as they considered him. Power's quips about destroying Albania, wondering if two heads are better than one, and declaring victory if two American lives are left to one Soviet after World War III are not the ravings of a madman but rhetorical jabs at his enemies, informing them and the audience that Power found their intellectual posturing ridiculous. His behavior was vain and slightly unprofessional, perhaps, but was not the action of an insane sadist.

Shortly after Power's death, Lt. Gen. Hewett Wheless defended his reputation during an oral history interview. The interviewer opined, "I know some people had some rather scary moments with [Power]. I remember a RAND team came in one time and only got about 2 minutes from him before he blew up and literally threw them out because he felt that they were off base on some particular item he felt he was the expert on. Strategic bombing and planes, plans and so forth. He felt he and his people were the world's expert on." Wheless interjected, "I think you do a little disservice when you said that. He was willing to listen to anyone and of course I knew him well. . . . I knew when to argue with him and when not to because there were times you could talk to Power and times when you couldn't." No matter what the subject, Wheless explained, "After a few days you could work back to a subject and he was never closed minded. If you could convince him to change his mind, he'd change it. But he had to be convinced."[112] Sometimes, Wheless admitted,

> he was a little bit hard-headed, but so many times—and this incident you put there is typical of Power—you see, because RAND . . . would come back to us and superficially, you see, hell we lived with this kind of stuff, he had seen the details, and come in and make some

superficial statement with no proof at all—an opinion—and this irritated Power more than anything. He spent his life in it [nuclear operations]. We'd studied it in detail. We chewed the pieces of it all the way. And unless you lived through it, like you'd make a remark, "Why don't you radio them in the air and try to change coordinates?" If you ever put a force in the air and try to change it at that time you were dead! The only thing that would happen is that you'd ensure that you'd screw it up. There was no way you could do that. We had a philosophy on our wing in Guam and we kept it all the way through SAC. Once a crew left the briefing room you NEVER changed the instructions. Call the whole mission off, anything you want, but you never try to change individual instructions. There is no way to do it and ensure that it'll be right.[113]

The interviewer then asked if there was a war between the civilian theorists and the SAC practitioners, commenting, "You know, the government spawned a number of these think outfits, think tanks, and it seemed to me at least that they never really got a welcome out at SAC. They'd be tolerated, certainly listened to, but were never given a lot of support." Wheless again countered, "Well, that was their own fault I think because say we'd listen to anybody out there that had an idea. . . . We were always inclined to listen to people that may have a new idea we hadn't thought of. There weren't many we hadn't thought of, though, because we [had] thoroughly gone over this time after time hours at each point, our training program, our operational program, our war plan."[114]

The interviewer, not getting what he'd hoped from him, asked Wheless to recount the story of the visit of President's Eisenhower's scientific advisers (led by George Kistiakowsky). Wheless replied:

Well, I took him out there and I called Power up, as you say they weren't always welcome, in this kind of voice. I said I'd like to bring [Kistiakowsky] out. He was at the SAC briefing so far and we'd take him to the war plan briefing and all this and we were sitting in the discussion period and Power was giving his philosophy of operations and somebody in the group stood up and said, "General Power, what makes you think you're an expert on this and that you know more than anyone else and that you are doing all the talking?" General Power stopped and said, "Let me tell you something. I didn't ask you to come out here. General Wheless asked me to give you this briefing. I assumed you came out here to listen to my story, my choice. It's evident you don't want to listen so to hell with it. The airplane's waiting. Feel free to walk out." Now this was an insult, really. Well, the guy sat back down and his neck got red, I was sitting right next to him. But it was a stupid remark [for the civilian] to make. That's why we went there, to listen to him [Power]. Now you can agree or disagree with him but you don't have to insult him. Now this is one of the reasons that this appearance that you talk about came out because this happened time and time again.[115]

This incident probably occurred when Kistiakowsky was sent to Omaha in 1960 to observe the SIOP being developed, and it was likely during this visit that Power questioned Kistiakowsky's patriotism.[116]

The "SAC side" of meetings between the civilian theorists and Power provides a necessary corrective to the one-sided histories written from the Whiz Kids' perspective. Wheless' testimony plays far less into most historians' biases. Other sympathetic opinions of Power's style exist from those men who worked with him closest.

Zimmerman would have agreed with Wheless that Power was not closed minded: "Overseas he always took the same four and five members of the staff. We conducted 'think' sessions, discussing issues and problems that we probably would not have taken the time to discuss at SAC HQ. We visited overseas SAC installations, and at night we would have no-holds-barred discussions. General Power was only another participant. He insisted that we not be influenced, or remain quiet, because of his position."[117] Zimmerman also commented on Power's humanity: "General Power had a reputation for being tough on his staff. Any wrath he imposed on them was usually well merited. He had a warm compassion for his troops."[118] That compassion is exemplified by his work on the Cardinal Spellman school in Omaha, the private Catholic school largely built from Thomas and Mae Power's efforts to provide religious schooling to the Catholic members of SAC.

Popular histories are not the only culprits behind the Power caricature. Eric Schlosser notes that the mental instability of SAC officers became a recurrent theme in Soviet propaganda from the late 1950s until the end of the Cold War. "According to a Pentagon report obtained by an East German newspaper and discussed at length on Radio Moscow," Schlosser reported, "67.3 percent of the flight personnel in the United States Air Force were psychoneurotic. The report was a communist forgery. But its bureaucratic tone, its account of widespread alcoholism, sexual perversion, opium addiction, and marijuana use at SAC, seemed convincing to many Europeans worried about American nuclear strategy."[119] Apparent evidence of Soviet claims occurred on 13 June 1958 when an Air Force mechanic stole a B-45 bomber from Alconberry Air Base, England, and took it for a joyride for a few minutes until crashing the jet and killing himself. The incident fed the population's worry that one rogue SAC officer could really be all that was necessary to start World War III.

Shortly after this Soviet propaganda was released, popular fiction using similar scenarios began to appear. Former Royal Air Force officer Peter George wrote the novel *Red Alert* in 1958 during the debate over Power's airborne alert. More than 250,000 copies of *Red Alert* were sold in the United States, and with that publication "the Strategic Air Command would increasingly be portrayed as a refuge for lunatics and warmongers, not as the kind of place you would find Jimmy Stewart."[120]

Tellingly, *Red Alert* influenced many civilian nuclear thinkers. Thomas Schelling bought forty copies and sent them to colleagues because the "book gave a good sense of what could go wrong."[121] SAC professionals like Power considered *Red Alert* and its filmed version, *Fail Safe*, as ridiculous dreck. Unfortunately, Stanley Kubrick's *Dr. Strangelove, or How I Stopped Worrying and Learned to Love the Bomb*, devastated Power's reputation with the character of Brig. Gen. Jack D. Ripper. The fictional Ripper, who single-handedly starts World War III, superficially shared many of the same traits as Power—foremost an intense hatred of communism. When the Whiz Kids penned their memoirs and historians wrote their books, many felt the best way to interpret Power was by invoking the memory of the General Ripper character.

Some also accused Power of being an arrogant and aristocratic commander. Although Thomas Power was quite different from his sisters, he almost assuredly got his aristocratic bent from them. While they were flippant and outgoing children who were sent to boarding school to curtail their flamboyancy, Tommy was a studious and meek child. When his sisters married early to cope with their father's abandonment of the family, Tommy instead abandoned his hopes for college to go to work in construction to support his destitute mother. While both sisters were divorcées and had multiple marriages, Thomas was devoted to his wife Mae for life. Where both sisters were known for their joie de vivre, many remember Thomas as being single-mindedly dedicated to mission. It seems that no brother could be more different from a family member than Thomas from his sisters.

Nonetheless, he learned a great deal from them, especially Dorothy. Power's growth as an officer from a working-class son of Irish immigrants into an aristocratic officer comfortable in high society came from the influence of his sister Dorothy. As a young lieutenant just beginning his flying career, Tommy often flew with his wealthy brother-in-law Harry Hall, who enjoyed stunt flying as much as Thomas did. Perhaps through Dorothy and her husband's contacts in Virginia society, young but relatively poor Thomas met and successfully courted Mae Ayre, a refined and elegant young British lady. When his sister entered English royalty, perhaps Power started to believe that he—a critical officer in the defense of the free world—also deserved some of the trappings of aristocracy.

From its beginning at least through the early part of World War II, Power had a professional but unremarkable career with no particularly noteworthy prospects. It was only by impressing General Yount as a staff officer that Power was given a combat assignment in 1944. Even with Power's command of the 314th Bombardment Wing on Guam for the last few months of the war, he seemed like just another young brigadier general, of which there were many by the war's end. Even though Power's efficiency reports had been steadily improving through the war, it was only by impressing Curtis LeMay on Guam, including by designing and leading the firebombing of Tokyo, that Power came to the forefront of the Air Force. In this way, just like LeMay, Power made his career with pluck and combat performance.

But Power was not LeMay. Lt. Gen. Francis Griswold, who served as Power's vice commander in chief of SAC from 1957 to 1961, differentiated LeMay and Power: "General LeMay's appeal was personal and General Power's appeal was to duty. For General LeMay you wanted to do it. For General Power you felt you should do it."[122] Perhaps some misinterpreted Power's style in appealing to duty as evil. However, Power demanded perfection from his men because they held the power of life and death, of civilization and the human race, in their hands. He may have had a taste for ridicule when he did not like someone, but Gen. Jack D. Ripper of *Dr. Strangelove* was a caricature of Power, not the man himself.

Simple ignorance is probably the reason that Power's reputation as a caricature has been unchallenged for so long. However, it may also have some element of willful ignorance, because the caricature in some ways aided the modern Air Force and the ascendance of the "fighter mafia." Discrediting Power also discredited SAC and the bomber barons. Vietnam-era tactical reconnaissance pilot Marshall Michel wrote in his 2002 book *The Eleven Days of Christmas* that by the mid-1960s, LeMay's "nuclear-only force, and his absolutist approach seemed hopelessly out of date." Additionally, "McNamara and his highly educated Defense Department staff, known to the military as 'Whiz Kids,' began to ask the senior Air Force leadership for detailed rationales for their decisions. LeMay's unwavering answer was 'this is our judgment, based on our lifetime of expertise and our combat experience,' a response that did not impress McNamara or Kennedy. . . . What the new administration wanted was flexible conventional forces to do battle with the charismatic revolutionaries of the Third World on their own terms." Although focusing on LeMay, Michel supported his derisive summary of the "SAC way" by dutifully reporting that "LeMay's successor at SAC, General Powers [*sic*], was only a high school graduate."[123]

Venerating the educated Whiz Kids and dismissing the "out of date" bomber barons strongly legitimizes the fighter pilot "pragmatist" take-over of the Air Force after Vietnam. Only the fighter pilots could provide the flexible conventional forces necessary to fight Third World revolutionaries, those "limited wars" that Power so detested as a focus of U.S. national security. The Power caricature was a great justification for the fighter pilots to assume Air Force leadership after Vietnam.

But the fighter pilots benefitted so much more from the Whiz Kids than just discrediting the bomber barons. By abandoning Power's war-winning nuclear capability and embracing mutually assured destruction, the fighter pilot–dominated Air Force could ignore its nuclear forces after Vietnam and spend its budget on tactical airpower. The Air Force then began to focus on realistic training at Red Flag and fighter weapons school and on operational-level doctrine such as AirLand Battle, virtually ignoring SAC. Once the Cold War was over, the fighter pilots merged SAC and Tactical Air Command into Air Combat Command—keeping the trappings of TAC and removing SAC symbols altogether.

The new fighter pilot–dominated Air Force fit the foreign policy adventurism post–Cold War politicians demanded. Instead of attempting to limit U.S. involvement in small wars as Power recommended, the military has seen an endless barrage of such wars. The Air Force, when engaged in independent operations, has been focused on coercion, or attempting to persuade "an opponent to stop an ongoing action or to start a new course of action by changing its calculations of costs and benefits," rather than deterrence.[124] The Air Force might retort that SAC's "big stick" would have been as useless in the limited wars and coercive diplomacy of Bosnia, Kosovo, Somalia, Iran, and Afghanistan, which have occupied the U.S. military since the 1990s, as its nuclear weapons were in Vietnam. However, as historian Carl Builder noted, "SAC wasn't conceived to defeat an enemy air force; it was designed to fulfill the Nation's highest security objective directly—to deter a nuclear attack by the visible threat of unacceptable damage through a well-coordinated retaliatory strike. . . . [it] might seem simplistic today . . . [but it] arose from strategic thinking."[125] To many critics, especially from the realist school of international relations, U.S. foreign policy since the end of the Cold War has exhibited very little strategic thinking.

Foreign policy adventurism had run amok, aided by an operationally minded Air Force that has continued to "fly and fight" in all of those adventures but has been hard-pressed to "win." By attempting to keep the status quo by coercion of developing countries for small stakes—and suffering the loss of thousands of troops and trillions of dollars doing so—instead of seeking to deter potential peer competitors from challenging U.S. might through conservation of that might, the United States has squandered its "unipolar moment." It must now contend with new peer states seeking to challenge its waning dominance. Power warned us that would happen if we indulged in strategically irrelevant limited wars. SAC, as a powerful tool of deterrence, was almost entirely useless as a coercive tool for limited wars. A significant portion of SAC's strategic strength may have never been truly identified or understood: it was incapable of fighting in any war other than for the highest stakes possible, and therefore it deterred not only an external enemy, but also internal foreign policy adventurism by denying politicians the tools of military coercion. Peace was SAC's profession. Peace is anathema to today's fighter pilot–dominated Air Force. America has been weakened by forgetting that peace is the true military profession.

Perhaps a revived Strategic Aerospace Command, such as Power envisioned, could provide key services to the competitiveness of the United States in great power competition. A new focus on deterrence of peer adversaries rather than coercion could keep the United States away from the destructive limited wars that have plagued it for decades. For the new, emerging nuclear powers of the second nuclear age such as North Korea and Iran, Power's concept of deterrence through overwhelming war-winning nuclear superiority could be revived and incorporated into U.S. strategy, as some nuclear theorists have advised.[126] Additionally, the new Space Force could take inspiration from Power and move boldly into space with a military force dedicated to deterrence rather than coercion. The Space Force, with "peace as their profession," could deter aggression—in space or anywhere else. The force could also assist in developing the technology and logistical infrastructure necessary for U.S. industry to develop space to its full potential, thus increasing national economic power to assist in great power competition and keep America strong. Power suggested exactly this course over a half-century ago.

All of Power's strategic writings, speeches, and beliefs are as relevant now as they were in the Cold War. Perhaps none are as relevant as one of the final thoughts in *Design for Survival* on the nature of deterrence:

> While it takes military superiority to *win* wars, it takes far more to *prevent* wars. Military strength for war becomes political strength for peace only when it is supported by the sum total of every deterrent inherent in a strong and united nation. Deterrence is a sound economy and prosperous industry. Deterrence is scientific progress and good schools. Deterrence is effective civil defense and the maintenance of law and order. Deterrence is the practice of religion and respect for the rights and convictions of others. Deterrence is a high standard of morals and a wholesome family life. Deterrence is honesty in public office and freedom of the press. Deterrence is all these things and many more, for only a nation that is healthy and strong in every respect has the power and will to deter the forces from within and without that threaten its survival.[127]

A 1965 *Reader's Digest* article described the Powers' home: "In the house on Pecos Road [Power] has a study and there, surrounded by his scrapbooks, pictures, and mementos of a top brass military career, he can continue his writings. There's a framed copy of his favorite poem, Kipling's 'If,' on the wall."[128] In this poem, we can see what Thomas Power thought he had to be. Almost every stanza is directly relevant to Power's Air Force career. Like Kipling's young subject, Power needed to keep his head about him through the storms of the Air Corps mail operations. He had to keep from hating when others hated and doubted him over SAC's mission. He had to ensure his alert crews were never tired by waiting. He heard the truth of deterrence through strength he had spoken be twisted by knaves. He dreamed of empires in space but never made the dreams his master. He focused on ensuring that, in the unforgiving minute, SAC would, with sixty seconds' worth of distance, run to defeat the Soviet Union if America had to risk everything on one turn of pitch and toss.

Thomas Power intended to be tough, to be the man Kipling yearned youth would be. He also expected SAC to exemplify such men. And that required the utmost of morality, because outsiders could perceive the actions required to toughen such men as anything but moral. Power wrote of the men of SAC, "history tells us that battle-seasoned troops win victories because they have been tested under fire. We shall not have the opportunity to test our crews under fire and must, therefore, continually and persistently seek out any weakness in the individual which may cause suspect of failure to carry out his duties under fire."[129]

When confronted with a public increasingly accusing Strategic Air Command of being the very demon it was designed to contain, Power offered only the short but direct reply, "We've been handling these weapons a long time and we haven't killed a soul. . . . I think our actions have shown the world that these weapons are in mature, moral hands."[130]

One day, while teeing off on the first hole at St. Andrew's in Scotland, the general reminisced to no one in particular, "If I had my life to live over, I can't think of much I would change."[131] Thomas Sarsfield Power had succeeded in becoming the man he felt was necessary.

NOTES

———•••———

Chapter 1. Introduction

1. This scene is a dramatization of the briefing described by an unknown member of the audience at Power's speech who wrote a summary memorandum entitled "Presentation by General Thomas S. Power, CINCSAC, on SAC's Strategic Role," 28 April 1963. Author unknown, U.S. Strategic Command History Office.
2. Norman Polmar, ed., *Strategic Air Command: People, Aircraft, and Missiles* (Annapolis, MD: Nautical and Aviation Publishing Company of America, 1979), 85.
3. "Power on SAC's Strategic Role."
4. For a representative popular account of Power, see Richard Rhodes, "The General and World War III," *New Yorker*, 19 June 1995, 56.
5. Stephen Budianski, *Air Power: The Men, Machines, and Ideas that Revolutionized War, from Kitty Hawk to Iraq* (New York: Penguin Books, 2004), 366.
6. Thomas M. Coffey, *Iron Eagle: The Turbulent Life of Curtis LeMay* (New York: Crown Publishers, 1986), 276.
7. Edward Kaplan, *To Kill Nations: American Strategy in the Air-Atomic Age and the Rise of Mutually Assured Destruction* (Ithaca, NY: Cornell University Press, 2015), 2.
8. Dale Hayden, "The Search for Space Doctrine's War-Fighting Icon," *Air and Space Power Journal*, November–December 2014, 61.
9. Richard Rhodes, *Dark Sun: The Making of the Hydrogen Bomb* (New York: Simon & Schuster, 1995), 571.

Chapter 2. From Flying Cadet to Aerospace Commander

1. Catholic Parish Registers, The National Library of Ireland, Dublin, Ireland, Microfilm No. 02454/08.

2. "Petition for Naturalization, Thomas Stack Power," 3 September 1918, U.S. District Court of New York, Southern District, vol. 104, record no. 25665.

3. Interview with Joel Dobson, 3 June 2017.

4. Dobson interview.

5. Gene Coughlin, "Atlantic Romances of Dorothy Power," *Cincinnati Enquirer*, 10 December 1950.

6. "So the American Girl Won the British Hero's Son," *San Bernardino County Sun*, 15 August 1937.

7. "So the American Girl Won."

8. "So the American Girl Won."

9. "So the American Girl Won."

10. Telephone conversation, Joel Dobson and Mark Nusembaum, New York County Clerk's office, 27 September 2016. Notes presented by Mr. Dobson to author.

11. "Thomas S. Power, Biography of Commanding Officer," in *Narrative History of 314th Bombardment Wing August 1944*, AFHRA reel C0149, pdf 543–44. See also John G. Hubbell, "Tough Tommy Power—Our Deterrent-in-Chief," *Reader's Digest*, May 1964, 72. In *Command and Control* (New York: Penguin Press, 2013), 179, Eric Schlosser writes that Power had dropped out of high school in the early 1920s and returned to graduate after working construction. Power historian Joel Dobson noted that in numerous military documents, Power implied that he graduated from high school, but he stated he had no diploma in his Atomic Energy Commission paperwork, where the penalty for giving false information was probably much more severe. The Horace Mann School (the descendant of Barnard Prep) no longer maintains records from the time of Power's attendance and could not confirm whether Power graduated. Power Papers, reel 34157, frame 1616.

12. "Biography–Thomas S. Power," Power Papers, reel 34157, frame 1578.

13. Kenneth Leish, interview, "Reminiscences of General Thomas S. Power," July 1960, AFHRA, call no. K146.34.

14. "Four-Star General," unpublished article, Power Papers, reel 34157, frame 1456.

15. Hubbell, 72.

16. Leish, 2.

17. "Four-Star General."

18. Bruce Ashcroft, *We Wanted Wings: A History of the Aviation Cadet Program* (Randolph AFB, TX: Headquarters Air Education and Training Command, 2005), 21.

19. Hubbell, 72.

20. J. E. Chaney, "The Selection and Training of Military Airplane Pilots," *U.S. Air Services*, March 1928, 18.

21. Chaney, 20.

22. Chaney, 18–19.

23. Leish, 3.

24. *Air Corps Newsletter*, 29 October 1928, 395.

25. Chaney, 19.

26. Leish, 3.

27. Report of Physical Examination, Thomas S. Power, 10 January 1930.

28. Howard E. Hall, *Air Corps Newsletter*, 26 April 1929, 160.

29. Hall, 160.

30. Leish, 4.

31. Leish, 4.

32. *Brooklyn Daily Eagle*, 12 May 1927.

33. Thomas S. Power, "Two More Members of the Caterpillar Club," *Air Corps Newsletter*, 17 October 1929, 353.

34. "Service Record of Thomas S. Power, 20 Sept. 1944," Power Papers, reel 34157, frame 1580.

35. Leish, 5.

36. "Personnel Report—Officer Air Corps, Thomas Power," April 1929; "Personnel Report, August 1929," AFHRA, call no. 167.4115–8.

37. "Thomas Sarsfield Power," Power Papers, reel 34157, frame 1572; Hubbell, 73.

38. Leish, 5.

39. "Second Bombardment Group Has Busy Month," *Air Corps Newsletter*, 17 October 1929, 353.

40. "AAF Officers Qualification Record—Thomas S. Power," Power Papers, reel 34157, frame 1581.

41. *Air Corps Newsletter*, 21 December 1929, 448.

42. *Air Corps Newsletter*, 10 April 1931, 145–46.

43. *Air Corps Newsletter*, 30 June 1931, 236.

44. W. F. Craven and J. L. Cate, eds., *The Army Air Forces in World War II*, vol. 6, *Men and Planes* (Washington, DC: Air Force History Office, 1946), 461.

45. "Gee Bee Junior Sportsters," http://goldenageofaviation.org/geebeec
.html.

46. Chanute Field, "Activity Report for the Month of October, 1931,"
10 November 1931, 2, AFHRA, reel B2113, pdf 1181.

47. "Officer Efficiency Report, Thomas S. Power, 30 September 1931–30 June
1932."

48. *Air Corps Newsletter,* 19 July 1932, 286.

49. Roland Birinn, "The 1932 Aerial Machine Gun and Bombing Matches,"
U.S. Air Services, November 1932, 10.

50. "Physical Examination for Flying, Thomas S. Power," 18 July 1932.

51. "Thomas S. Power Personnel Report, June and July 1933," Power Papers,
reel 34157, frame 1568.

52. Ralph L. Hoyt Jr., "Civilian Conservation Corps," http://www.rindgehis
toricalsociety.org/?page_id=276.

53. Maj. B. Q. Jones, "Report of the Eastern Zone, Army Air Corps Mail
Operations February 10, 1934 to May 25, 1934," Headquarters Eastern
Zone Army Air Corps Mail Operations, Mitchell Field, Hempstead, NY,
1934, 6.

54. Jones, 9.

55. "The Four-Star General."

56. George Bradham, "Army Fliers Good Mail Carriers," *Greensboro Daily
News,* 28 April 1934.

57. John L. Frisbee, "AACMO—Fiasco or Victory?" *Air Force Magazine,*
March 1995, 79.

58. "Personnel Report, Air Corps, Thomas Power," February 1929–
September 1933, AFHRA, call no. 167.4115–8.

59. Leish, 5.

60. Leish, 5–6.

61. Leish, 6.

62. Leish, 6–7.

63. Jones, appendix C (IV), 1–3.

64. "Thomas Sarsfield Power."

65. Rebecca Hancock Cameron, *Training to Fly: Military Flight Training,
1907–1945* (Washington, DC: Air Force Museums and History Program,
1999), 266–67.

66. "Thomas Sarsfield Power."

67. *Air Corps Newsletter,* 15 August 1935, 18.

68. "Annex III: Basis of Air Corps Requirements," n.d., 22, AFHRA, reel
A1378, pdf 1922.

69. "Gen Thomas Power Dies at 65," *New York Times*, 8 December 1970.
70. Leish, 7.
71. Robert B. Gagney, "Boating in the Philippines," *Air Corps Newsletter*, 15 August 1935, 8.
72. *Air Corps Newsletter*, 15 September 1937, 4.
73. Letter, P. P. Bishop to T. S. Power, 10 March 1937, Power Papers, reel 34157, frame 1672.
74. *Air Corps Newsletter*, 15 September 1937, 4.
75. Letter, Power to Chief of the Air Corps, 8 February 1937, Power Papers, reel 34157, frame 1620.
76. Letter, Dixon to Power, Power Papers, reel 34157, frame 1622–23.
77. Leish, 8.
78. "Officer Efficiency Report, Thomas S. Power, 13 February 1936–30 June 1936."
79. "Officer Efficiency Report, Thomas S. Power, 6 November 1936–28 February 1937."
80. "Officer Efficiency Report, Thomas S. Power, 1 March 1937–30 June 1937."
81. Alfred Emile Cornebise, *The United States 15th Infantry Regiment in China, 1912–1938* (Jefferson, NC: McFarland and Company Press, 2004), 215–16.
82. Leish, 8.
83. Leish, 8–9.
84. Power biography fragment, n.d., Power Papers, reel 34157, frame 1564; *Air Corps Newsletter*, 15 April 1940.
85. Robert T. Finney, *History of the Air Corps Tactical School 1920–1940* (Washington, DC: Air Force History and Museums Program, 1998), 79.
86. Finney.
87. Finney, 80–81.
88. "Officer Efficiency Report, Thomas S. Power, 3 April 1940–29 June 1940."
89. Graduation photos, AFHRA, reel A2732 pdf 513.
90. Mike Worden, *Rise of the Fighter Generals* (Maxwell AFB, AL: Air University Press, 1998), 142.
91. Letter from Gillham to Brant, 1 April 1941, Power Papers, reel 34157, frame 1670.
92. "Officer Efficiency Report, Thomas S. Power, 1 July 1937–20 February 1938."
93. *Air Corps Newsletter*, 15 April 1941, 16.
94. Leish, 9.

95. Signal Corps message to commander, Moffett Field, 20 January 1942, 532pm, Thomas S. Power Official Military Record.

96. "Thomas Sarsfield Power."

97. "Officer Efficiency Report, Thomas S. Power, 1 July 1942 to 31 December 1942."

98. "Officer Efficiency Report, Thomas S. Power, 1 January 1943 to 30 June 1943."

99. Leish, 9.

100. "Aircrew Data—Thomas S. Power," Power Papers, reel 34157, frame 158.

101. Office of Information Services, "Highlights of the Second Air Force," n.d., AFHRA, reel A4093, pdf 887.

102. "Officer Efficiency Report, Thomas S. Power, 1 July 1943 to 31 December 1943."

103. "Aircrew Data," Power Papers, reel 34157, frame 1582.

104. "War Diary 304th Bombardment Wing (Heavy) 1 March 1944–31 March 1944," 20 April 1944, 2, AFHRA, reel C0110, pdf 1269.

105. Leish, 9.

106. Leish, 10.

107. Leish.

108. "Aircrew Data."

109. Robert S. Ehlers Jr., *The Mediterranean Air War* (Lawrence: University Press of Kansas, 2015), 384–85.

110. "304th Headquarters History Narrative," AFHRA, reel C0110, pdf 1341, 1376.

111. Ehlers, 401.

112. "Officer Efficiency Report, Thomas S. Power, 1 January 1944 to 30 June 1944."

113. Memo, 25 April 1944, AFHRA, reel C0110, pdf 1261, 1295.

114. "Historical Records," Headquarters 304th Bomb Wing, 1 April–30 April 1944, 5–6, AFHRA, reel C0110, pdf 1297–98.

115. Biography fragments, Power Papers, reel 34157, frame 1561.

116. 314th Bombardment Wing, "Staff Meeting Minutes," 1 September 1944, 1–2, AFHRA, reel C0149, pdf 896–97.

117. 314th Bombardment Wing, "Narrative History for August 1944," 5, AFHRA, reel C0149, pdf 508.

118. 314th Bombardment Wing, "Staff Meeting Minutes," 4 September 1944, 1, AFHRA, reel C0149, pdf 912.

119. Curtis E. LeMay and MacKinlay Kantor, *Mission with LeMay: My Story* (Garden City, NY: Doubleday, 1965), 340.

120. "Aircrew Data."
121. "Narrative History of Headquarters," 314th Bombardment Wing, 1 December 1944–28 February 1945, AFHRA, call no. WG-314-HI Dec 44–Feb 45, vol. 1, 1.
122. Leish, 12.
123. Leish, 12–13.
124. Leish.
125. Leish.
126. Leish, 13, emphasis added.
127. Gene Gurney, *Journey of the Giants* (New York: Coward-McCann, 1961), 209.
128. Leish, 13–14, emphasis added.
129. Gurney, 208–9.
130. Leish, 13–14.
131. Coffey, 158–59.
132. Richard B. Frank, *Downfall: The End of the Imperial Japanese Empire* (New York: Random House, 2001), 63.
133. Warren Kozac, *LeMay* (Washington, DC: Regnery Publishing, 2009), 213, 217.
134. LeMay, 10.
135. Ralph H. Nutter, *With the Possum and the Eagle: The Memoirs of a Navigator's War over Germany and Japan* (Denton: University of North Texas Press, 2002), 239–40.
136. Nutter, 240.
137. Nutter.
138. Nutter, 240–1.
139. Nutter.
140. Nutter, 242.
141. LeMay, 10.
142. LeMay, 565.
143. Edwin P. Hoyt, *Inferno: The Firebombing of Japan March 9th–August 15th, 1945* (New York: Madison Books, 2000), 37.
144. 314th Bombardment Wing, "Consolidated Mission Report: Meeting-house 2, 9–10 March 1945," 18 March 1945, AFHRA, reel C0150, pdf 565.
145. Leish, 14–16.
146. Hoyt, 37.
147. Barrett Tillman, *Whirlwind: The Air War Against Japan 1942–1945* (New York: Simon and Schuster, 2011), 152.
148. Leish, 16.

149. Leish, 14–16.
150. Leish.
151. LeMay, 10.
152. Hoyt, 37.
153. "XXII Bomber Command Tactical Mission Report, Mission 40 Flown 10 March 1945," 5–6, AFHRA, call no. 702.35. Years later in the Leish interview, Power claimed he lost a full quarter of his wing. Leish, 17.
154. Tillman, 152–53.
155. Hoyt, 37–38.
156. Headquarters, XXI Bomber Command, "General Orders No. 41," 14 March 1945, AFHRA, reel C0150, pdf 556.
157. Headquarters, 314th Bombardment Wing, "Unit History for March 1945," 22–29, AFHRA, reel C0150, pdf 258–67.
158. "Commendation," 29 March 1945, AFHRA, reel C0150, pdf 252.
159. "Commendation," 20 March 1945, AFHRA, reel C0150, pdf 763.
160. Letter, Thomas Stack Power to Power, 9 March 1945, Power Papers, reel 34154, frame 485.
161. Telex, "Personal to LeMay for Power from Norstad," message no. G-14-22, Letters of General Thomas S. Power, AFHRA, reel 34154, frame 505.
162. Coffey, 276; "Form for a Special Rating of General Officers, Thomas S. Power," by Curtis E. LeMay, 20 April 1945.
163. "Commendation—Power," Power Papers, reel 34157, frame 1646.
164. Thomas Power, introduction in Gurney, 12.
165. Leish, 18.
166. AFHRA, reel A7112 pdf 887.
167. AFHRA, reel A7112, pdf 1437.
168. Leish, 19.
169. Leish, 19–20.
170. Leish, 17.
171. Memorandum for Thomas S. Power, Temporary Duty Travel, 27 May 1948.
172. Biography, 9 March 1948, Power Papers, reel 34154, frame 677.
173. Biography, 9 March 1948, Power Papers, reel 34154, frame 680.
174. Leish, 20–21.
175. Letter, Ackerman to Power, 3 November 1948, Power Papers, reel 34154, frame 756.
176. Letter, Power to Ackerman, 10 November 1948, Power Papers, reel 34154, frame 762.
177. Coffey, 276–77.

178. Hewitt T. Wheless, interview, 18 December 1970, AFHRA, call no. K146.051–5, tape 1, IRIS 01107131. Transcription by author.
179. Wheless.
180. Letter, Fulcher to Power, 19 November 1954, Power Papers, reel 34154, frame 1361.
181. Letter, Power to Stratemeyer, 10 August 1950, Power Papers, reel 34154, frame 961.
182. George E. Stratemeyer, *The Three Wars of Lt. Gen. George E. Stratemeyer: The Korean War Diary*, ed. William T. Y'Blood (Washington, DC: Air Force History and Museums Program, 1999), 96.
183. Stratemeyer, 384n76.
184. Conrad C. Crane, *American Airpower Strategy in Korea: 1950–1953* (Lawrence: University Press of Kansas, 2000), 70.

Chapter 3. Constructing the Aerospace Force

1. Air Force Regulation 23–8, *Organization-Field: Air Research and Development Command*, 28 July 1954, 1.
2. Michael E. Brown, *Flying Blind: The Politics of the U.S. Strategic Bomber Program* (Ithaca, NY: Cornell University Press, 1992), 167.
3. Letter, Power to Director of Requirements, HQ USAF, 30 March 1953, AFHRA, call no. K243.01V4, 1 January to 30 June 1959, emphasis added.
4. "AMC-ARDC Executive Responsibilities for Aircraft Programs," 5 April 1954, AFHRA, IRIS 484772, pdf 17.
5. Jacob Neufeld, *Ballistic Missiles in the United States Air Force, 1945–1960* (Washington, DC: Office of Air Force History, 1989), 104.
6. Neufeld, 107.
7. Neufeld, 104.
8. Neil Sheehan, *A Fiery Peace in a Cold War: Bernard Schriever and the Ultimate Weapon* (New York: Random House, 2010), 157–58.
9. Sheehan, 251.
10. Sheehan, 250.
11. Sheehan, 252.
12. Sheehan.
13. Sheehan, 253.
14. Sheehan, 260.
15. Sheehan.
16. Gen. Bryce Poe II, U.S. Air Force oral history interview, 7 November 1987, 143, AFHRA, call no. K239.0512–1729v1.
17. Poe interview, 157.

18. Poe interview.
19. Robert L. Perry, *Origins of the USAF Space Program 1945–1956*, AFSC Historical Publications, Series 62-24-10 (Los Angeles AFB: Air Force Space Systems Division, 1961), 41.
20. Perry, 42.
21. Perry.
22. Perry, 43.
23. Perry, 44.
24. Perry.
25. Perry.
26. ARDC System Requirement SR No. 5, 17 October 1955, in *Document History of WS-117L 1946 to Redefinition* (Los Angeles AFB: Air Force Systems Command, n.d.), no. 68, AFHRA, call no. K243.012–34v1.
27. Operations Order 4–55, HQ Air Research and Development Command, 9 December 1955, in *Orbital Futures: Selected Documents in Air Force Space History*, vol. 1, ed. David N. Spires (Peterson AFB, CO: Air Force Space Command, 2004), 518–19.
28. Memorandum, Terhune to Sheppard, 3 November 1954, in *Document History of WS-117L*, no. 35.
29. Memorandum (Draft), Schriever to Power, "Interactions Amongst Ballistic Missile and Satellite Programs," n.d., 1–2, AFHRA, call no. 168.7171-82.
30. Schriever to Power, 3–4.
31. Schriever to Power, 15.
32. Schriever to Power, 16.
33. Schriever to Power.
34. Schriever to Power, 19.
35. Schriever to Power, 18.
36. Schriever to Power, 20.
37. Schriever to Power.
38. Memorandum, Schriever to Terhune, 15 April 1955, in *Document History of WS-117L*, no. 47.
39. Douglas Aircraft Company, "Preliminary Design of an Experimental World-Circling Spaceship," Report No. SM-11827, 2 May 1946, 10.
40. Neufeld, 201.
41. Stephen M. Rothstein, *Dead on Arrival? The Development of the Aerospace Concept, 1944–58* (Maxwell AFB, AL: Air University Press, November 2000), 54.

42. Sheehan, 266.
43. Rothstein, 54.
44. David N. Spires, *Beyond Horizons: A Half Century of Air Force Space Leadership* (Peterson AFB, CO: Air Force Space Command, 1996), 37–38.
45. Spires.
46. I. B. Holley Jr., *Technology and Military Doctrine* (Maxwell AFB, AL: Air University Press, August 2004), 1.
47. Holley, *Technology and Military Doctrine*, 2.
48. Holley, *Technology and Military Doctrine*, 2.
49. I. B. Holley Jr., *Ideas and Weapons* (New Haven, CT: Yale University Press, 1953), 156.
50. Holley, *Technology and Military Doctrine*, 142.
51. Holley, *Technology and Military Doctrine*, 9.
52. Holley, *Technology and Military Doctrine*, 10.
53. Thomas S. Power, "The Air Atomic Age," in *The Impact of Air Power*, ed. Eugene Emme (Princeton, NJ: Van Nostrand Company, 1959), 686–87.
54. Power, "Air Atomic Age," 690.
55. *Chronology of Early Air Force Man in Space Activity 1955–1960*, AFSC Historical Publications Series 65-21-1 (Los Angeles AFB: Air Force Systems Command, 1965), 1.
56. Letter, Thomas Power to Honorable Roger Lewis, 9 May 1955.
57. Clayton Christensen, *The Innovator's Dilemma: When New Technologies Cause Great Firms to Fail* (Boston: Harvard Business Press, 2016).
58. Letter, Power to Lewis, 9 May 1955.
59. Letter, Power to Gen. Nathan F. Twining, 2 August 1955.
60. "Air Chief of Staff Twining Accepts Russian Invitation to View Moscow Air Show," *Stanford Daily*, 31 May 1956.
61. "9 Will Accompany Twining to Moscow," *New York Times*, 14 June 1956, 54.
62. "Twining and Aides Off for Moscow," *New York Times*, 22 June 1956, 1.
63. "Twining Finishes His Soviet Visit," *New York Times*, 1 July 1956, 12.
64. "It Was a Rough Party Soviets Gave Twining," *New York Times*, 11 July 1956, 3.
65. Letter, Power to Zhukov, 9 July 1956, Power Papers, reel 34154, frame 1571.
66. "The Stalingrad-Moscow Express," *Combat Crew*, September 1956, 4–5.
67. "Excerpts from Twining's Report to Senate on Soviet Visit," *New York Times*, 11 July 1956, 12.

68. "Twining Warns Congress of New Soviet Weapons," *New York Times*, 11 July 1956, 13.

69. *Soviet Total War: "Historic Mission" of Violence and Deceit*, vol. 1, House Un-American Activities Committee, Washington, DC, 23 September 1956, 399–402.

70. *Soviet Total War*, 402–3.

71. *Soviet Total War*, 403.

72. Thomas S. Power, "A Message from ARDC," *Aviation Week* 65, no. 6 (6 August 1956), 70.

73. *History of Air Research and Development Command*, 1 July–31 December 1955, vol. 1, V-177–V-178, AFHRA, call no. K243.01v1, IRIS 484779.

74. Letter, Power to Yates, 7 October 1955, in Alfred Rockefeller, *History of Evolution of the AFBMD Advanced Ballistic Missile and Space Program 1955–1958* (Los Angeles AFB: AFBMD, 11 February 1960), 5.

75. *History of ARDC*, V-178.

76. Claude Witze, "Industry Role in New Weapons Increases," *Aviation Week* 65, no. 6 (6 August 1956), 86.

77. *History of ARDC*, V-178.

78. *History of ARDC*, V-179–V-180.

79. *History of ARDC*, V-180.

80. *History of ARDC*, V-181–V-182.

81. *History of ARDC*, V-184.

82. *History of ARDC*.

83. *History of ARDC*, V-186.

84. *History of Air Research and Development Command*, 1 July–31 August 1956, vol. 1, IX-528, AFHRA, call no. K243.01

85. *History of ARDC*, 1 July–31 December 1955, vol. 1, V-186–V-187.

86. Witze, 88.

87. *History of ARDC*, 1 July–31 December 1955, vol. 1, V-187–V-188.

88. Witze, 86, 89–80.

89. Witze, 88.

90. Witze, 86.

91. Dwayne Day, "Take Off and Nuke the Site from Orbit (It's the Only Way to Be Sure . . .)", *The Space Review*, 4 June 2007, http://www.thespacere view.com/article/882/1.

92. Tab E—Air Force Study Program, n.d., AFHRA, call no. K168.8636–4, 46/00/00–60/02/15.

93. Tab E—Air Force Study Program.

94. ARDC LRP 61–76, *Air Research and Development Command Long Range Research and Development Plan 1961–1976* (U), n.d., CO-85017, AFHRA, call no. K243.8636–1, 1961–76.

95. ARDC LRP 61–76, 9.

96. ARDC LRP 61–76.

97. ARDC LRP 61–76, 11–12.

98. ARDC LRP 61–76, 12.

99. ARDC LRP 61–76.

100. ARDC LRP 61–76, 13.

101. *Military Lunar Base*, 1 January 1961, AFHRA, call no. K140.8636–2.

102. *Military Lunar Base*.

103. *Military Lunar Base*.

104. Memorandum, Hartman to Director, Space Flight Development, 2 April 1959, 3.

105. Hartman to Director, 1.

106. Hartman to Director, 3.

107. Hartman to Director.

108. S. E. Singer, "The Military Potential of the Moon," *Air University Quarterly Review* (Summer 1959): 44.

109. Singer, 45.

110. *Military Lunar Base Program or S.R. 183 Lunar Observatory Study*, vol. 1, April 1960, I-5.

111. Singer, 51.

112. Letter, Wheless to ARDC, "The Air Force Space Program," 10 November 1964, 1 (Kirtland AFB, NM: Air Force Research Laboratory Historians Office, Orion Archives).

113. Wheless to ARDC, 3.

114. *History of Air Research and Development Command*, 1 January–31 December 1958, *ARDC and the National Space Program*, I-17, AFHRA, call no. K243.01v1, January-December 1958, vol. 1.

115. *ARDC and the National Space Program*, I-17.

116. *ARDC and the National Space Program*, I-17–I-18.

117. *ARDC and the National Space Program*, I-1–I-2.

118. *History of the Air Research and Development Command*, 1 January–30 June 1955, iii, AFHRA, call no. K234.01v1.

Chapter 4. Power as CINCSAC

1. Alwyn T. Lloyd, *A Cold War Legacy: Strategic Air Command 1946–1992* (Missoula, MT: Pictorial Histories Publishing Company, 2000), 255.

2. Donald W. Klinko, unpublished draft biography of Gen. Thomas S. Power, n.d., I-1, Air Force Global Strike Command Historian's Office.

3. Klinko, I-2.

4. Klinko.

5. Richard G. Hubler, *SAC: The Strategic Air Command* (New York: Duell, Sloane, and Pearce, 1958), author's note.

6. "Quotes: General Thomas S. Power," compiled by Strategic Air Command, 1 December 1961, VIII-2.

7. Klinko, I-1.

8. Campbell Craig, *Destroying the Village: Eisenhower and Thermonuclear War* (New York: Columbia University Press, 1998).

9. "Quotes," I-3.

10. General Power, remarks to New York civic leaders at Offutt AFB, NE, 10 October 1963, in Strategic Air Command Recording Service Archives, AFHRA, call no. K416.153–4 (2 parts).

11. Power, remarks.

12. Klinko, II-1. See David A. Rosenberg, "The Origins of Overkill: Nuclear Weapons and American Strategy, 1945–1960," *International Security* 7, no. 4 (Spring 1983): 3–71, for a classic account of the "overkill" thesis.

13. Lloyd, 260–61.

14. Thomas S. Power, "How Much Can Missiles Really Do?" *Air Force Magazine*, September 1956, 105–6.

15. Thomas S. Power, "Ballistic Missiles and the SAC Mission," *Air Force Magazine*, April 1958, 76.

16. Power.

17. Power, emphasis original.

18. Power.

19. Thomas S. Power, "SAC and the Ballistic Missile," in *The United States Air Force Report on the Ballistic Missile*, ed. Kenneth Gantz (Garden City, NY: Doubleday, 1958), 175.

20. Power, "Ballistic Missiles and the SAC Mission," 76.

21. Power, "SAC and the Ballistic Missile," 178–89.

22. Power, 184.

23. Power, 177.

24. Power.

25. Power, 178.

26. Power, 175–76.

27. Klinko, II-4.

28. Thomas S. Power, *Design for Survival* (New York: Coward-McCann, 1964), 131.
29. Foreign Broadcast Information Service (FBIS), "Soviet Propaganda on the Nature of the Nuclear War Threat," 25 June 1958, 26.
30. FBIS, 3, footnote.
31. Klinko, II-6.
32. Klinko.
33. Pat Frank, "These Men Must Stop Russia's ICBM," *This Week Magazine*, 24 November 1957, 8.
34. Power, remarks to New York civic leaders.
35. "The Man the Kremlin Fears Most," *U.S. News and World Report*, 2 May 1958, 62.
36. Power, *Design for Survival*, 131–32.
37. FBIS, 7.
38. FBIS.
39. FBIS, 8.
40. FBIS.
41. Thomas S. Power, memorandum, "To Each Member of the SAC Alert Force," 9 November 1957.
42. Letter, Power to White, "Strategic Air Command Space Policy," 13 August 1958, in *Orbital Futures: Selected Documents in Air Force Space History*, ed. David N. Spires, vol. 1, (Peterson AFB, CO: Air Force Space Command, 2004), 27.
43. Power, "SAC Space Policy," 27.
44. Power.
45. Power.
46. Power.
47. Power.
48. Thomas S. Power, "Strategic Aspects of Space Operations," *Air Force Magazine and Space Digest*, November 1958, 80.
49. Power.
50. Power, 82.
51. Power.
52. Power.
53. In . . . *the Heavens and the Earth: A Political History of the Space Age* by Walter McDougall (Baltimore: Johns Hopkins University Press, 1985), Power is mentioned only twice—for his deterrence statements and his disdain for civilian intellectuals.

54. Power, remarks to New York civic leaders.

55. Letter, Power to Arnhym, Power Papers, reel 34156, frame 356.

56. Memorandum, Leach to Luehman, Power Papers, reel 34156, frame 609.

57. Letter, Power to Speer, 28 August 1959, Power Papers, reel 34156, frame 663.

58. "McElroy's Flimsy Excuse," *Greenville News*, 30 August 1959, Power Papers, reel 34156, frame 652.

59. "Get the General's Book Off the Shelf; Public Needs to Know about Defense," *Denver Post*, 11 September 1959, Power Papers, reel 34156, frame 668, emphasis original.

60. Letter, Leach to Power, 8 September 1959, Power Papers, reel 34156, frame 681.

61. Letter, Random House to Power, 24 September 1959, Power Papers, reel 34156, frame 703.

62. Robert Hotz, editorial, *Aviation Week*, 13 April 1959, 2.

63. Klinko, III-4.

64. "Power Airs SAC Deterrent Capability," *Aviation Week*, 20 April 1959, 66–93.

65. "Power Airs SAC Deterrent Capability," 71.

66. Klinko, III-7.

67. "Power Airs SAC Deterrent Capability," 80.

68. Power, remarks to New York civic leaders.

69. Power.

70. "Power Airs SAC Deterrent Capability," 91.

71. "Power Airs SAC Deterrent Capability," 81–83.

72. *Public Papers of the Presidents of the United States: Dwight D. Eisenhower, 1960*, 145.

73. Letter, Gardner to Power, 4 February 1960, Power Papers, reel 34155, frame 107.

74. Letter, Unknown to Power, 2 February 1960, Power Papers, reel 34155, frame 77.

75. Klinko, III-8.

76. Klinko.

77. Klinko, III-10.

78. George E. Lowe, *The Age of Deterrence* (Boston: Little, Brown, and Company, 1964), 192–93.

79. Desmond Ball, *Politics and Force Levels: The Strategic Missile Program in the Kennedy Administration* (Berkeley: University of California Press, 1980), 11.

80. Ball.

81. See Power Papers, reel 34157, frames 728–59, for a comparison of the original speech, its handwritten amendments, and the final speech as delivered.

82. Letter, Tunney to Power, 22 January 1960, Power Papers, reel 34155, frame 20.

83. Letter, Shea to Power, 21 January 1960, Power Papers, reel 34155, frame 23.

84. Lowe, *Deterrence*, 205–6.

85. Klinko, III-12.

86. Klinko, III-12.

87. Klinko, III-12.

88. Lowe, *Deterrence*, 217–18.

89. Letter, Hotz to Power, 27 June 1960, Power Papers, reel 34155, frame 196.

90. Letter, Power to Hotz, 29 June 1960, Power Papers, reel 34155, frame 195.

91. Lt. Gen. Paul K. Carlton Jr., USAF (ret.), interview with author, 13 December 2016.

92. Worden, 142.

93. Letter, Power to White, 15 October 1960, Power Papers, reel 34155, frame 300.

94. Letter, Power to McBrayer, 12 December 1960, Power Papers, reel 34155, frame 340.

95. Letter, Power to Bartlett, n.d., Power Papers, reel 34155, frame 582.

96. Letter, Bartlett to Power, 15 December 1961, Power Papers, reel 34155, frames 583–84.

97. Letter, Bartlett to Power.

98. Letter, Schwiebert to Power, 25 January 1962, Power Papers, reel 34155, frames 618–23.

99. Letter, Arnhym to Power, 10 January 1962, Power Papers, reel 34155, frame 588.

100. Letter, Luehman to Power, n.d., Power Papers, reel 34155, frame 590.

101. Letter, Power to Luehman, 10 January 1962, Power Papers, reel 34155, frame 587.

102. See Worden for a classic treatment of the "fighter pragmatists" versus the "bomber barons."

103. Letter, Spaatz to Power, 30 March 1961, Power Papers, reel 34155, frame 405.

104. Letter, Eaker to Power, 26 October 1961, Power Papers, reel 34155, frame 541.

105. Letter, Power to Eaker, 30 October 1961, Power Papers, reel 34155, frame 540.

106. Lloyd R. Leavitt, *Following the Flag: An Air Force Officer Provides an Eyewitness View of Major Events and Policies during the Cold War* (Maxwell AFB, AL: Air University Press, 2010), 238–39, emphasis original.

Chapter 5. Planning for Armageddon

1. Edward Drea et al., *History of the Unified Command Plan 1946–2012* (Washington, DC: Joint Chiefs of Staff, 2013), 2.

2. Headquarters Strategic Air Command, History and Research Division, *History of the Joint Strategic Target Planning Staff: Background and Preparation of SIOP-62*, B-82767, 2.

3. *History of the JSTPS*, 4.

4. Glenn A. Kent et al., "The Single Integrated Operational Plan," in *Thinking About America's Defense: An Analytical Memoir* (Santa Monica, CA: RAND, 2008), 24.

5. For an example of Admiral Burke's thoughts on Power, see "Admiral Burke's Conversation with Secretary Franke, 12 Aug 60," declassified document, https://nsarchive2.gwu.edu//nukevault/ebb275/14.pdf.

6. *History of the JSTPS*, 7.

7. *History of the JSTPS*, 8.

8. *History of the JSTPS*, 9.

9. *History of the JSTPS*, 10.

10. *History of the JSTPS*, 11.

11. *History of the JSTPS*, 12.

12. *History of the JSTPS*, 14.

13. *History of the JSTPS*, 15.

14. *History of the JSTPS*, 20.

15. Walter S. Poole, *The Joint Chiefs of Staff and National Policy 1961–1964*, History of the Joint Chiefs of Staff, vol. 8 (Washington, DC: Office of Joint History, 2011), 27.

16. *History of the JSTPS*, 17.

17. *History of the JSTPS*, 20.

18. *History of the JSTPS*, 21.

19. *History of the JSTPS*, 23.

20. *History of the JSTPS*, 24.

21. Rosenberg, 8.

22. R. Cargill Hall, "Civil-Military Relations in America's Early Space Program," in *The U.S. Air Force in Space: 1945 to the Twenty-First Century*,

ed. R. Cargill Hall and Jacob Neufeld (Washington, DC: Air Force History and Museums Program, 1998), 29.

23. Hall, 29.
24. Rosenberg, 8.
25. Kent, 27.
26. Kent, 26–27.
27. Kent, 27.
28. *History of the JSTPS*, 25.
29. *History of the JSTPS*, 26.
30. *History of the JSTPS*, 27–28.
31. John H. Rubel, *Doomsday Delayed: USAF Strategic Weapons Doctrine and SIOP-62* (New York: Hamilton Books, 2008), 25. Emphasis original.
32. Craig, 161.
33. Thomas S. Power, "The Myth of the Overkill," *Combat Crew*, October 1963, 4–5.
34. See Kent, 35–36, for an example of the behavior of the Whiz Kids when confronted by a SIOP defender who engaged them with the mathematics behind the JSTPS planning factors.
35. Rubel, 27.
36. Rubel, 23.
37. Rubel, 25.
38. Rubel, 29.
39. Kent, 28.
40. *History of the JSTPS*, 28.
41. *History of the JSTPS*, 16.
42. *History of the JSTPS*, 16–17.
43. Letter, Gates to Power, 19 January 1961, Power Papers, reel 34155, frame 353.
44. *History of the JSTPS*, 17.
45. *History of the JSTPS*, 18.
46. Letter, A. A. Arnhym to Dr. Norman Auburn, Power Papers, reel 34155, frame 979.
47. Poole, 32.
48. Kent, 30.

Chapter 6. SAC's Finest Hour

1. *Strategic Air Command Operations in the Cuban Crisis of 1962*, vol. 1, Historical Study No. 90, B-91816, 5, https://nsarchive2.gwu.edu/nsa/cuba_mis_cri/dobbs/SAC_history.pdf.

2. *SAC Operations in the Cuban Crisis*, 6.
3. *SAC Operations in the Cuban Crisis*, 7.
4. *SAC Operations in the Cuban Crisis*, 8.
5. "Message to Combat Crews," Power Papers, reel 34155, frames 820–22.
6. *SAC Operations in the Cuban Crisis*, 11.
7. *SAC Operations in the Cuban Crisis*, 30.
8. *SAC Operations in the Cuban Crisis*, 32.
9. *SAC Operations in the Cuban Crisis*, 33.
10. John F. Kennedy, Address on the Cuban Crisis, October 22, 1962, https://sourcebooks.fordham.edu/mod/1962kennedy-cuba.html.
11. *SAC Operations in the Cuban Crisis*, 35.
12. *SAC Operations in the Cuban Crisis*.
13. *SAC Operations in the Cuban Crisis*, 36.
14. *SAC Operations in the Cuban Crisis*, 37.
15. *SAC Operations in the Cuban Crisis*, 39.
16. *SAC Operations in the Cuban Crisis*, 43.
17. *SAC Operations in the Cuban Crisis*, 42.
18. *SAC Operations in the Cuban Crisis*, 43.
19. *SAC Operations in the Cuban Crisis*, 46.
20. *SAC Operations in the Cuban Crisis*, 51.
21. *SAC Operations in the Cuban Crisis*, 62.
22. Worden, 82–83.
23. Gen. Horace M. Wade, oral history interview, 10 October 1978, AFHRA, K239.0512–1105, 305.
24. *SAC Operations in the Cuban Crisis*, 62.
25. *SAC Operations in the Cuban Crisis*, vii.
26. Letter, Galer to Power, 30 October 1962, Power Papers, reel 34155, frame 833.
27. Raymond L. Garthoff, *Reflections on the Cuban Missile Crisis* (Washington, DC: Brookings Institution, 1989), 62.
28. Leavitt, 250–51.
29. *SAC Operations in the Cuban Crisis*, 65.
30. Michael Dobbs, *One Minute to Midnight: Kennedy, Khrushchev, and Castro on the Brink of Nuclear War* (New York: Random House, 2008), 277–78.
31. Kristen Inbody, "Montana Plays Cold War Role with Malmstrom's 'Ace in the Hole,'" *USA Today*, September 21, 2014, https://www.usatoday.com/story/life/my-montana/2014/09/21/montana-plays-cold-war-role-malmstromsace-hole/15911403/.

32. Dobbs, *One Minute to Midnight*, 279.

33. *SAC Operations in the Cuban Crisis*, 73.

34. *SAC Operations in the Cuban Crisis*, 74.

35. *SAC Operations in the Cuban Crisis*, 73.

36. *SAC Operations in the Cuban Crisis*, 75.

37. *SAC Operations in the Cuban Crisis*, 72.

38. Vandenberg Air Force Base launch history, http://www.spacearchive .info/vafblog.htm.

39. Scott Sagan, *The Limits of Safety: Organizations, Accidents, and Nuclear Weapons* (Princeton, NJ: Princeton University Press, 1993), 79.

40. *SAC Operations in the Cuban Crisis*, 22.

41. *SAC Operations in the Cuban Crisis*, 23.

42. *SAC Operations in the Cuban Crisis*, 24.

43. *SAC Operations in the Cuban Crisis*.

44. *SAC Operations in the Cuban Crisis*, 25.

45. Michael Dobbs, "Missing Over the Soviet Union," https://nsarchive2 .gwu.edu/nsa/cuba_mis_cri/dobbs/maultsby.htm.

46. Dobbs, "Missing Over the Soviet Union."

47. *Strategic Air Warfare*, Office of Air Force History, 15 June 1984, AFHRA, call no. K239.0512–2115, 220.

48. "Obituary—Colonel Charles Maultsby," *Tucson Citizen*, 21 August 1998.

49. Chris Adams, *Deterrence: An Enduring Strategy* (New York: iUniverse, 2009), 202.

50. Adams, 202–3.

51. *SAC Operations in the Cuban Crisis*, 59.

52. *SAC Operations in the Cuban Crisis*, 60.

53. *SAC Operations in the Cuban Crisis*.

54. *SAC Operations in the Cuban Crisis*, 61.

55. *SAC Operations in the Cuban Crisis*, 48.

56. President John F. Kennedy, Remarks in Omaha Upon Presenting a Special Flight Safety Plaque to the Strategic Air Command, 7 December 1962, http://www.presidency.ucsb.edu/ws/index.php?pid=9042.

57. *SAC Operations in the Cuban Crisis*, 76.

58. *SAC Operations in the Cuban Crisis*, 77.

59. *SAC Operations in the Cuban Crisis*, 78.

60. *SAC Operations in the Cuban Crisis*, 26.

61. *SAC Operations in the Cuban Crisis*, 27.

62. *SAC Operations in the Cuban Crisis*, 94.

63. *SAC Operations in the Cuban Crisis*, 95.

64. *SAC Operations in the Cuban Crisis*, 97.
65. *SAC Operations in the Cuban Crisis*, 100.
66. *Strategic Air Warfare*, 209–11.
67. *Strategic Air Warfare*, 220–22.

Chapter 7. Destiny Derailed

1. George Dyson, *Project Orion: The True Story of the Atomic Spaceship* (New York: Henry Holt and Company, 2002), 23.
2. Douglas Aircraft Company, "Preliminary Design of an Experimental World-Circling Spaceship," 7.
3. Scott Lowther, "The Large Orions: As Close as We've Come to a Starship," *Aerospace Projects Review* 2, no. 2 (March–April 2000): 27.
4. Lowther.
5. Lowther.
6. Donald M. Mixson, *Military Implications of the Orion Vehicle*, TN-59–26 (Kirtland AFB, NM: Air Force Special Weapons Center, July 1959), 1, AFHRA, call no. K242.04–10, July 1959.
7. Mixson, 1.
8. Mixson.
9. Mixson, 2.
10. Mixson, emphasis original.
11. Mixson, 2–3.
12. Mixson, 3.
13. Mixson.
14. Frederick F. Gorschboth, *Counterforce from Space*, TN-61-17 (Kirtland AFB, NM: Air Force Special Weapons Center, 1 August 1961).
15. Joint Message Form, COMDR AFSWC, Kirtland AFB, NM, to HQ SAC, Offutt AFB, NE, 28 August 1959, in author's personal collection.
16. Thomas S. Power, "Strategic Earth Orbital Base, Strategic Air Command Qualitative Operational Requirement," 21 January 1961.
17. Power, "Strategic Earth Orbital Base."
18. Power, "Strategic Earth Orbital Base."
19. Power, "Strategic Earth Orbital Base."
20. Power, "Strategic Earth Orbital Base."
21. Power, "Strategic Earth Orbital Base."
22. "Personnel File, Donald M. Mixson," National Personnel Records Center, St. Louis, MO, in author's personal collection.
23. Mixson, personnel file.

24. Thomas S. Power, "Strategic Air Command," *Air Force Magazine*, September 1960, 71.

25. Power.

26. Lloyd, 264.

27. Mark Erickson, *Into the Unknown Together: The DOD, NASA, and Early Spaceflight* (Maxwell AFB, AL: Air University Press, 2005), 280.

28. Gerald T. Cantwell, *The Air Force in Space Fiscal Year 1963* (Washington, DC: Air Force Historical Division Liaison Office, December 1966), 5.

29. Cantwell.

30. Launor F. Carter, *An Interpretive Study of the Formulation of the Air Force Space Program* (Washington, DC: Headquarters USAF, 4 February 1963), 7.

31. Robert S. McNamara, "Current Views of the Secretary of Defense," draft staff summary, testimony to Senate Armed Services Committee, 11 September 1963.

32. Cantwell, 7.

33. See Brent Ziarnick, "Starfleet Deferred: Project Orion in the 1962 Air Force Space Program," *Journal of the British Interplanetary Society* 68 (2015): 17–25, for a full treatment.

34. Letter, Power to Brown, 3 November 1962, in *History of the Strategic Air Command*, July 1962–June 1963, vol. 8, AFHRA, call no. K426.01–92v8.

35. Letter, Brown to Power, 15 November 1962, in *History of SAC*, July 1962–June 1963, vol. 8, emphasis original.

36. Letter, Wheless to Ferguson, "Air Force Space Plan," 14 March 1962.

37. Letter, Power to LeMay, "Orion Program," 20 February 1962, in Papers of Gen. Thomas D. White, National Archives, Washington, DC.

38. Power to LeMay.

39. Power to LeMay.

40. Power to LeMay.

41. Gen. Thomas S. Power, "The Strategic Air Command—Past, Present, and Future," address to Union League Club of New York, 10 April 1962, 14.

42. Power, 14.

43. Power, 16–18.

44. Dyson, 261.

45. Frederick Gorschboth, interview with author, 15 October 2014.

46. For a description of Dyson's criticisms of RAF Bomber Command, see Randall T. Wakelam, *The Science of Bombing* (Toronto, Canada: University of Toronto Press, 2009), 38, 66–67, 150–52.

47. Dyson, 285–86.

48. Dyson, 219.
49. Dyson.
50. Dyson, 220.
51. Dyson, 221.
52. Harold Brown, oral history interview, JFK no. 6, 9 July 1964, John F. Kennedy Presidential Library, 26–28.
53. Brown, 26–27.
54. Lowther, 51.
55. Thomas S. Power, "Military Aspects of Manned Spaceflight," speech to the Second Annual Manned Spaceflight Meeting, Dallas, Texas, 24 April 1963, Power Papers, reel 34157, frame 998.
56. Memorandum, Hinkle to Director of Information, Strategic Air Command, 16 April 1963, Power Papers, reel 34157, frame 997.
57. Power, "Military Aspects of Manned Spaceflight."
58. Thomas S. Power, testimony, "Military Aspects and Implications of Nuclear Test Ban Proposals and Related Matters," Hearings Before the Preparedness Investigating Subcommittee of the Committee on Armed Services, United States Senate, Eighty-Eighth Congress, First Session, 12–27 August 1963, 779.
59. Power, testimony, 789.
60. Power, testimony, 782.
61. Power, testimony, 780.
62. Power, testimony, 782.
63. Power, testimony, 810.
64. Power, testimony, 813.
65. Brown, oral history interview, JFK no. 5, 38.
66. Letter, Power to HQ, USAF, "Nuclear Pulse Propulsion (ORION)," 14 October 1963.
67. Letter, Power to HQ, USAF.
68. Letter, Power to HQ, USAF, emphasis original.
69. Letter, Power to HQ, USAF.
70. Thomas D. White, "Strategy and the Defense Intellectuals," Saturday Evening Post, 4 May 1963, 10.
71. Letter, Power to White, 3 May 1963, in Personal Letters of Thomas D. White, AFHRA, call no. 168.7004–73, 63/02/19—63/05/04.
72. Brown, oral history interview, JFK no. 1, 1964, 38.
73. Brown.
74. Power, remarks at Milestone Dinner, 4 March 1962, Power Papers, reel 34157, frame 891.

75. Letter, Hope to Power, Power Papers, reel 34155, frame 668.

76. "SAC: The Big Stick," review, Power Papers, reel 34155, frame 736.

77. Letter, Wilson to Power, n.d., Power Papers, reel 34155, frame 733.

78. Letter, McKnew to Power, Power Papers, reel 34155, frame 741.

79. List of quotes, Power Papers, reel 34155, frame 759.

80. Letter, Zuckert to Power, 29 January 1963, Power Papers, reel 34155, frame 884.

81. Letter, Taylor to Power, 16 April 1963, Power Papers, reel 34155, frame 965.

82. Letter, McNamara to Power, 1 July 1963, Power Papers, reel 34155, frame 1038.

83. Letter, Auburn to Power, 6 June 1963, Power Papers, reel 34155, frame 1028.

84. Letter, Arnhym to Auburn, 28 May 1963, Power Papers, reel 34155, frame 979.

85. Letter, Parres to Power, 12 June 1963, Power Papers, reel 34155, frame 1009.

86. Letter, Cousins to Power, 18 September 1963, Power Papers, reel 34155, frame 1174.

87. Letter, Ellis to Power, 16 September 1963, Power Papers, reel 34155, frame 1090.

88. Letter, Zuckert to Power, 30 November 1963, Power Papers, reel 34155, frames 1241–42.

89. Letter, Cowles to Power, 17 February 1964, Power Papers, reel 34155, frame 1358.

90. Letter, Power to Cowles, 28 February 1964, Power Papers, reel 34155, frame 1357.

91. Letter, Caffery to Power, 27 February 1964, Power Papers, reel 34155, frames 1364–66.

92. Letter, Linn to Power, 10 April 1964, Power Papers, reel 34155, frame 1423.

93. Letter, George to Power, 11 April 1964, Power Papers, reel 34155, frame 1431.

94. Letter, Bruno to Power, 14 April 1964, Power Papers, reel 34155, frame 1424.

95. Letter, Lacour to Power, 25 May 1964, Power Papers, reel 34155, frame 1489.

96. Letter, Necrason to Power, 14 September 1964, Power Papers, reel 34155, frame 1660.

97. Letter, Spivak to Power, 17 April 1964, Power Papers, reel 34155, frame 1460.
98. Letter, Power to Spivak, 6 May 1964, Power Papers, reel 34155, frame 1459.
99. Letter, Power to Bender, 19 May 1964, Power Papers, reel 34155, frame 1519.
100. Letter, Brandt to Power, 5 May 1964, Power Papers, reel 34155, frame 1510.
101. Letter, Brandt to Power, 18 May 1964, Power Papers, reel 34155, frames 1506–7.
102. Letter, Loomis to Brandt, 20 May 1964, Power Papers, reel 34155, frames 1503–4.
103. Letter, McCormick to Brandt, 2 June 1964, Power Papers, reel 34155, frame 1560.
104. Theresa Wulf, "Air Force Efforts Silenced Spellman School's Critics," *Bellevue Leader* (Belleview, NE), 24 June 1989, 1–2.
105. Wulf.
106. Wulf.
107. "Cardinal Spellman 1963–1975 Scrapbook Photo Album," Cardinal Spellman School, n.d., 33.
108. "Gen. Power, Wife, Cited by Vatican," unknown newspaper, 10 July 1964, in "Cardinal Spellman 1963–1975 Scrapbook Photo Album," 36.
109. Letter, Power to Spellman, 17 July 1964, Power Papers, reel 34155, frame 1593.
110. Letter, Power to Various Recipients, 10 November 1964, Power Papers, Reel 34156, frames 796–98.
111. "General Power of SAC," WLS Chicago, 1 December 1964, Power Papers, reel 34157, frame 349.
112. Letter, Brandt to Power, 18 November 1964, Power Papers, reel 34156, frame 860.
113. Thomas S. Power, medical records, 26 June 1964.
114. Letter, Townsend to Niess, 18 September 1952, Gen. Thomas S. Power, medical records.
115. Letter, LeMay to Power, 10 November 1964, Power Papers, reel 34156, frame 785.
116. Lloyd, 346.
117. Lloyd.
118. Lloyd, 348.

Chapter 8. The War of Remembrance

1. "The Four-Star General," Power Papers, reel 34157, frame 1458.
2. "The Four-Star General," frames 1458–59.
3. Letter, Power to Besse, 14 October 1949, Power Papers, reel 34154, frame 902.
4. Letter, Power to Prashker, 3 December 1964, Power Papers, reel 34156, frame 911.
5. Letter, Arnhym to Power, 28 January 1965, Power Papers, reel 34156, frame 936.
6. Letter, Goodwyn to Power, 30 December 1964, Power Papers, reel 34156, frame 912.
7. Letter, Arnhym to Power, 29 December 1964, Power Papers, reel 34156, frame 917.
8. Letter, Ryan to Power, 23 December 1964, Power Papers, reel 34156, frame 900.
9. Letter, Schlatter to Power, n.d., Power Papers, reel 34156, frame 961.
10. Letter, McConnell to Power, 2 February 1965, Power Papers, reel 34156, frame 970.
11. Letter, Wheless to Power, 4 February 1965, Power Papers, reel 34156, frame 972.
12. Letter, Brennan to Power, 17 September 1963, Power Papers, reel 34155, frame 1176.
13. Letter, Power to Brennan, 26 September 1963, Power Papers, reel 34155, frame 1175.
14. Letter, Power to Brennan, 14 December 1964, Power Papers, reel 34156, frames 877–79.
15. Letter, Brennan to Power, 21 December 1964, Power Papers, reel 34156, frames 892–93.
16. Letter, Schelling to Brown, 27 January 1965, Power Papers, reel 34156, frames 930–31.
17. Letter, Brennan to Power, 26 February 1965, Power Papers, reel 34156, frame 956.
18. Letter, Arnhym to Power, 11 January 1965, Power Papers, reel 34156, frame 932.
19. Letter, Harper to Power, 31 March 1965, Power Papers, reel 34156, frame 1064.
20. Letter, Lewis to Power, 2 February 1965, Power Papers, reel 34156, frame 965.

21. Letter, Lewis to Power, 3 May 1965, Power Papers, reel 34156, frame 1107.
22. Letter, Wood to Power, 23 July 1965, Power Papers, reel 34156, frame 1147.
23. Letter, Todt to Power, 6 April 1965, Power Papers, reel 34156, frame 1082.
24. Letter, Sefton to Power, 31 May 1966, Power Papers, reel 34156, frame 1218.
25. Letter, Loosbrock to Power, 10 February 1965, Power Papers, reel 34156, frame 977.
26. Letter, Arnhym to Power, 14 March 1965, Power Papers, reel 34156, frame 1058.
27. Letter, Arnhym to Power, 25 April 1965, Power Papers, reel 34156, frame 1081.
28. Transcript, *Meet the Press*, 21 March 1965, Power Papers, reel 34157, frame 172.
29. *Meet the Press*, frame 177.
30. *Meet the Press*.
31. *Meet the Press*, frame 178.
32. *Meet the Press*, frame 179.
33. *Meet the Press*.
34. *Meet the Press*, frame 181.
35. *Meet the Press*.
36. *Meet the Press*, frame 184.
37. *Meet the Press*, frame 186.
38. Letter, Blum to Power, 21 March 1965, Power Papers, reel 34156, frame 1016.
39. Letter, Ormsby to Power, 21 March 1965, Power Papers, reel 34156, frame 997.
40. Letter, Klayman to Power, March 1965, Power Papers, reel 34156, frame 1012, emphasis original.
41. Letter, Vanerlann to Power, 22 March 1965, Power Papers, reel 34156, frame 1014.
42. Letter, Eaker to Power, 24 March 1965, Power Papers, reel 34156, frame 1005.
43. Letter, Payne to Power, 24 March 1965, Power Papers, reel 34156, frame 1010.
44. "Bombing by SAC in Vietnam Urged by Force's Ex-Chief," *New York Times*, 23 March 1964, 4.
45. Letter, Widener to Power, 26 March 1965, Power Papers, reel 34156, frame 1070, emphasis added.

46. James D. Atkinson, "Design for Survival," book review, *Military Affairs* 29, no. 2 (Summer 1965): 95.
47. Ronald Steel, "Hitting the SAC," *New York Review of Books*, 20 May 1965.
48. Hanson W. Baldwin, "The Creed of Strength," *New York Times*, 21 March 1965
49. Letter, Montgomery to Power, 17 May 1965, Power Papers, reel 34156, frame 1113.
50. Bernard Montgomery, *A History of Warfare* (New York: William Morrow and Co., 1983), 12.
51. "New York Times Adult Hardcover Best Seller Listings," http://www.hawes.com/pastlist.htm.
52. Letter, Power to Johnson, 7 May 1965, Power Papers, reel 34156, frame 1108.
53. Letter, Smith to Power, 24 May 1965, Power Papers, reel 34156, frame 1111.
54. Letter, Power to Robinson, 28 May 1965, Power Papers, reel 34156, frame 1101.
55. Phyllis Schlafly and Chester Ward, *Strike from Space* (Alton, IL: Pere Marquette Press, 1965), 3.
56. Schlafly and Ward, 189–90.
57. Power, "*Strike from Space* Enclosure," n.d., Power Papers, reel 34156, frame 1217.
58. Letter, Grow to McManus, 30 July 1965, Thomas S. Power medical records.
59. Letter, Hebert to Power, Power Papers, reel 34156, frame 1181.
60. Letter, Todt to Power, 14 January 1966, Power Papers, reel 34156, frame 1183.
61. "Fish or Cut Bait," *St. Louis Globe-Democrat*, 15–16 January 1966, Power Papers, reel 34156, frame 1189.
62. Letter, Porter to Power, 16 February 1966, Power Papers, reel 34156, frame 1196.
63. Letter, Desert Four Republican Women's Club to Power, 23 May 1966, Power Papers, reel 34156, frame 1219.
64. Letter, Reagan to Power, 23 May 1967, Power Papers, reel 34156, frame 1283.
65. Letter, Nixon to Power, 9 February 1967, Power Papers, reel 34156, frame 1258.
66. Letter, Ellsworth to Power, 1 May 1967, Power Papers, reel 34156, frame 1288.

67. Letter, Lincoln to Power, 14 July 1967, Power Papers, reel 34156, frame 1290.

68. Interview with General Power, n.d., Power Papers, reel 341567, frame 208.

69. Letter, Storz to Power, 17 February 1967, Power Papers, reel 34156, frame 1263.

70. Letter, Fisher to Power, 26 January 1967, Power Papers, reel 34156, frame 1253.

71. Letter, Thomas to Power, 31 May 1967, Power Papers, reel 34156, frame 1282.

72. Letter, Schlafly to Power, 11 March 1968, Power Papers, reel 34156, frame 1345.

73. Power, notes on Fourth Report, n.d., Power Papers, reel 34157, frame 81.

74. Power notes on No. 10, 25 August 1967, Power Papers, reel 34157, frame 99.

75. Letter, Fisher to Power, 4 August 1967, Power Papers, reel 34156, frame 1295.

76. Letter, Lincoln to Power, 4 October 1967, Power Papers, reel 34156, frame 1304.

77. Letter, Nixon to Power, 26 October 1967, Power Papers, reel 34156, frame 1305.

78. Letter, Lincoln to Power, 22 November 1967, Power Papers, reel 34156, frames 1314–16.

79. Letter, Lincoln to Power, 8 February 1968, Power Papers, reel 34156, frame 1331.

80. Power, handwritten notes, February 1968, Power Papers, reel 34156, frame 1335.

81. Letter, Schlafly to Power, 25 March 1968, Power Papers, reel 34156, frames 1346–47.

82. Letter, Power to Meyer, LeMay Review, 27 May 1968, Power Papers, reel 34156, frame 1370.

83. Letter, Neal to Power, 5 April 1968, Power Papers, reel 34156, frame 1358.

84. Letter, Twining to Power, 4 June 1968, Power Papers, reel 34156, frame 1378.

85. Letter, Lincoln to Power, 30 July 1968, Power Papers, reel 34156, frame 1392.

86. Letter, Compton to Power, 20 September 1968, Power Papers, reel 34156, frame 1454.

87. Letter, Schlafly to Power, 10 April 1968, Power Papers, reel 34156, frame 1356.

88. Letter, Compton to Power, 20 September 1968, Power Papers, reel 34156, frame 1460.

89. Letter, Compton to Power, frame 1457.

90. Letter, Compton to Power, frame 1471.

91. Letter, Lincoln to Power, 9 November 1968, Power Papers, reel 34156, frame 1485.

92. Letter, Knudsen to Power, 2 December 1968, Power Papers, reel 34156, frame 1487.

93. Dr. Thomas Hughes first offered this insight.

94. Letter, Power to American Security Council Press, 12 June 1968, Power Papers, reel 34156, frame 1373.

95. Letter, Power to Braun, 1 August 1968, Power Papers, reel 34156, frame 1414.

96. Letter, Power to Buckley, 1 August 1968, Power Papers, reel 34156, frame 1422.

97. Letter, Reagan to Power, 19 August 1968, Power Papers, reel 34156, frame 1413.

98. Letter, Burke to Fisher, 23 August 1968, Power Papers, reel 34156, frame 1431.

99. Thomas S. Power, "Topics—In Defense of the Pentagon," *New York Times*, 23 May 1970, 21.

100. "General Thomas S. Power, 1905–1970," *Air Force Magazine*, January 1971, 17.

101. Budianski, 366.

102. Fred Kaplan, *The Wizards of Armageddon* (New York: Simon and Schuster, 1983), 245.

103. Carroll L. Zimmerman, *Insider at SAC: Operations Analysis Under LeMay* (Manhattan, KS: Sunflower University Press, 1988), 70.

104. Leavitt, 238.

105. Kaplan, 245–46.

106. Kaplan, 271–72. Rubel related that Power's Albania comment was during the SIOP meeting at Offutt Air Force Base in December 1960, when Thomas Gates was secretary of defense. Kaplan says Power mentioned Albania in February 1961, after Robert McNamara had taken the position. It is unclear who provided Power's quote for Kaplan, but Rubel was

interviewed for *Wizards of Armageddon*. It is as likely that Rubel's and Kaplan's accounts are of the same incident as the possibility that Power commented on Albania in two separate meetings.

107. Budianski, 366–67.
108. Rhodes, 56.
109. Wade interview, 10 October 1978, 308.
110. Wade interview, 310.
111. Zimmerman, 79.
112. Gen. Hewett T. Wheless, SAC oral history interview, AFHRA, call no. K416.051–5, tape 1.
113. Wheless interview.
114. Wheless interview.
115. Wheless interview.
116. Hall and Neufeld, 29.
117. Zimmerman, 92.
118. Zimmerman, 93.
119. Schlosser, 189.
120. Schlosser, 189–90.
121. Schlosser, 275.
122. Melvin G. Deaile, *Always at War: Organizational Culture in Strategic Air Command, 1946–62* (Annapolis, MD: Naval Institute Press, 2018), 190–91.
123. Marshall L. Michel III, *The Eleven Days of Christmas: America's Last Vietnam Battle* (San Francisco: Encounter Books, 2002), 9.
124. Robert A. Pape, *Bombing to Win: Air Power and Coercion in War* (Ithaca, NY: Cornell University Press, 1996), 12.
125. Carl H. Builder, "Keeping the Strategic Flame," *Joint Force Quarterly* (Winter 1996–97): 82.
126. See *On Limited Nuclear War in the 21st Century*, ed. Jeffrey A. Larson and Kerry M. Kartchner, (Stanford, CA: Stanford Security Studies, 2014).
127. Power, *Design for Survival*, 253. Emphasis original.
128. "The Four-Star General," frame 1458.
129. "The Role of Man in Strategic Air Command," n.d., Power Papers, reel 34155, frame 811.
130. "The Four-Star General," frame 1460.
131. Zimmerman, 93.

BIBLIOGRAPHY

Primary Sources

Air Force Historical Research Agency Archives
Air Force oral history interviews, call no. K239.0512.
Thomas S. Power Papers, call no. 168.7155, reels 34154–57.

Government Documents and Testimony
McNamara, Robert S. "Current Views of the Secretary of Defense." Draft staff summary. Testimony to Senate Armed Services Committee, 11 September 1963.

Power, Thomas S. Testimony to Senate. "Military Aspects and Implications of Nuclear Test Ban Proposals and Related Matters." Hearings before the Preparedness Investigations Subcommittee on Armed Services, United States Senate, 88th Congress, First Session, 12–27 August 1963.

Soviet Total War: "Historic Mission" of Violence and Deceit, Vol 1. Washington, DC: House Un-American Activities Committee, 23 September 1956.

United States Space Launch Competitiveness Act of 2015. H.R. 2262, 114th Congress, 1st Session, 25 November 2015.

Interviews and Oral Histories
Brown, Harold. Oral history interview for John F. Kennedy Presidential Library, 25 June 1964, 9 July 1964. https://www.jfklibrary.org.

Gorschboth, Frederick F. Interview with author, 15 October 2014.

Articles
"9 Will Accompany Twining to Moscow." *New York Times,* 14 June 1956.

"Air Chief of Staff Twining Accepts Russian Invitation to View Moscow Air Show." *Stanford Daily,* Stanford, CA, 31 May 1956.

Air Corps Newsletter. Multiple issues, 1927–45. Air Force Historical Support Division. https://www.afhistory.af.mil/History/Air-Corps-Newsletter/.

Birinn, Roland. "The 1932 Aerial Machine Gun and Bombing Matches." *U.S. Air Services*, November 1932.

Bradham, George. "Army Fliers Good Mail Carriers." *Greensboro Daily News*, 28 April 1934.

Chaney, J. E. "The Selection and Training of Military Airplane Pilots." *U.S. Air Services*, March 1928.

Coughlin, Gene. "Atlantic Romances of Dorothy Power." *Cincinnati Enquirer*, 10 December 1950.

Douglas Aircraft Company. "Preliminary Design of an Experimental World-Circling Spaceship." Report SM-11827, 2 May 1946.

Gagney, Robert B. "Boating in the Philippines." *Air Corps Newsletter*, 15 August 1935.

"General Thomas Power Dies at 65." *New York Times*, 8 December 1970.

"General Thomas S. Power, 1905–1970." *Air Force Magazine*, January 1971.

Hubbell, John G. "Tough Tommy Power—Our Deterrent-in-Chief." *Reader's Digest*, May 1964.

"It Was a Rough Party Soviets Gave Twining." *New York Times*, 11 July 1956.

Power, Thomas S. "A Message from ARDC." *Aviation Week* 65, no. 6, 6 August 1956.

———. "Ballistic Missiles and the SAC Mission." *Air Force Magazine*, April 1958.

———. "How Much Can Missiles Really Do?" *Air Force Magazine*, September 1956.

———. "The Mystery of Overkill." *Combat One*, October 1963.

———. "Strategic Air Command." *Air Force Magazine*, September 1960.

———. "Strategic Aspects of Space Operations." *Air Force Magazine and Space Digest*, November 1958.

———. "Two More Members of the Caterpillar Club." *Air Corps Newsletter*, 17 October 1929.

"So the American Girl Won the British Hero's Son." *San Bernardino County Sun*, 15 August 1937.

"Twining and Aides Off for Moscow." *New York Times*, 22 June 1956.

"Twining Finishes His Soviet Visit." *New York Times*, 1 July 1956.

"Twining Warns Congress of New Soviet Weapons." *New York Times*, 11 July 1956.

White, Thomas D. "The Inevitable Climb to Space." *Air University Quarterly Review*, Winter 1958–59.

———. "Strategy and the Defense Intellectuals." *Saturday Evening Post*, 4 May 1963.

Books

Air Force Space Command. *Resiliency and Disaggregated Space Architectures*. Peterson AFB, CO: Air Force Space Command, 2016. https://www.afspc.af.mil/Portals/3/documents/AFD-130821-034.pdf?ver=2016-04-14-154819-347.

Cantwell, Gerald T. *The Air Force in Space Fiscal Year 1963*. Washington, DC: USAF Historical Division Liaison Office, December 1966.

Emme, Eugene, ed. *The Impact of Air Power on National Defense*. Princeton, NJ: Van Nostrand Company, 1959.

Kent, Glenn A., et al. *Thinking About America's Defense: An Analytical Memoir*. Santa Monica, CA: RAND, 2008.

Gantz, Kenneth F., ed. *The United States Air Force Report on the Ballistic Missile*. Garden City, NY: Doubleday, 1958.

Garthoff, Raymond L. *Reflections on the Cuban Missile Crisis*. Washington, DC: Brookings Institution, 1989.

Headquarters Strategic Air Command, History and Research Division. *History of the Joint Strategic Target Planning Staff: Background and Preparation of SIOP-62*. B-82767. https://nsarchive2.gwu.edu//nukevault/ebb236/SIOP-62%20history.pdf.

Leavitt, Lloyd R. *Following the Flag: An Air Force Officer Provides an Eyewitness View of Major Events and Policies during the Cold War*. Maxwell AFB, AL: Air University Press, 2010.

LeMay, Curtis E., and MacKinlay Kantor. *Mission with LeMay: My Story*. Garden City, NY: Doubleday, 1965.

Michel, Marshall L. *The Eleven Days of Christmas: America's Last Vietnam Battle*. San Francisco: Encounter Books, 2002.

Nutter, Ralph H. *With the Possum and the Eagle: The Memoir of a Navigator's War over Germany and Japan*. Denton: University of North Texas Press, 2002.

Power, Thomas S. *Design for Survival*. New York: Coward-McCann, 1964.

Public Papers of the Presidents of the United States: Dwight D. Eisenhower (1960–61). Washington, DC: Government Printing Office, 1999.

Spires, David N., ed. *Orbital Futures: Selected Documents in Air Force Space History*. Peterson AFB, CO: Air Force Space Command, 2004.

Strategic Air Command. *Strategic Air Command Operations in the Cuban Crisis of 1962*. Vol I, Historical Study No. 90, B-91816. https://nsarchive2.gwu.edu/nsa/cuba_mis_cri/dobbs/SAC_history.pdf.

Stratemeyer, George E. *The Three Wars of Lt. Gen. George E. Stratemeyer: The Korean War Diary*. William T. Y'Blood, ed. Washington, DC: Air Force History and Museums Program, 1999.

Zimmerman, Carroll L. *Insider at SAC: Operations Analysis Under LeMay*. Manhattan, KS: Sunflower University Press, 1988.

Secondary Sources

Articles

Atkinson, James D. "Design for Survival." *Military Affairs* 29, no. 2, Summer 1965.

Baldwin, Hanson W. "The Creed of Strength." *New York Times*, 21 March 1965.

Builder, Carl H. "Keeping the Strategic Flame." *Joint Force Quarterly*, Winter 1996–97.

Correll, John T. "The Faded Vision of 'Military Man in Space.'" *Air Force Magazine*, November 2015.

Frank, Pat. "These Men Must Stop Russia's ICBM." *This Week Magazine*, 24 November 1957.

Frisbee, John L. "AACMO—Fiasco or Victory?" *Air Force Magazine*, March 1995.

Hayden, Dale. "The Search for Space Doctrine's War-Fighting Icon." *Air and Space Power Journal*, November–December 2014.

Hoyt Jr., Ralph L. "Civilian Conservation Corps." http://www.rindgehistorical-society.org/?page_id=276.

Lowther, Scott. "The Large Orions: As Close as We've Come to a Starship." *Aerospace Projects Review* 2, no. 2, March–April 2000.

Rhodes, Richard. "The General and World War III." *New Yorker*, 19 June 1995.

Rosenberg, David A. "The Origins of Overkill: Nuclear Weapons and American Strategy, 1945–1960." *International Security* 7, no. 4, Spring 1983.

Singer, S. E. "The Military Potential of the Moon." *Air University Quarterly Review*, Summer 1959.

"Space: An American Necessity." *Life Magazine*, 30 November 1959.

"The Stalingrad-Moscow Express." *Combat Crew*, September 1956.

Steel, Ronald. "Hitting the SAC." *New York Review of Books*, 20 May 1965.

Witze, Claude. "Industry Role in New Weapons Increases." *Aviation Week* 65, no. 6, 6 August 1956.

Books

Adams, Chris. *Deterrence: An Enduring Strategy*. New York: iUniverse, 2009.

Ashcroft, Bruce. *We Wanted Wings: A History of the Aviation Cadet Program*. Randolph AFB, TX: Air Education and Training Command, 2005.

Brown, Michael E. *Flying Blind: The Politics of the U.S. Strategic Bomber Program*. Ithaca, NY: Cornell University Press, 1992.

Budianski, Stephen. *Air Power: The Men, Machines, and Ideas that Revolutionized War, from Kitty Hawk to Iraq*. New York: Penguin Books, 2004.

Cameron, Rebecca Hancock. *Training to Fly: Military Flight Training, 1907–1945*. Washington, DC: Air Force Museums and History Program, 1999.

Christensen, Clayton M. *The Innovator's Dilemma: When New Technologies Cause Great Firms to Fail*. Cambridge, MA: Harvard Business School Press, 2016.

Coffey, Thomas M. *Iron Eagle: The Turbulent Life of Curtis LeMay*. New York: Crown Publishers, 1986.

Cornebise, Alfred Emile. *The United States 15th Infantry Regiment in China, 1912-1938*. Jefferson, NC: McFarland and Company Press, 2004.

Craig, Campbell. *Destroying the Village: Eisenhower and Thermonuclear War*. New York: Columbia University Press, 1998.

Crane, Conrad C. *American Airpower Strategy in Korea: 1950–1953*. Lawrence: University Press of Kansas, 2000.

Craven, W. F., and J. L. Cate, eds. *The Army Air Forces in World War II*. Volume VI, *Men and Planes*. Washington, DC: Air Force History Office, 1946.

Deaile, Melvin G. *Always at War: Organizational Culture in Strategic Air Command, 1946-62*. Annapolis, MD: Naval Institute Press, 2018.

Dobbs, Michael. *One Minute to Midnight: Kennedy, Khrushchev, and Castro on the Brink of Nuclear War*. New York: Random House, 2008.

Drea, Edward, et al. *History of the Unified Command Plan 1946-2012*. Washington, DC: Joint Chiefs of Staff, 2013.

Dyson, George. *Project Orion: The True Story of the Atomic Spaceship*. New York: Henry Holt and Company, 2002.

Ehlers Jr., Robert S. *The Mediterranean Air War*. Lawrence: University Press of Kansas, 2015.

Erickson, Mark. *Into the Unknown Together: The DOD, NASA, and Early Spaceflight*. Maxwell AFB, AL: Air University Press, 2005.

Finney, Robert T. *History of the Air Corps Tactical School 1920-1940*. Washington, DC: Air Force History and Museums Program, 1998.

Frank, Richard B. *Downfall: The End of the Imperial Japanese Empire.* New York: Random House, 2011.

Gurney, Gene. *Journey of the Giants.* New York: Coward-McCann, 1961.

Hall, R. Cargill, and Jacob Neufeld, eds. *The U.S. Air Force in Space: 1945 to the Twenty-First Century.* Washington, DC: Air Force History and Museums Program, 1988.

Holley Jr., I. B. *Ideas and Weapons.* New Haven, CT: Yale University Press, 1953.

———. *Technology and Military Doctrine.* Maxwell AFB, AL: Air University Press, 2004.

Hoyt, Edwin P. *Inferno: The Firebombing of Japan March 9th–August 15th, 1945.* New York: Madison Books, 2000.

Hubler, Richard G. *SAC: The Strategic Air Command.* New York: Duell, Sloane, and Pearce, 1958.

Kaplan, Edward. *To Kill Nations: American Strategy in the Air-Atomic Age and the Rise of Mutually Assured Destruction.* Ithaca, NY: Cornell University Press, 2015.

Kaplan, Fred. *The Wizards of Armageddon.* New York: Simon and Schuster, 1983.

Klinko, Donald W. Unpublished draft biography of General Thomas S. Power. Barksdale AFB, LA: Air Force Global Strike Command History Office, n.d.

Kozak, Warren. *LeMay.* Washington, DC: Regnery Publishing, 2009.

Larson, Jeffrey, and Kerry Kartchner, eds. *On Limited Nuclear War in the 21st Century.* Stanford, CA: Stanford Security Studies, 2014.

Lloyd, Alwyn T. *A Cold War Legacy: A Tribute to Strategic Air Command, 1946–1992.* Missoula, MT: Pictorial Histories Publishing Company, 2000.

Lowe, George E. *The Age of Deterrence.* Boston: Little, Brown, and Company, 1964.

McDougall, Walter. *. . .the Heavens and the Earth: A Political History of the Space Age.* Baltimore: Johns Hopkins University Press, 1985.

Montgomery, Bernard Law. *A History of Warfare.* New York: William Morrow and Co., 1983.

Neufeld, Jacob. *Ballistic Missiles in the United States Air Force, 1945–1960.* Washington, DC: Office of Air Force History, 1989.

Pape, Robert A. *Bombing to Win: Air Power and Coercion in War.* Ithaca, NY: Cornell University Press, 1996.

Perry, Robert L. *Origins of the USAF Space Program 1945–1956.* AFSC Historical Publications Series 62-24-10. Los Angeles AFB: Air Force Space Systems Division, 1961.

Polmar, Norman, ed. *Strategic Air Command: People, Aircraft, and Missiles.* Annapolis, MD: Nautical and Aviation Publishing Company of America, 1979.

Poole, Walter S. *The Joint Chiefs of Staff and National Policy 1961–1964.* History of the Joint Chiefs of Staff, Vol. 8. Washington, DC: Office of Joint History, 2011.

Rhodes, Richard. *Dark Sun: The Making of the Hydrogen Bomb.* New York: Simon and Schuster, 1995.

Rosen, Stephen. *Winning the Next War: Innovation and the Modern Military.* Ithaca, NY: Cornell University Press, 1991.

Rothstein, Stephen M. *Dead on Arrival? The Development of the Aerospace Concept, 1944–58.* Maxwell AFB, AL: Air University Press, November 2000.

Rubel, John H. *Doomsday Delayed: USAF Strategic Weapons Doctrine and SIOP-62.* New York: Hamilton Books, 2008.

Sagan, Scott. *The Limits of Safety: Organizations, Accidents, and Nuclear Weapons.* Princeton, NJ: Princeton University Press, 1993.

Schlafly, Phyllis, and Chester Ward. *Strike from Space.* Alton, IL: Pere Marquette Press, 1965.

Schlosser, Eric. *Command and Control.* New York: Penguin Press, 2013.

Sheehan, Neil. *A Fiery Peace in a Cold War: Bernard Schriever and the Ultimate Weapon.* New York: Random House, 2010.

Spires, David N. *Beyond Horizons: A Half Century of Air Force Space Leadership.* Peterson AFB, CO: Air Force Space Command, 1996.

Tillman, Barrett. *Whirlwind: The Air War Against Japan 1942–1945.* New York: Simon and Schuster, 2011.

Worden, Mike. *Rise of the Fighter Generals.* Maxwell AFB, AL: Air University Press, March 1998.

INDEX

ABOUT THE AUTHOR

————•●•————

Brent D. Ziarnick is an assistant professor at the Air Command and Staff College, Maxwell Air Force Base, Alabama. He has been published in *Wired*, *Politico*, and *The Hill* on space subjects. He is a graduate of the U.S. Air Force Academy and the School of Advanced Air and Space Studies.